WITHDRAWN

Waking
from the
Dream

ANCHOR BOOKS
DOUBLEDAY
New York
London Toronto Sydney
Auckland

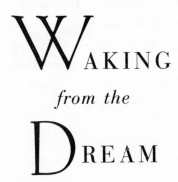

Waking

from the

Dream

*My Life in the Black
Middle Class*

Sam Fulwood III

⚓

AN ANCHOR BOOK

PUBLISHED BY DOUBLEDAY

a division of Bantam Doubleday Dell Publishing Group, Inc.

1540 Broadway, New York, New York 10036

ANCHOR BOOKS, DOUBLEDAY, and the portrayal of an anchor are
trademarks of Doubleday, a division of Bantam Doubleday Dell
Publishing Group, Inc.

The names of some individuals have been changed at their request.

Book design by F. J. Levine

Library of Congress Cataloging-in-Publication Data
Fulwood, Sam.
    Waking from the dream: my life in the Black middle class / Sam
Fulwood III.—1st Anchor Books ed.
        p.   cm.
    1. Fulwood, Sam.   2. Afro-Americans—Cultural assimilation.
3. Middle class—United States.   4. Afro-Americans—Biography.
I. Title
E185.97.F93A3   1996
305.896′073—dc20   95-40930
                                                                  CIP

ISBN 0-385-47822-4
Copyright © 1996 by Sam Fulwood III
All Rights Reserved
Printed in the United States of America
First Anchor Books Edition: April 1996

1   3   5   7   9   10   8   6   4   2

For Aunt Willa,

God rest her soul, who
admonished me to take
my nose out of books and
to go outdoors and play.

I have a dream that my four little children will one day live in a nation where they will not be judged by the color of their skin, but by the content of their character. I have a dream today.

THE REVEREND
MARTIN LUTHER KING, JR.
August 28, 1963

Assimilation is freedom to move, to participate, to belong on your terms, not someone else's . . . It is a certain kind of comfort zone in which you function. I don't enjoy that comfort zone—not even in 1995, not even as the James B. Duke Professor of History at Duke University.

JOHN HOPE FRANKLIN
July 2, 1995

CONTENTS

Prologue

BLUE-CHIP BLACK

I first became aware that being black was special on a spring day in 1968 when I was eleven years old. That day I heard our principal's voice suddenly crackling over my classroom's intercom, summoning me to her office. I was a sixth grader at Oaklawn Elementary School, a segregated black school in Charlotte, North Carolina, and Mrs. Gwen Cunningham, our principal, wanted to chat about my future.

She was a proper and proud black woman who was convinced, on the advice of my teachers, that I should be among the first students from her elementary school to attend a white junior high school the following year. This was an honor, she declared.

I didn't want to do it. I wanted to stay with my friends and go to the junior high school in our neighborhood. But Mrs. Cunningham deflected all my arguments. As if I needed additional persuading, she stated, "I am absolutely certain that you can hold your own with the best [white students] at Ranson Junior High."

Suddenly, I was different from my friends and classmates. It was my duty to my race to blaze a path for other blacks to follow. Mrs. Cunningham didn't know it, but she had set my life on a new course. I had been tapped into the fraternity of blue-chip blacks, an unofficial grouping of the best our race had to offer. One by one, we were culled from the masses to lead the way toward improved racial understanding.

I evolved that day into a race child. I believed I would, in due time, illuminate the magnificent social changes wrought by racial progress. Overt racial barriers were falling and I, the son of a minister and a schoolteacher, fully credentialed members of Charlotte's black middle class, thought my future would be free of racism and free of oppression. I believed I was standing at the entrance to the Promised Land.

Now, as the twentieth century exhausts itself, I am awakening from my blind belief in that American dream. I am angrier than I've ever been.

Lest anyone misunderstand me, this is a new and troubling sensation. I was bred to cheerfully embrace the integration of the races, not to retreat into a segregated world in despair. I was among the vanguard group of black men and women for whom legal segregation was less a cruel reality and more a historical (some say forgotten) fact. Nobody ever called me a nigger.

But now, for the first time in my life, I am facing those questions that I've spent a lifetime avoiding: Is American society the race-blind haven that black people of my parents' generation had hoped it would become? If not, what alternative do we have?

Although racial tensions continue to escalate, few blacks or whites seem willing to spend the resources—both fiscal and human—to ease the strain of living separate lives. Rather, a form of Balkanization is occurring, with race and class separating us. My generation—the "new black middle class," according to at least one sociologist—is so disillusioned by the persistent racism that continues to define and limit us that we are abandoning efforts to assimilate into the mainstream of society.

I came of age as the Great Society of the 1960s closed—a period defined as the "years of the black" by author and scholar David Bradley in his seminal essay in the May 1982 issue of *Esquire.* Bradley called it a "fascinating epoch" during which benevolent, wealthy and white liberals, driven by the guilt of their forefathers' sins and the rantings of Afro'd, heat-packing, shades-wearing militants, persuaded politicians and activists to swallow an expensive set of social programs meant "to conceal evidence of a scandalous past or present."

I have kept a clipping of Bradley's autobiographical essay—titled "Black and American, 1982: There Are No Good Times to Be Black in America, but Some Times Are Worse Than Others"—ever since it was published. At that time, I was embarking on my career as a reporter for my hometown newspaper with the naive notion that my ambition and ability would carry me to unlimited vistas. I was convinced that someday I would respond to Bradley, challenging his pessimism and extolling my triumph. I would declare that the Reverend Martin Luther King, Jr.'s great vision had been fulfilled in my generation. Mine would be the first in this nation's history to be judged "by the content of their character," not "by the color of their skin."

Sadly, more than a decade later, I must admit that Bradley, a professor of English at Temple University, was right to say that it is impossible "to give a socially meaningful description of who I am and what I've done without using the word black." This is painful because it means I must accept his corollary: "Nothing I shall ever accomplish or discover or earn or inherit or buy or sell or give away—nothing I can ever do—will outweigh the fact of my race in determining my destiny."

As a child of the black bourgeoisie, I matured in the post–civil rights era and was a primary beneficiary of the protest generation. That placed me among the most ardent believers in the American Dream. Today, we sons and daughters who were trained to run the next lap, after the historic heroism of those who faced the dogs, water hoses and brutal cops, are turning away from our parents' noble expectations of an integrated America. Many middle-class black executives are moving out of their corporate roles to create fulfilling jobs that serve black customers. Black colleges are experiencing a renaissance. Black organizations—churches, fraternities, sororities and professional groups—are attracting legions of new members. And, most surprising to me, upscale blacks are moving to neighborhoods that insulate them from the slings and arrows of the larger society.

Four years ago, I lived in the conspicuously affluent middle-class black suburban neighborhood of Brook Glen, about fifteen miles from downtown Atlanta. My neighbors were proud of their large homes and loved to entertain. One warm summer evening, a backyard gathering fell suddenly silent as a car, marked with a local realtor's logo and containing a white couple, cruised slowly through the subdivision. Finally, one of my neighbors spoke up. "What are they looking for?" he asked bitterly. "I hope they don't find anything they like. Otherwise, there goes the neighborhood." The message was clear: whites would ruin the sanctuary of our community.

Many of the middle-class black Americans who have come to accept this reality appear to fit neatly within the system among their white peers. They own the symbols of success. They drive bright, shiny cars, live in the suburbs and send their children to private academies. But deep inside, they are unhappy, knowing they are not accepted as equals by their white colleagues or acquaintances. And so they retreat into a self-protective buppie cocoon, separate from poor blacks and all whites.

I know all about this bubble. It is where I live, reluctantly, but more comfortably than anywhere else I could imagine. Despite what my heart wants to believe, I can't escape the thought that white America, which stopped short of embracing middle-class blacks at the moment we most wanted inclusion, may already have lost its opportunity. The refusal of the larger society to accept us, on our own terms, combined with our unwillingness to return to the ghetto, is likely to result in even more isolation, frustration and desperation. And, worst of all, more anger.

Lately, I have wondered what to tell my six-year-old daughter, Amanda, about all this. She is developing an awareness of her own racial and class identity, and soon she will be asking difficult questions about her place in society. Only a year ago, she shocked her mother and me by declaring that when she grows up, she intends to "be white" like one of her classmates.

For the moment, simple answers satisfy her. But clearly, the time is coming when I will need something more. All I know now is that I will not repeat the blind beliefs of my youth. My daughter will not be a second-generation blue-chip black, laboring under the mistaken belief that race will one day be coincidental, unimportant or ignored in her life.

Chapter One

SLEEPING AND DREAMING

I grew up believing I lived in a near-perfect world. God in Heaven was perfection, and I had the closest thing on Earth, in Charlotte, North Carolina. I lived with my father, mother and brother on a quarter-acre lot in a single-story, five-room redbrick house in a subdivision called McCrorey Heights. A community of 130 homes, McCrorey Heights was a place where preachers, schoolteachers, principals, college professors, doctors, dentists, lawyers, police officers and homemakers lived comfortably. These people were all Negroes—or black people, as they were slowly, laboriously beginning to think of themselves, though "colored" still slipped easily off many older people's tongues. This community was a new frontier, built to accommodate the expanding tastes and pocketbooks of an educated black middle class whose housing options were limited by the living legacy of Jim Crow.

In the spring, my neighborhood could have been the suburban setting for a Hollywood movie. Dogwood trees opened their buds, unfurling a blazing display of pink and white, while sweet and sticky sap oozed from pines and huge emerald hands sprouted from oak trees. It was the early 1960s, and I played ball in the streets and raced through wooded lots with other neighborhood kids. This was a world where all the girls had Barbie dolls, the boys G.I. Joes, and every kid owned roller skates and bicycles. We played oblivious to the powerful forces of race and class from which our families shielded us.

My parents had been born and raised in neighboring small towns in rural Union County, North Carolina, during the first quarter of the century. By the time they married in 1950, both had finished college and had begun their careers. Daddy, like his father, was a Presbyterian minister. Momma, like her father and all but one of her six siblings, was an elementary school teacher. These were ideal pedigrees for Southern black society's elite.

So in 1950, the Reverend S. L. Fulwood, Jr., and his bride, the former Hallie Massey, purchased our family home and came to live in McCrorey Heights. Back then, the community was no more than a muddy tract on what had been a municipal landfill just inside the Charlotte city limits. McCrorey Heights was hidden behind a city waterworks plant on Beatties Ford Road, a major artery that once served as a Colonial-era path linking the western edge of Charlotte to a commercial waterway running through the Piedmont foothills. Just outside our subdivision was Biddleville, an old and distinguished streetcar suburb for blacks, named in honor of Major Henry Jonathan Biddle, a white Union Army officer whose wealthy widow bequeathed a large sum of money to establish a Presbyterian school for the recently freed slaves in Charlotte. Biddle Institute, chartered in 1867, became Johnson C. Smith University in 1875. The college built a cluster of stately wood-and-masonry homes to house its black professors—who in time would instruct three generations of my family, starting with my paternal grandfather and continuing with my father and my brother.

My parents knew what they were doing by choosing to live in this Ozzie and Harriet enclave of black Charlotte. It would grow with Charlotte's black middle class and provide a buffer against the hostile world outside. Though I doubt the idea ever crossed their minds, McCrorey Heights was the buppie cocoon of their day.

I was born August 28, 1956. My brother, George, arrived a year and a half later, in January 1958. During the late 1950s and early '60s, when my parents were raising their children, Charlotte was as segregated a place as any in the region, but the city fathers preferred not to highlight the hard-edged racism so many other Southern towns openly displayed. In the years surrounding my birth, Charlotte rarely drew attention to its racial hierarchy. There were no fire hosings of black protesters, no redneck police chiefs thumping heads in public, no German shepherds snapping at the ends of taut leashes.

There was one exception. In September 1957, an academically gifted light-brown-skinned fifteen-year-old girl from Biddleville, Dorothy Counts, tried but failed to integrate the all-white Harding High School. Her father was the Reverend Herman Counts, a professor of religion and philosophy at Johnson C. Smith University and a Presbyterian preacher colleague of my father's. NAACP activists and lawyers were eager to focus the country's attention on how slow the Southern school systems were to implement the Brown decision, and Dr. Counts agreed to allow his daughter to be their test case. In fact, she was one of four black students "handpicked for their ability and character" to integrate the city's schools in the wake of the 1954 Supreme Court decision *Brown* v. *Board of Education of Topeka, Kansas.*

The three other students successfully attended other formerly all-white elementary and junior high schools that year despite some tense moments and some precipitous moves by white city leaders. But student and parent opposition to Dorothy Counts took a nasty turn. I have never understood why her case posed more of a problem than the other integrationists' efforts. But who can ever fully explain why race bothers some people more than others? Regardless, Charlotte was suddenly the image of white Southern resistance to integration, something civic leaders so desperately wanted to avoid. The most unflattering sight of all—from the city's point of view—was the compelling photograph of the proud, stoic girl, eyeglasses on a cord around her neck and white ribbon fluttering down her checkered dress, arriving for her first day of classes at an all-white school. In that photograph, Dorothy appears to glide with the poise and grace of a swan as an ugly, white mob of Brylcreem-slicked schoolboys shout epithets at her. After Dorothy's fourth day at Harding, the taunts and threats of physical violence proved too much for her, prompting the Counts family to withdraw her from Harding High.

Later, when civil rights activists of the 1960s staked out public streets and Woolworth lunch counters as their battlegrounds, Charlotte's business leaders remembered the lesson of Dorothy Counts. They met in private with civil rights leaders and white community figures to plead for civility as they struggled to respond piecemeal to the rising demands of black citizens. These business leaders wanted no more Dorothy Counts photographs, no televised images of burning and looting in their streets and no scenes of the police repression that would certainly follow any Negro outbursts. They wanted none of this because they feared negative publicity would cripple Charlotte's emerging economic development. They had worked so hard to build the city's banking towers and trucking firms that they would not let anything stop Charlotte's growth as a regional, perhaps even national, financial center.

Black people of means, like the preachers and teachers and doctors and postal workers and small business owners settling in McCrorey Heights, purchased their homes in carefully selected crannies where they and their families could work for upward mobility and racial progress. There, these black families existed in relative comfort and isolation, beyond the oppressive purview of whites. Affluent white people, who made the big decisions about Charlotte's future, lived far across town. Whites who lived closer never invaded our space; they were too preoccupied with the problems of their own hardscrabble, working-class existence. Our paths never crossed. I knew next to nothing about them, and they knew even less about me.

For the middle-class denizens of McCrorey Heights, affluence meant a college education, a professional job with the government or with a business catering to black consumer needs, marriage to another employed person, and home ownership. It had little to do with heredity or legacy, as in other parts of the country, where the black bourgeoisie was an older and more sophisticated elite. Nearly everyone in our neighborhood had migrated from rural communities outside Charlotte, just like my parents. Many had initially rented in more densely populated central city areas, gathering their resources to settle in the suburbs. Nor was colorism, the clumping together of black folks along lines demarcated by skin tone, an issue in McCrorey Heights. There, a virtual rainbow coalition of black folks lived without petty dissensions wrought by the historic divide between house and field slaves.

Though both my parents knew how narrow life had been for black people of their generation, they never complained about—or even mentioned—the inherent unfairness and inequality they must have observed growing up black. Perhaps, I suspect, they didn't talk about it because they were more blessed than most of their colored contemporaries.

My paternal grandparents, the Reverend S. L. Fulwood, Sr., and his prim schoolteacher wife, Rosa, a graduate of Barber-Scotia Teachers' College in nearby Concord, North Carolina, must have cut quite a figure among the poorer black sharecroppers and domestics living cheek by jowl in Waxhaw, a tiny backwater outpost, where for the rank and file of its black residents, just making a living was challenge enough.

But not for my family. Though my grandparents were far from wealthy, they wanted for less than other colored people. In their time and in that place, ministers and schoolteachers were just about as revered as any colored folks could be. Indeed, the labors of this country preacher, who died many years before I was born, and his schoolmarm wife established the values and attitudes that placed my father and his sons on upwardly mobile courses.

Momma's people, the Masseys of Monroe (Union County's county seat), like Daddy's family in rural Waxhaw, were well placed at the apex of the social constellation of Negro families. For years, my grandfather, John L. Massey, taught school in a rural one-room shack, where he did his best to educate the colored children of his community. 'Fessor Massey, as the townsfolk knew him, was a pecan-brown-skinned man with the stern and serious countenance that men of his race and generation maintained so as to deflect all manner of trouble that could swoop down unexpectedly from sources beyond their control. He was a frugal, proud man with deep Methodist convictions, fearful of the Lord and protective of his family. His wife, the former Lundella Sadler, was much younger than her husband. She died in her thirties after having given birth to three daughters and four sons. "I never heard her call him anything other than 'Mr. Massey,' " said my mother, who was a teenager when her mother died.

To provide for his large family, 'Fessor Massey moonlighted as a porter on the Southern Railroad line that ran through the big cities and countless hick towns along the eastern seaboard between Boston and Miami. Between his teacher's salary and piecemeal railroad pay, he amassed enough money to purchase several plots of land in Newtown, the densely populated black area of Monroe sectioned off from white neighborhoods by the ever-present railroad tracks.

Sometime in the late 1880s, 'Fessor Massey managed to jump the tracks to Quality Hill, which was well on the other side of town. At the corner of Windsor and Bragg streets, he constructed a marvelous two-story Victorian frame house with a spacious porch that wrapped around the front. Now a historic landmark in Monroe, this six-bedroom palace was not far from similar, albeit much grander, homes owned by white folks.

Scuttlebutt among black folks in Monroe had it that my grandfather was able to live in such grand style because he had profited from a great fire that consumed the railroad office. According to this never-proved rumor, as the flames licked at the old wooden structure, my grandfather realized that all bookkeeping records would be destroyed and walked off with a canvas bag containing an undisclosed sum of cash. He kept the money, the colored folks whispered.

Whether the story was true or not, none of us really knew. But the mere fact that it existed explained a great deal about the closely knit, highly secretive Massey clan, who seemed to consider anyone outside the family a danger. Momma often related how her mother refused to allow her to play with neighbors. "If we asked to go over to someone's house, she would order us to scrub the floors along that long hall upstairs," she said. "Whenever we wanted to do things like the other young people in the area, she often refused. It got to the point we wouldn't ask to go anywhere, preferring to invent games and play among ourselves rather than to have her find more chores for us to do. I used to think that was the meanest thing in the world for her to do, but as I grew older, I began to understand why she did that. She was looking after our best interests."

With much the same mysterious protectiveness, my mother attempted to look after the best interests of her own children. Like her mother, she was wary of our accepting invitations to parties and to play at the neighbors', knowing that such acts required reciprocation. "Friends cost you," she would say. "I don't want to be in debt to friends."

I often failed to understand her logic and was confused by her seemingly arbitrary rules. I tried to make sense of the often indecipherable homilies that she passed out as explanations. Momma's discipline was like that too. "No child of mine is going to grow up like a weed," she used to mutter over and over, like some strange mantra, as she flailed upon George or me with a switch or leather belt for having transgressed some household rule. Such whippings, however, were rare, as we so hated them that we went to great lengths to avoid inciting her wrath. We simply did whatever she expected, often without having to be told.

My earliest memory of Daddy is of him dressed in his black robe and preaching about God from the pulpit of Allen Temple Memorial Church in a small rural community of factory workers in the North Carolina foothills. He spoke in calm, reasoned tones without the pulpit-thumping and strutting favored by the Baptist preachers down the road. Stylistically, he resembled a homespun philosopher teaching a classroom of believers. His congregation—schoolteachers and day laborers in their Sunday hats and once-a-week suits, reeking of mothballs—listened quietly, reverently and with great appreciation to his story about one of God's faithful prophets:

"There's nothing wrong with asking God questions. Questions can be good, especially if you're seeking understanding. You see, that's what Habakkuk was doing in the Old Testament. He was seeking understanding. He would never dare question the righteousness of God."

"Yes," someone from the choir softly moaned. *Daddy paused to allow the word to hiss across the congregation.*

"It be's like that sometimes," Daddy continued. *"We want understanding, but we can't understand God's work on our terms, on demand. God doesn't work on our terms. He works on His own time. We have to wait for His time and His plans to unfold around us. That's what He was trying to tell ol' Habakkuk when He said, 'I am doing a work in your days that you would not believe if told.'*

"See, Habakkuk couldn't understand why God, who is so powerful, so kind and so loving to His people, would let loose the evil of the Chaldeans—what do the Scriptures call them, let me read that to you 'cause it's important to understand just what God Himself thought of them: 'For lo, I am rousing the Chaldeans, that bitter and hasty nation.' God called them a bitter and hasty nation. They were. They were ruthless. They were mean. They were ill-tempered. And God set them loose upon His own people, whom He loved. But more than that, these Chaldeans were powerful. The Bible says they had quick, strong horses that flew like eagles and were fiercer than night wolves.

"Church, listen to the Word: 'They all come for violence: terror of them goes before them. They gather captives like sand. At kings they scoff, and of rulers they make sport. They laugh at every fortress, for

they heap up earth and take it. They sweep by like the wind and go on, guilty men, whose own might is their god!'

"*Habakkuk just could not understand why. 'Why, Lord, My God, My Holy One,' he asked God of the Everlasting to Everlasting. And he was seeking understanding.*"

I liked that sermon. But I had no idea what it was all about. Decades would pass before I understood Habakkuk's questions or accepted them as a parable for my life. Back when I first heard this story, I was one in the congregation, watching the spell my father cast over the church. I was proud because that was Daddy up there, at the center of attention, on that stage he called a pulpit. As far as I could see, Daddy owned that church, a birthright waiting for me one day in the distant future.

Often, after one of Daddy's Sunday sermons and the extended glad-handing that followed, some parishioner would invite our family over for a dinner of fried chicken (it was always fried chicken: "Reb'm Fulwood, I know how you love chicken," someone would say, and Daddy would pat his extended belly and reply with mock surprise, "What would make you think such a thing?"), macaroni and cheese, string beans, tomatoes, biscuits, iced tea and apple pie. Our family would be seated and served, the host family standing by as we ate and praised their cooking. Momma didn't care much for those Sunday dinners. She politely picked at her plate and, with great effort, finished her meal. Food wasn't good to her unless she had witnessed—and critiqued—its preparation. In later years, she would refuse to eat in restaurants where she did not know whose hands had touched her food.

My mother and father wrapped us in their protective world, one that was supportive and nurturing and isolated from unknown evils. It was a paradox of sorts: while they expected that their children's lives would expand more fully than their own, they also drew us into a defensive web of their own construction.

The forces of racism and classism, negative and threatening, were already operating outside my notice to confine my life choices. I just did not know it then because my parents in their well-built fortress shielded me from those invisible limits.

My parents gave only passing consideration, like their brief conversations about the weather or local happenings in the daily papers, to the historic rumblings afoot in their city, across the South and throughout the United States. Just beyond their picture windows and outside their cozy nest, the wave that would eventually propel my life was gathering force. Later, I came to question all they failed to teach me about race and class and my place in America.

But for the moment, I accepted the bubble my parents had fashioned for me.

They imbued in me the belief that the evil of the outside world could be made to disappear by an act of Protestant willpower. If I worked hard and believed strongly enough in God, the inherent fairness of humanity would reveal itself to me and nothing would be impossible.

If something happened that required my parents' serious attention, it would be defined as "house business" and Momma and Daddy would huddle out of our sight and hearing. When they emerged, whatever had been said would be presented to George and me as a fait accompli. Similarly, my parents never talked to my brother and me explicitly about sex; they simply ordered us to keep our pants zipped, stay away from fast girls, and there would be no trouble. No questions were answered and no discussions ensued. Indeed, George and I were sheltered from the lingering traces of Jim Crow and taught to regard what little bit of it peeked into our hooded eyes as the fleeing tail of a dying beast.

Despite their best efforts, however, racial issues intruded upon us anyway. Sometime in the early 1960s—I don't remember when exactly—my family and I were going by Clark's Department Store. George noticed the bright red, blue and green neon lights in the store's parking lot. That's where the donkeys, tethered to a pole in the asphalt, slowly paced in a hay-filled circle. Other kids were riding the animals. We begged our parents to let us ride too.

As George and I waited with Momma at a safe distance, Daddy

approached a booth where a teenaged white attendant collected money and dispensed tickets. Daddy never repeated what the white boy said to him, but the message was clear: he wasn't going to permit two black boys to ride. As good, decent and law-abiding Negroes, my parents accepted the snub without argument or question. Rather, they turned to leave, acquiescing with the same aplomb as if they had been sadly informed by an itinerant greengrocer that he had no tomatoes. As the family walked back to our car with George and me in full-throated retreat, my parents' obvious embarrassment was reasonably composed and veiled—until George (I am sure it was George) asked Daddy why they wouldn't let us ride.

"The people who own the animals don't want colored people riding them," he said. His voice was even, matter-of-fact. "Only whites."

"Well, we can come back tomorrow," George announced in the imperious voice that only a child can summon. "We can wear false faces. Maybe then they'll let us ride."

Daddy's explanation of why we could not ride the donkeys was baffling to me. How could something as insignificant as the color of my skin be the reason for turning me away from the rides?

If that was so, then I was proud of George for offering what seemed a reasonable compromise. False faces, the kind worn on Halloween, ought to satisfy the white attendant. But Momma burst into tears at the mere thought of her little ones hiding behind plastic masks for a ride on a funky donkey. It was the first time I remember seeing her cry and it propelled Daddy into a rare flash of anger.

"You're not wearing any false faces and you're not riding the damn donkey," he said. "So forget it. This never happened."

I was not prepared for any of this. It was the first time I was made aware of the fact that white people had any power to deny my wishes. Until this point, I had no sense that white people, simply because they were white, had anything I wanted or coveted.

Thanks to the world created by my parents, I knew only varying shades of blackness. I felt no shame or trepidation about white people, because they were simply not part of my world. I did not consider "white is right" a meaningful concept. White people were the images I saw flickering on the television set in the den: Lucy and Ricky; Tarzan and Jane; Hoss and Little Joe on *Bonanza;* Ed Sullivan; George Jetson and Fred Flintstone. I knew they were white, but I also knew they were not real, flesh-and-blood people, because they came and went when Daddy or Momma summoned them into the room with a twist of the TV dial and they disappeared just as magically. They did not speak directly to me or my experiences. Therefore, I concluded, white people existed only in some other, irrelevant dimension.

The sudden and dramatic social changes that transpired during my childhood made it easier in later years for my family to joke about the donkey episode. They turned that indignity, one among many my parents must have endured, into a comedy of manners. Laughter was a weapon of survival: anything that was so side-splittingly funny could never be taken seriously enough to pose any danger to my soul.

On another occasion, I recall Momma commenting to Daddy about a truckload of poor, lint-headed rural white folks who gestured at us (I can only assume it was a middle-finger salute) as they sped past in their clay-encrusted pickup.

"There go the millionaires," she said, unaware that I had heard her comment.

"Where?" I said, looking around in hopes of a rare sighting. "I don't see any rich people."

"Hush, boy," Daddy said with a wink and giggle toward Momma.

I was a teenager before I caught the drift of her irony, and I finally figured out she was implying that poor white trash considered themselves "millionaires" in comparison to all black folks, whatever their economic status. But neither Momma nor Daddy would ever explain their shared meaning of "millionaires" to me.

That, I now understand, was their way of *gittin' over* on white folks. They struck back at racism with peals of laughter, and it was a lesson I carried into adulthood. That they could laugh seemed proof, once I was old enough to ponder such things, that racism should not be taken seriously or personally. Even as the economic woes of the 1970s and greedy insensitivities of the '80s laid waste my idealism, I held fast to that dream. I believed hard work and good wishes would persuade the world that I was a worthy member of America's mainstream. Somehow, I remained certain that when I turned thirty-five, no one would care about the color of my skin. All that would matter was whether I carried a green, gold or platinum American Express card.

In my childhood world, I was my parents' son, safe and secure, happy to be who and where I was. Anything negative or threatening to my identity did not exist. This state of blissful ignorance is what I remember most about growing up in Charlotte, a sense that my life had merit, not because it was sanctioned by white people but because I was loved by my family.

When I learned to drive the family's Deuce and a Quarter, Momma was precise in her instructions. She said, "Remember to always drive on the right-hand side. You can go anywhere you want and nothing will hit you if you stay on your side of the road." Funny how those directions stuck with me. It was a metaphor for the way she lived her life and how she expected me to live mine. She had stayed in her place. If I stayed in my place, I could go anywhere, accomplish anything. It sounded, like all that rushed by during my young life's journey, so perfect.

Early in the summer of 1963, however, the Civil Rights Movement did nudge against my life. One day, George and I trouped along with Daddy to one of his many meetings at Johnson C. Smith University. While he consulted with a group of his friends, George and I raced across the campus's green lawn. I do not remember anyone explaining that Daddy was there for an advance planning meeting to support a proposed March on Washington called by civil rights leaders. These ministers, some of them white but most black like Daddy, were deciding how to board and feed the marchers—who would travel up from Atlanta in bus caravans to the outskirts of Charlotte, then disembark for a dramatic parade into the Westside-Biddleville area before the waiting news cameras. It was quite a task and these ministers were setting their agendas and making sure Charlotte did its part to be hospitable.

Daddy was no civil rights crusader. In fact, he was one of many black preachers involved only on the fringes of the Civil Rights Movement, preferring instead to minister from the comparative safety of his pulpit and provide for the daily, practical and nonthreatening spiritual needs of his congregation. He espoused a brand of black Christian theology that was heavy on self-help and light on street activism.

The significance of his presence at the university that summer's day escaped George and me. Just another of Daddy's boring meetings, an excuse for the Fulwood boys to evade close supervision for an hour or two of play. Of more immediate interest to us was the upcoming family vacation—a trip to the New York World's Fair.

Leaving Charlotte in the middle of the night, Daddy drove us north in his new sky-blue Ford station wagon, with the rear seats folded down to make a bed for George and me. Momma packed sandwiches, soda pop and doughnuts. They did not want to take chances. If we kids were asleep when we left home, we would wake to brown-bagged car treats and there would be no need to stop along the way in the unfriendly, segregated territories of rural North Carolina and Virginia. Of course, nothing like this was spelled out to us. As far as we knew, the home-packed goodies were part of the journey, a special treat reserved for vacations and other family excursions.

We did stop at every orange-roofed Howard Johnson on the New Jersey Turnpike heading into New York, first for ice cream, then for saltwater taffy or some other delicacy. This was Daddy's way of making up for the separate-but-unequal public accommodations below the Mason-Dixon Line. Freed from social restraints, he took full advantage of the opportunity to shower George and me with roadside treats.

Our itinerary allowed for us to stay with Momma's Cousin Mable on Long Island and spend a few days in Baltimore with Daddy's sister, Aunt Anne, and her husband, Uncle Frank, on the return trip. Nobody paused to consider stopping over in Washington, where preparations of another sort were developing. In fact, I remember nothing being said to me or George about the March on Washington. But as we passed through the capital, we saw crowds and buses on the Mall between the Lincoln Memorial and the Washington Monument.

I do not know why my parents avoided our participation as a family in the march. It was not as though they were unaware of or unmoved by that defining moment in the Civil Rights Movement. With the benefit of hindsight, I suspect my folks were social surfers, content to reap the benefit of others' protests. I guess they felt one more set of faces in that crowd would not make a decisive difference—racial changes were coming regardless. For whatever reasons, they just didn't feel compelled to share that moment in history with their children.

Years later, after the March on Washington became the historic milestone it remains today, my parents would remark almost as an afterthought that we had been nearby, in Baltimore, at about the time Dr. Martin Luther King, Jr., was delivering his "I Have a Dream" speech. This was said in order to link a Fulwood family moment to King's historic oration, which by our calculations transpired at nearly the same point that Cousin Frankie and her childhood friends were singing "Happy Birthday" to me.

Chapter Two

First Contact

Like any black kid who came of age in the South in the late 1960s, I heard stories of how it was when my parents were children. How they had to walk to a decrepit one-room schoolhouse as white kids chugged past aboard yellow school buses. It was always stressed that hard times had made colored people hearty, better able to withstand adversity and greatly appreciative of the luxuries that we kids took for granted.

"Why, there's a toilet on every floor of that school you're going to attend," Daddy once said, tossing a sly smile toward me. "We never had nothing like that. Went into the outhouse behind the school. Or into the woods. Didn't know about no fancy indoor toilets. That's what they had at the white schools, I reckon. Never went inside one to know for sure."

Daddy rarely spoke of his childhood or how it had been for him to grow up in the racially segregated rural South. Instead, he talked about the normal aspirations of middle-class black parents, especially those who wanted the best for their kids. I remember, for example, Daddy reading the comics to me every morning to help me learn my ABC's. Newspapers, magazines and books littered our house. Long before I entered the first grade, I already knew what was going to happen to Dick and Jane and their dog, Spot; I had read it for myself at least a year before and was also proficient in Dr. Seuss.

Where I would attend first grade, like everything else of import in my childhood, was a matter of house business. I'd been told that all children had to go to school when they turned six, but I was hardly aware that where you went was decided, in part, by who you were. Bundling me off to school was an important step for my parents because it represented my first prolonged exposure outside our home.

So, in August 1961, I enrolled at Biddleville Elementary, a sprawling split-level public school set hard by the railroad tracks and directly across Beatties Ford Road from the entrance to McCrorey Heights. Biddleville was actually Momma's second choice. She had wanted me to attend Our Lady of Consolation, a private Catholic elementary school for black people. But the school had limited spaces for non-Catholics, and Momma had waited too long to enroll me.

There was nothing extraordinary about Momma's attempt to put me in a private school. The segregated black public schools were less desirable than the Catholic schools. Black families who could afford it eagerly spent money on a "good" education for their children. "Whatever you put in your head, nobody can ever take away from you," Momma used to say. "I want you to learn all you can. An education will stay with you for the rest of your life."

I enjoyed attending Biddleville, partly because I developed a powerful crush on my first-grade teacher, Mrs. Pittman. As the year progressed, I grew certain that Mrs. Pittman loved me back. She doted on my reading ability and praised the huge block letters I crafted so carefully on those thick sheets of writing paper with the blue lines. By the middle of the second grade, I was over my childish affair with Mrs. Pittman, realizing that teachers were kind to everybody.

The next year, 1964, I transferred to Oaklawn Elementary, a new all-black school where I spent the rest of my grade school years. I was a good student, earning more A's than B's, and never any C's. I liked all my teachers, especially Mrs. Wheeler, who taught an advance group of sixth graders. Matronly, stern and serious about learning, she reminded me of Momma and her sisters, Aunt Willa and Aunt Kate, women who seemed to care about teaching hardheaded chaps to count, read and obey.

I assumed that my success in school was the product of good home training and my earnest study habits. The whole truth included something more. Others were working behind the scenes to support me. I know them now as the Negro Community Guardians, a term I invented for all the black teachers I had from Mrs. Pittman to Mrs. Wheeler, as well as folks I didn't even know who worked on my behalf. Self-appointed race women and men, they stayed on the lookout for what was good for our people. Many of the Guardians had worked for a long time in black public schools, using hand-me-down books and materials. They were eager to prepare others for success in the new, integrated world. Members of their small tactical, elite army issued orders to young people like me so we could blaze a path among privileged whites and acquit our race with distinction. The Guardians applied their firm discipline with love because we stood as a tribute to their skills. These teachers were masters at building poise among their promising students.

One day when I was in the sixth grade, Principal Gwen Cunningham summoned me to her office. Mrs. Cunningham, who was always immaculately dressed and smelled as though she took baths in a huge vat of floral perfume, handed me some papers.

"Samuel, do you know Dorothy Counts?" she said.

"No, ma'am."

"Well, you should know who she is. She lived in your neighborhood and is very famous."

"I don't know her," I said, wishing I did.

"Well," she said, shifting strategies, "your father and mother know her and her parents. Dorothy Counts attempted to desegregate the public schools just before you were born. Your parents probably have told you all about this. Does it sound familiar?"

I nodded. Well, yes, I had a glimmer of understanding of what Mrs. Cunningham was trying to say. But what did this have to do with me?

"I want you to take these home," she said, pointing to the papers. "Have your parents read them and sign on the last page.

"I've talked with your teacher. Mrs. Wheeler says you're one of the best students in her class and she thinks you should go to Ranson Junior High next year. I think you and your parents should be very proud."

Now I realized something *was* wrong. It was more serious than having to stay after school for running down the halls or, worse, getting a paddling for picking a fight or playing hooky. It was bigger than any of that. Mrs. Cunningham was redirecting my life, suggesting I go to a WHITE junior high school. I had been looking forward to going to Northwest Junior High, where some of my friends were already in the seventh grade. They walked to school together each morning, talking about sock hops and football games and à la carte lunches. I wanted to be with my friends. This was no honor, as Mrs. Cunningham seemed to be implying. It was a disaster.

"Who else is going?" I asked.

"Well, there are a number of students from your sixth-grade class that we are recommending. Maybe five or six of you. But you shouldn't be concerned with that. I am absolutely convinced that you can hold your own at Ranson. This is very important and you should feel confident that you can do your best even if white children are in the same classroom. You know, Samuel, that is going to be what will happen in the future anyway and you are just as well prepared for that day as you will be in the future."

I realized suddenly that I was being viewed differently from my friends and classmates: I could "hold my own." In a sense, Mrs. Cunningham was making it clear that my life was no longer entirely my own. She was conscripting me on behalf of all colored people. With her perfect diction and precise words, she made a lucid argument: "You are not your own little boy anymore. You belong to us."

I applied to Ranson, but the school board rejected my request. The one-paragraph letter offered no explanation, except to say that the school had filled its allotment of spaces for black students by the time my application arrived.

Momma was furious at the high-handed way the decision was made, but I shrugged it off. The delay gave me time to collect myself for some future onslaught of white students. There was no rush, I figured, because I was one of the chosen ones and would remain so. I had done as Mrs. Cunningham and Mrs. Wheeler requested by applying to Ranson. I could now get ready for the seventh grade at all-black Northwest Junior High, armed with the knowledge that I would be ready for the job the moment I was needed.

Mrs. Cunningham had set my life on a new mission, one I accepted because she made me feel special, needed and chosen. I could not refuse. I could not fail. So much would depend on my success. A baton had been passed and my role would be to hurdle what few overt racial barriers remained. I, among the favored in Charlotte's black middle class, began at that point to anticipate my future, my emerging self-awareness the end result of a process that had begun several years earlier. I felt like a woolly caterpillar about to burst from its cocoon as a beautiful winged butterfly.

About the time I was entering Oaklawn, middle-class black folks around my Westside neighborhood were anticipating all the potential riches of racial integration because a thirty-two-year-old dark-skinned civil rights attorney named Julius Chambers had sued to integrate the Charlotte-Mecklenburg school system. I, of course, was happily unaware of any impending changes.

Chambers was suing on behalf of Vera and Darius Swann, who had returned to Charlotte in 1964 after spending more than a decade abroad, most of it as Presbyterian missionaries in India. Because of their years living in multiracial communities, the Swanns considered American-style white supremacy "a distant and nearly inexplicable aberration." Convinced that integration had the power to redeem white people, they had decided long before they returned to Charlotte to buck segregation practices that interfered with their desires. That opportunity arose when they tried to enroll their six-year-old son, James, in a supposedly integrated elementary school that happened to be the one closest to their home in the Biddleville community. But James came home from his first day of school with a polite, apologetic, but firm note from the principal. James could not attend classes there and was ordered to report the next day to rickety old Biddleville Elementary.

In response to the suit Chambers filed on behalf of the Swanns, the Charlotte-Mecklenburg public school system accelerated the pace of voluntary desegregation by crafting a "freedom of choice" proposal that made it easier for parents to send their children to schools where they would be in a racial minority. To do this, however, the school system would need buses to move students from one racially isolated neighborhood to another.

The mere filing of the Swann suit changed the atmosphere in my community, convincing all the people who surrounded me that racially integrated schools were now closer than a mere speck on the horizon. The long-delayed promise of racial equality was coming. And the Negro Community Guardians began to look for promising black students to march headfirst into a white world. I was one of those students.

I was now fully aware that race was a factor in my life and I wanted to prevail in my unique role as a Negro ambassador. That meant making choices to ensure I excelled in school. I signed up for the advanced credit courses at Northwest Junior High, where I entered the seventh grade in late summer 1968. By the midterm of my eighth-grade year, I was well known to my classmates as a pretentious, overachieving student, fond of aggressive class participation. I belonged to the Junior Honor Society, Student Council, Glee Club, and was a trainer for the seventh-grade basketball team.

I wanted to be equipped to "hold my own." I would do even better than that: I would succeed with grace and skill. I wanted to do my people proud.

I remembered Momma and Daddy and other old folks talking about the way they would proudly gather around the radio to listen as Joe Louis, the heavyweight "champeen" of the world, "whupped" one after another Great White Hope. I, too, would knock out all comers, like the Brown Bomber, with a nod, smile and gracious word. "I glad I win," Louis said after every victory. I could not wait to say it too: "I glad I win." Only, I would use proper English.

At Northwest Junior High, Clarence "Pop" Moreland, the stern and formal principal, had a profound and enduring impact on me. Pop was an old-fashioned black educator. He had taught in tumbledown one-room clapboard schoolhouses, where sinewy boys chopped firewood for the potbellied stove and Vaseline-groomed girls brought pop bottles for him to refund, with the money set aside for classroom needs. That's how Moreland got his nickname, an endearing one that reflected both his paternal concern and his skinflint practicality. Pop was greatly respected at Northwest by students and teachers alike, partly because nothing seemed to rattle him and partly because of his strict belief in rules about our behavior.

He had the habit of summoning us to unscheduled schoolwide assemblies, which he called "fireside chats," patterned after FDR's old radio broadcasts. Here, Pop pontificated on the state of the world and race relations, exhorting us as black students to study twice as hard because we could expect only half as many rewards in life as even more poorly prepared white kids. I hated the assemblies because Pop demanded rapt attention, calling out the names of any students he spotted napping or nodding or chewing gum. His rambling orations continued for an hour or more, and it took more fortitude than I could muster to remain alert in that stuffy auditorium.

Yet some of what he said has stayed with me through the years— little things that are even more relevant now than when he was on the auditorium stage. I remember, for example, one lecture that began with a detailed anecdote about his visiting an S&W Cafeteria in uptown

Charlotte. He talked about how he had stood in line, tray in hand, and ordered his meal. He said he was so proud to pay for it with money he had earned from teaching. But the proudest part, he said, "was the fact that none of the white people left because I walked in." That was proof of changing times and we needed to be ready for more changing times, said Pop Moreland.

During my two years at Northwest Junior High, civil rights lawyers were locked in their protracted fight with the Charlotte-Mecklenburg school board. Negotiations to compel the schools to desegregate with "all deliberate speed" bogged down in legal maneuvering and confrontation. While the courts wrestled with the legality of the existing "freedom of choice" plan, the lawyers and board members agreed to an interim step. For the 1969–70 school term, some of the system's teachers would be reassigned by race. Practically speaking, this meant that Northwest would receive an influx of white teachers for my eighth-grade term and that some of the black teachers (we suspected the better ones) would be shipped off to teach in all-white schools.

Like most of my classmates, I had had limited exposure to white people and had never taken instructions from a white teacher. For all of our apprehension, which was high, the white teachers "bused" into our soon-to-be integrated school were far more concerned about us than we were about them. They were soft-spoken and stiff in their teaching style, a radical departure from the hands-on, caring approach to which I had grown accustomed.

For all the tension during that year, I can remember only one really disturbing moment. On the day we received midterm grades, my algebra teacher, an excitable young white woman fresh from practice classes and with obviously limited exposure to black students, received stone-faced stares from much of the class after she distributed the report cards. She had failed half the class, based on their work through the first six weeks. I had my usual A, but for many of my classmates, it was the first time they had ever seen an F on their report cards.

She explained that the grade was meant as a warning, not a permanent record of achievement. But the "flunked" students demanded she change their grades. She declined.

Someone in the rear of the class cursed her. Another student, also seated somewhere in the back, shouted "Look out!" just as an ignited firecracker sailed toward the teacher's desk at the front of the room. There was no explosion, but the missile spouted a gray-blue plume of sulfurous smoke that quickly filled the room.

The teacher, apparently thinking it was a bomb, screeched and rushed into the hall as the students scattered. I ran toward the open windows at the rear of the room to inhale the outside air. Almost immediately, Pop appeared in the doorway with a fire extinguisher. He ordered us to have our parents sign the report cards and bring them to his office for his personal verification. "What makes any of you think you can bully a teacher into giving you a grade you didn't earn?" he said. He was not shouting, but his voice was edged with rage.

This was a power play and show of support for the now terrified teacher. But it did little to mollify her. Not very long after, she "retired" from Northwest.

I wasn't happy when, just as I was preparing to enter the ninth grade, court-ordered busing went into effect in Charlotte. All summer, the school board had met, proposing elaborate plans for busing students across town to different schools. I was assigned to McClintock Junior High. I knew this was a big, big deal for everyone, black and white students alike. But now, more than ever, I wanted things to remain as they had always been. I wanted to remain at Northwest. I still wanted it to be an all-black school. I was afraid of integration because I didn't know how much it would change everything. But there was nothing I could do about it. Change had come and I had been prepped to be ready for this moment and I was ready—reluctant but ready.

On September 9, 1970, I rode a bus for the first time twenty miles across Charlotte to attend classes at McClintock Junior High in a neighborhood much like my own, except it was white. This would be my first contact with an alien race. No more delays—I had finally been enlisted for classroom warfare against white students. The white students I had been warned about and prepped for assumed Romulan-like stature, fueled by an imagination fed on *Superboy* comic books and *Star Trek* episodes. Everybody said they were fierce and shrewd, that I had to be at the top of my game at all times and on guard for treachery and deception.

When the buses arrived at McClintock, carrying the kids from Mc-Crorey Heights and another middle-class enclave adjacent to my neighborhood, I was shocked to find a group of students with hostile *black* faces. They had loud voices and aggressive manners. None of them carried notebooks or little book bags. A couple of the boys dribbled a basketball. One boy sucked on a Kool cigarette and slowly puffed out a series of perfect smoke rings. And surely, the girl wearing a silk bandanna that only partially covered pink sponge rollers cared little about fitting in or belonging at McClintock. And what of the girl who was talking to her loudly and intrusively? I caught only the drift of her conversation, but even that was too much, something about what her momma had said to her daddy. I forced myself not to look or listen after I heard her say "Motherfuck this . . ." and saw her hand close into a fist that swung toward her friend's jaw.

Klingons! I was expecting Romulans. But here was another group altogether I had not thought about or prepared for. Klingons!

Somebody had made a mistake, I thought. Surely these black students were not the best academic fighters available, let alone concerned about being the best they could be in the presence of whites. Obviously not, but why not? Had no one—their parents, Sunday school teachers, anyone—told them about the need to excel, to do their best? Didn't they have a Mrs. Wheeler, a Mrs. Cunningham or a Pop Moreland who picked them for this assignment and drilled them into a crack army of best black warriors?

The white kids comported themselves more like us, the McCrorey Heights/Oaklawn Park bunch, Westside Charlotte bourgeois blacks. By comparison, they seemed far less threatening and much less remarkable than I had imagined. I adjusted to this shock by limiting my dealings with the loud black kids, whom I later learned lived in inner-city housing projects.

Every day, Mr. Leete, our white principal at McClintock, called over the intercom for "inner-city students" to board their buses, meaning that the buses for all of us black students were ready to depart. I never noticed any hidden meaning in his words. But Billy Lindsay, a small outspoken kid who sat next to me in homeroom and rode the same bus that I did, bristled at Mr. Leete's announcement. After a month or so, he couldn't contain himself any longer. As our bright yellow school bus made its return voyage to our homes, bounding over the enormous social gaps between our middle-class black enclave and the school on the other side of town, he turned to me and said, "It ain't right the way he refers to us."

"What are you talking about, Billy?" I asked.

"I don't like the way Mr. Leete refers to the black kids as 'inner-city students,' like we all come from the same ghetto," he said. "I had half a mind to march into his office and tell him we don't all live in the inner city. We're the only ones riding the buses. Why does he have to call us inner-city? It's because we're black and he doesn't want to say that. I'm going to complain and make him stop. We aren't like those *ignorant niggers.*"

But the principal's slight had never meant anything to me. Far more significant was the actual source of intrablack student friction: those black proletarian rebels who delighted in disruptive confrontations. They were not happy to be at the school and wanted all—teachers, classmates, anyone within earshot—to know it. I hated them for being so rude and obnoxious, imposing their disinterest in school and hostility toward the system on everyone else.

To be honest, I hated them for another reason. Even when they were not around, their presence stalked me. We had little in common. But our shared accident of birth—being born black in America—compelled a comparison. By merely being a dark disruption, they drew attention to themselves and, indirectly, to me. All anyone saw was blackness. And it was confusing to some whites, like the classmates who would invariably declare me different for reasons they could not comprehend. "You're not like other black people," one of them would blurt out, expecting me to explain the contradictions.

Those words, spoken in honest, observant candor, stung as if someone had singed my cheeks with a white-hot poker. In time, I would hear these words or some variant over and over, never finding the right response and perpetually feeling the heat. Every time, I would feel the pain of being judged by the least of my race, never the best. Someone who misbehaved was the standard for black people, and my demeanor, which was not similar to theirs, was a deformity that had to be explained away and I never had the words to do so.

"No," I said to my earnest white classmate, "I am not like *all* black people." Other words did not come, words to shout down my embarrassment at the loud blacks for heaping their ignorance of shame upon me, words to drown out the chagrin caused by intrusive whites who forced me to feel a compulsion to distance myself from "other black people," words to decipher just who I was and who were the ones with the rude behavior. I just did not know what to say, so I said as little as possible, changing the subject or dumbly excusing myself to go off alone in confusion and frustration.

That was the problem with the white students. They drew attention to the obvious, to something that anyone with half a brain could figure out on his own.

Eddie Nanney was an exception. He was one of the first white kids I met, since he sat next to me in homeroom. About a head taller than I, Eddie had the bearing of Jack Armstrong, the All-American Boy. He had attended McClintock for all of his junior high years and was popular with both the white students and teachers; he was an A student and a member of the football and basketball teams.

I liked Eddie because he asked the right questions and had enough poise to see complexity and absurdity in our shared dilemma. He was also willing to make the experiment succeed. I saw myself in him and decided he was a worthy and honorable adversary, the kind of person I had expected to find at a white school.

During the school year, Eddie and I made a point of debating whether Archie Bunker's comments on *All in the Family* were so offensive as to warrant banning the show from the airwaves.

"But that is what you people think of us blacks," I once said during homeroom. "Archie called the black person a jungle bunny because that's the way he thinks. I think people ought to see that because it's reality."

"But you would be offended if I called you that," Eddie shot back. He had come armed with ammunition for this debate, a newspaper clipping reporting that NAACP officials were demanding the show be withdrawn because it contained racist depictions harking back to *Amos 'n' Andy*, which the civil rights organization had successfully rallied against a generation earlier. "So why should *All in the Family* be on television if it is likely to upset people and if *Amos 'n' Andy* can't be shown?" he asked.

But getting along with Eddie cost me the friendship with some black classmates, who demanded, "Are you with us or are you an Uncle Tom?" Always that choice, never another option or anyone to turn to for advice. Which rules should I follow?

I wanted to fit in. I wanted other blacks to want to fit in as well. This was the burden of being a trailblazer. So once again I made a choice: I gathered an isolationist's courage and took a front seat in each of my classes. I would cast my lot with the high achievers, the whites and the few blacks who had registered for advanced credit courses in language arts and history. I would go it alone, if necessary. It would be worth the scorn and ridicule of the ignorant and uncaring masses. Successful completion of these courses, much like the honors curriculum in college, boosted your academic record. My being in these classes guaranteed that I would have a higher grade point average (status in the white-world rankings) than most of my black peers.

Most black students were tracked into vocational classes, with a heavy emphasis on developing skills in auto mechanics and metalworking, cooking and sewing. Those courses offered no "bonus" points redeemable on a college entrance application. After all, who really cared about academic standing at the corner filling station?

I knew better things were in my future. I did not consider myself to be "acting white" by excelling in my carefully selected courses. At most, it was coincidence, based on my exercise of free will, that directed me along the same path as upwardly mobile white students. Advanced credit classes assured me of competing with the best (black or white) students and would better my chances for future success.

There was the persistent, nagging downside to black peer ostracism. But I accepted stoically the abuse and ridicule that went with my choice: "You acting white." "Uncle Tom." "Fool. It don't matter, 'cause you ain't one of them." I was convinced of a future payoff, and besides, others were effusive in their praise. "If all my students were like you, how great it would be," one white teacher wrote in a note for me to show to my parents. "Sam has been a valuable addition to our class," another noted on a report card.

Praise from white people linked me to white peers. In this case, being a black student in an alien white school demanded adherence to a well-understood code: If the whiteys like it, then something is wrong with it. I knew I was breaking this rule, venturing off on my own. If this was the price of admission to a color-blind future, I reasoned, I would pay it.

My brother, George, took the opposite route. He felt the same yearnings. But the pressure of being the younger brother weighed heavily upon him. He rebelled.

Quietly and passively, at first, he tried to ignore the critical remarks from teachers and later his peers: "You're not like your brother." "No," he responded, "I am not. I am me." And then he set out to demonstrate just how different he could be. He cast his lot with the carefree dudes. When Sam studied, George played. Sam was so serious about life; George was happy-go-lucky. Sam was the introspective bookworm; George was the class clown and athlete.

As toddlers and younger children, we were "the Fulwood Boys," as one neighbor tagged us. George and I were inseparable, appearing identical in dress and manner. So this remarkable change was something neither of us understood. Yet both of us felt something like the pain of an invisible wedge slipping between us, splitting one brother from the other in ways we could only vaguely sense. Of course, we never talked about any of this, because conversation would have implied comprehension. Therefore, neither of us said what he felt, beyond the bickering common among all siblings.

On one occasion I asked George, apropos of nothing, if he gave any thought to the direction our lives would take as adults. It was the sort of issue that I silently pondered ad nauseam and that, as far as I could tell, George ignored as foolish.

"The future will take care of itself," he said. George's point stuck with me. His assessment was certainly accurate. The future comes regardless of whether we like it or not, whether we prepare for it or not. And that was fine with George.

"I don't live in the future like you," he said. "I live in the now."

But it wasn't good enough for me. It was clear to me, from then onward, that George and I would go in different directions. This realization pained me because we came from the same place. To my mind, we should go into the future together, with the same zeal for accomplishment. I imagined, but dared not say out loud, that the Fulwood Boys would rise in the world together.

But George was not dreaming my dreams. His life was defined by peer approval. By selecting this route, he was freed from the hovering shadow of an always striving older brother. Liberated, he could redefine himself on his own. While George was just as mindful of our parents' expectations of good grades and praise from teachers, his desire to satisfy them was subordinated to living the good life and avoiding any undue stress. Indifference to pressure for overachievement at school, plus acting out at home, served his purpose.

George's attitude, more than anything, annoyed me because I was convinced I was pursuing the correct route and he was not. I studied hard, obeyed the rules and lived within the expectations of parents, teachers and any authority figure who crossed my path. Meanwhile,

George's minor troublemaking—by junior high school, his grades slipped as he began to skip classes and run with a more mischievous crowd than I had ever dared cultivate—gave him no apparent worries.

I was troubled further because I wanted, on my own intellectual terms, what it seemed he achieved with minimal effort: popularity. The ringing telephone always seemed to be for him, with a call from a new girlfriend or an invitation to a party; it was always something social. He played halfback on the football team, point guard on the basketball team and saxophone in the concert band. His life seemed so free, secure and amusing. And I envied George.

George did fulfill the expectations of my parents. He finished Johnson C. Smith University, stayed close to home and today lives a conventional life. Along the way, he had loads of reckless fun.

I had never heard of an oratorical contest until the late winter of 1971, when each of us in Mrs. Viracola's speech and drama class was assigned to write and deliver a public lecture. I got an A for my efforts, prompting Mrs. V to register my name in the East Mecklenburg Optimist Club Oratorical Contest. "Give it a try," she suggested. "You may surprise yourself and succeed."

On a brisk March night, I escorted my parents to the contest site, a banquet room at Swain's Charcoal Steak House, located directly across from where the former Clark's Department Store had stood and, less than a decade earlier, George and I had been rebuffed in our attempts to ride donkeys. There were four other boys, accompanied by their proud parents. But other than the unseen cooks in the kitchen, my family comprised the only blacks inside the building.

I was neither hopeful nor frightened by this occasion. I had rehearsed my speech over and over in Mrs. V's class to the point where I could be roused from a deep sleep and recite it. In fact, the hard part had been writing the speech because the topic ("This I Believe") was so broad and I really did not know what I believed. But there I was now, sitting with Momma, Daddy and Mrs. V, everybody all dressed up and smiling, waiting for me to step to the lectern for a four-and-half-minute spiel on citizenship. I would speak third. I felt relieved when I heard each of the two boys who preceded me pause in midsentence to try to recollect a forgotten phrase.

When my name was announced, I wiped my moist hands on a white linen napkin and walked solemnly to the lectern. I imagined myself standing behind my father's pulpit as I began. Speaking in even tones that rose and dipped in the dramatic moments, I explained why society should respect young people, who have a lot to contribute to creating our nation's future—"For this I believe."

It was done. Two more speakers, and the judges retired to a private room for about fifteen minutes. When they returned, they announced the runners-up first. Then, with a wave of the first-place trophy in my direction, the club president declared, "The 1971 winner of the East Mecklenburg Optimist Club Oratorical Contest is Sam Fulwood."

I smiled a smile that was half as bright as those twin dazzlers on Momma's and Daddy's faces. On that night, I realized something more important than winning the contest, more important than beating four white kids. I had been present the first time my parents ever witnessed *in person* a black man, woman or child compete head-to-head with white folks and win! Even better, it was their own son. I had made them prouder to be black and American than at any time in their lives. I never forgot their sense of elation and sought to re-create it time and time again.

Three weeks later, I won the next round in the contest, beating four more white boys. But at the next level, the district competition in Gastonia, my oratorical victories ended. I finished fifth in a field of four white boys and myself. My sponsor, an insurance salesman, was livid over the outcome. He kept mumbling to me and my parents about "those rednecks in Gastonia." But as far as I was concerned, my winning two rounds defied the odds. I had beaten all of the white boys in two out of three falls. I had distinguished myself, my parents and black people by drawing positive attention to my ability to hold my own. Indeed, a few weeks before the district competition, Mrs. V called a reporter at the *Charlotte News* and convinced her to do a "human interest story."

A few days later, a memorial of my accomplishment was stretched across the bottom of the local news section's front page, together with a photograph of me, head jerked cockily at an angle, grinning from ear to ear.

I was not prepared for what happened the next day at school: the daily announcements mentioned the article. Mrs. Scott, my homeroom and French teacher, posted a copy on the wall. Other teachers smiled at me as I floated down the halls. A group of admiring classmates, put up to it by Reid Outen, a blond boy who took several classes with me, started cheering when I entered class. I felt uneasy at this acceptance from white students. I was unsettled because some black students, seeing the reaction of the whites, silently bored holes into the back of my skull with their hot and angry stares.

Chapter Three

GO ALONG TO GET ALONG

The day in early March 1973 began as so many others preceding it had—with a ride on a city-chartered bus to my junior-year classes at Garinger High School. As I left home that morning, the air blew unseasonably warm, even for the twilight of winter in the South. I was grateful for the coming of spring because it meant not having to bundle up in a thick overcoat. After three years of taking these daily bus rides, I was accustomed to the routine. Still, I hated being crammed into that musty bus. Wearing a heavy jacket or raincoat only made it more uncomfortable. It would be another year before Daddy would buy himself another car and give me the Deuce and a Quarter. Until then, I was trapped inside this metal tube.

"It's not going to rain," I said to one of my classmates who was already seated when I climbed aboard. "Why are you carrying that umbrella?"

"I might need it to protect me from more than the rain," he said.

"If some redneck cracker wants to start some shit, I'm not going to be empty-handed."

"That's crazy," I said. "You don't need that kind of protection. Just stay out of the way of trouble. Anyway, an umbrella ain't much of a weapon."

"Beats nothing," he replied.

I dreaded going to school that day. Tension, thick layers of racial antagonism, filled the air around us. I tried to ignore it, but could not. It was too strong, like the smell of cigar smoke trapped in stale air. I could almost taste it.

I got along well enough with my classmates, both black and white, by limiting my dealings with them. But I often felt exposed and uncomfortable. In large gatherings, where we were forced to integrate, I became diffident. Most of the time, I kept my own company, mingling in larger social situations only when necessary.

But on this dull, gray morning, the situation seemed ready to spin out of control. On the previous Friday, black and white students had hurled rocks and stones at one another on the West Mecklenburg High campus, located in a predominantly white and working-class part of the county. Police in riot gear were called to the school and classes were canceled. Local television news spent the weekend replaying footage of students running around and gesturing toward the cameras, and of school officials and community leaders speculating on whether violence would spread to other schools.

On Monday, it did. Classes at South Mecklenburg High, a suburban school in the wealthiest and whitest part of the county, were canceled after black and white students rumbled on the school grounds. Again, news reporters and police rushed to the scene. When the police warned that they might not be able to control the crowds if classes were held the next day, school officials shuttered the schools. That prompted one conservative and antidesegregation board member to condemn, in the papers and on television, the school board and its superintendent for their "permissive attitude," which had led to the disturbance. He suggested that black students were being coddled, and strongly implied that some of them should be expelled from the local high schools in order to restore order. Many black students decried his comments as racist. But such attitudes were gaining currency among white parents, and perhaps among their children.

This media speculation and black student anger made me want to spend all of Tuesday in bed with the covers pulled over my head, blocking out the world. If there had been any way to stay away from school, I would have found it. But Daddy was adamant. "If they're having school, then you're going," he said. While my parents expected us to attend classes, they provided no strategies for navigating the minefield that the city's public schools had become. They simply admonished George, who attended junior high school at a different campus, and me to just stay away from "bad people." To my parents, anyone (black or white) who seemed likely to cause trouble was *bad*, and I heeded their warnings by steering clear of them. I believed it was only a matter of time before the school violence, which seemed to skip like a hurricane from one Charlotte high school to another, slammed into Garinger. I did not know when, but I did not want to be anywhere in the vicinity on that day.

I had dodged all the usual schoolyard fights by going in the opposite direction whenever they occurred, or seemed about to occur, and these violence-avoiding (as opposed to nonviolent) moves served me well. But racial fights were different, requiring new stratagems to avoid bricks or punches carelessly thrown in the direction of people with opposing skin colors. So far, I felt lucky to have escaped with only fear and no bruises.

There had been racial dustups at most of the public schools every year since the start of court-ordered desegregation. Even at McClintock, there was a minor walkout by some of the black students to protest what was going on at the nearby high schools. But these full-scale fights, with guns and knives and bicycle chains, were something new, something out of *West Side Story*. I would do anything possible to circumnavigate them.

Racial tension at Garinger finally climaxed at a student assembly in the gym. An integrated rock-and-roll group called The Spurrlows was making the rounds of the city's high schools to sing of peace and brotherhood. Just after their concert ended with one of the band members urging people to love one another, knots of black and white students attacked each other at the gym exit. Within minutes, the television helicopters thumped the skies and helmeted cops stormed the campus.

Almost as quickly as the fights began, they ended. Sixteen students were injured in random fights, with seven suffering minor wounds taken to a nearby hospital. Two teachers were slightly roughed up. One student's car was flipped over and windshields were broken on several others parked in the student parking lot.

It was widely assumed by Garinger students that "outside agitators" from South Mecklenburg had come over to our campus to start trouble. Our principal, Dr. Jack Stern, was flabbergasted. "Conduct was excellent in assembly," he told reporters, "and then all hell broke loose."

I saw none of this. As soon as the concert ended, I went directly to my third-period French class. When I took my seat, Mrs. Sims seemed shocked to see me with books in hand. I was offended when she praised the class for showing up. "You all are wonderful students," she said. I swear Mrs. Sims was looking dead into my eyes, the eyes of the only black student in the room.

What the hell did she expect? Didn't she understand that I was in school to learn enough so I could get away from what was happening outside? Couldn't she see that foolish violence was the *last* thing I'd be interested in? I understood that she meant well, but I did not feel like a wonderful student. I felt cheated. Mini race wars were not part of my carefully scripted high school agenda. I wanted to get past high school to the productive part of life, where racial tension and antagonism would be forgotten. I did not want to get hurt in a schoolyard fight. More, I did not want anything on my record that crippled my chances of getting into college.

Almost from the first day of high school, my clique of Westside Charlotte friends focused on which colleges we would attend after high school. Any thought of not completing our education at a four-year college was as remote as dropping out of high school before graduation. To get into one of the better colleges, I figured I needed impressive grades and extensive participation in the right school activities.

Not once did I give even a passing thought to the idea of receiving affirmative action bonus points for being a black student, nor do I remember any teacher or classmate suggesting it. I considered the odds of my succeeding or failing in high school—and, later, in college and beyond—as tied to whether I excelled against the best and the brightest of my peers.

The fighting ruined all that.

High school became a tough proving ground where mastery of the system had little to do with the classroom and everything to do with behaving well and holding on to my racial identity. Everyone had a place and anyone daring to step outside the boundaries suffered penalties imposed by their classmates.

"Why are you hanging with all those faggot white people?" George asked me one evening after I arrived home from a rehearsal for the school play. He had noticed that I'd been driven home by a white student who was in drama club with me. "Don't you know what people say about you behind your back? Don't you care?"

"No," I said. "I don't care what people say about me and you shouldn't either."

"I just thought you didn't know what was being said," George said. "Forget I mentioned it. If it doesn't bother you, it certainly doesn't bother me."

But that was a lie. Fitting in concerned both of us. For George, it must have been embarrassing to overhear a snide comment about his brother being on the high school stage, "flitting" around, the only black up there.

I suspect George wanted to warn me and protect his own honor. I overheard those comments as well and pretended they did not matter. I would not change my plans to suit the conventions of peer pressure.

The Georgetown Players, as we called the drama club, was a haven for extroverted students, mostly juniors and seniors and, true, mostly white. I joined their troupe as a sophomore, and we got along much like a large family. I remember no exposed nerves or overt hostilities in our daily rehearsals and frequent travels to state drama festivals and competitions. This was a wonderful ensemble of students, who were also my friends.

With delusions of becoming the next Sidney Poitier, who portrayed dignified, self-sacrificing Negroes in the integrationist films of my childhood, I read for and received parts in most of the Garingertown Players' productions my sophomore year. In addition to the drama club, I looked for other groups to join that would impress college admissions officers. Next came *The Rambler*, the school newspaper, which I signed up for late in my sophomore year, worked on in my junior year and coedited in my senior year.

And, of course, there was student government, where all super-ambitious high school students learn the art of satisfying establishment standards of rectitude while remaining popular enough to garner the votes of their peers. I was elected twice to our Student Council, serving terms during my junior and senior years.

But even student politics did not escape the intrusion of racial engineering. When the school board ordered busing for desegregation, they did so according to a numerical formula that reflected Charlotte's 30 percent black population. They set the target enrollment for each of the city's ten public high schools at a 70–30 ratio of white–black students. This, of course, created a permanent minority of black students at every school, one that had no chance of electing black student leaders if the voting went along racial lines.

A committee of student leaders anticipated this problem and consulted with the school board. The deal they struck (and lobbied through the board) allowed each student body to be governed by a popularly elected nine-member executive committee. This committee would supplant traditional school officers.

To ensure racial equality, six seats would be filled by the three whites and the three blacks who received the most votes. The three other seats would go to whoever among the remaining candidates received the highest number of votes, without regard to race. The executive committee would then vote among themselves to select class officers.

Larry Alston and I were best friends throughout high school. We had known each other for so long we thought of ourselves as brothers. Larry had grown up with his grandparents and his mother in a house located not more than a block from Johnson C. Smith University. Larry's grandfather, who had died by the time he was in high school, was well known around the Smith campus as a handyman, quick with a hammer and knowledgeable about carpentry. He and many of the ministers on campus, including my father, would volunteer their time to renovate student housing or the homes of poor black folks in the city.

By the time we reached high school, Larry, a caramel-skinned fellow with a rounded, well-groomed Afro, and I were inseparable. We participated in many of the same school functions, especially student government. Larry was elected vice president of the student executive committee, and was also voted the best-looking guy in the senior class.

During the summer preceding our senior year, Larry and I spent a week camping at Lake Lure in the central part of North Carolina as part of a new human relations group called (in 1970s fashion) Project Aries, after the astrological sign of its founder, Rufus Washington. A black high school senior at Independence High, Washington had become so concerned about the tensions and fights in the public schools that he came up with an idea: train teams of students in each high school to be role models for the junior high students coming along the next year. Washington's idea found favor with a pair of white benefactors: Kitty Huffman, president of the Charlotte chapter of the National Conference of Christians and Jews, and Roy Alexander, head of the Charlotte-Mecklenburg County 4-H extension office. As a first step, the high school students were sent to a weeklong camp with the expectation that they would unite into an interracial group capable of working together. For Larry and me, this was the first time either of us had bunked away from home for so long and the first time we had lived surrounded by white people.

"I viewed that camping trip as a tremendous learning experience," Larry said years later. "But I learned more than I expected because not only did I get to meet some people who were different from ourselves, I got an opportunity to see how they were not so different. The people in Project Aries were a lot more openminded than the general school population. I think I grew and benefited from learning that more than anything else." Project Aries had another unexpected by-product—it brought Larry and me closer together.

Despite my participation in school-related activities—or perhaps, as I actually feared, because of them—I never considered myself a part of the black student in-crowd. I couldn't escape the social stigma of being a nerdy guy in glasses who made good grades and had a perfect attendance record. But I would not change my ways to be popular. Having Larry as a best friend made high school a lot more bearable. Not only did he share my ambitions for college, but he seemed thoroughly nonjudgmental in our relationship. He was also the more socially outgoing and engaging of the two of us. And this made us a mutually dependent team: while Larry received frequent invitations to parties, I had my own set of keys to Daddy's car.

If other black students chose other paths, that was their decision and their fates would reflect their choices. Yet it seemed they had so much more fun than I did. The shortest route to peer approval and popularity among the black students involved two attributes I never copped: a cool nickname and a girlfriend.

In our social constellation, there were the guys who appeared in my mind's eye as comets with an entourage of lesser lights and wannabes trailing behind them. These boys immediately got to play on the main basketball court or cruised around town in red Camaros with their AFBs—"always fine bitches," in the slang of the day. They answered to tough-guy names like Zeke, Red, Ice, Slick, Cool-T, Da Mack, Rip,

Sweet Pea (or just plain Sweets, for short), Head, Pluck. Some others simply responded to initials: JT, BP, QT.

I never had a chance with the best-looking and most desirable girls in competition with these guys—bad boys all, with their weird names, pimping gaits, stiff attitudes and mile-high hair. Guys like me had to settle for the remainders, typically found at church dances and Jack and Jill meetings. For reasons having mainly to do with personal terror and a few date-from-hell experiences, I seldom dated during high school. At those infrequent times when I screwed up the courage to ask someone special to a movie or a concert, some unspeakable tragedy would ruin my date. These cosmic accidents usually struck within hours of our appointed rendezvous, forcing me to change my plans or go out alone. That was exactly what happened on the night of my junior year prom, the worst social evening of my teenage years and the foundation for years of angst in my relationships with the opposite sex.

My date for the prom was a favored doe-eyed girl from the rural community surrounding Daddy's church. She went to school in another county and would be a mystery to everyone at my high school. I liked that idea, since I didn't have anyone to ask from Garinger and I did want to go to the dance. She and I had talked a lot on the telephone, but this would be our first real date. I secured the prom tickets, made dinner reservations and washed the Deuce and a Quarter.

I arrived at her house decked out in a pastel blue–and–white tuxedo, a long-collared blue shirt with black-tipped ruffles, and a floppy butterfly bow tie—all rented in the Charlottetown Mall from Gingiss Formal Wear, a place favored by pimply-faced boys for the dressy duds they wore on prom nights or at their own shotgun weddings. My date's parents seemed more shocked by the fact that the preacher's boy was stepping up to their dusty woodframe house than I was by the fact that she was not inside it. They offered no explanations, no apologies. Since I was the self-appointed chauffeur for Larry and our dates, I had to endure an embarrassing night of dancing with other people's partners in what was considered the biggest social event of the junior year calendar. Momma later told me I should have known better, since my date

probably could not afford a formal dress and most likely was too embarrassed to admit it. That made sense and I never called her to press
for an explanation or apology.

The best experience of my high school years took place at an off-
campus part-time job. During spring break in my sophomore year, I
wandered with my family into Webster's Men's Wear, a small and
brightly lit shop in Tryon Mall, about a mile from Garinger High.
Offhandedly, I approached the store manager, a chain-smoking white
man named Dave Morse, about the possibility of working there during
the summer.

"I can use someone right now," he said. "Are you available?"

Of course I was, and agreed to start the next day, a Saturday. I had
landed my first job and I was elated . . . until Momma heard about it.

Momma saw a threat in that store, something she could not articulate at the time but something she intuitively felt. "What do you need
to work there for?" She was angry, betrayed that I had not discussed it
with her before accepting the job. "I'm not so sure about this."

"I thought you would be glad I found a job," I said. "I like the idea
of getting out and making money, my own money, to buy things."

"You don't need any money. You have everything you need. You
don't know nothing about that place. It will take away from your
classes. You've got a lifetime to work. Why rush it?"

Years later, Momma explained to me that her objections had been
based on fear. My working at Webster's represented to her a final break
with the insular community Daddy and she had created. She also
feared that the older white men who worked in the store would provide
bad role models for my initiation into their world. "They might have
said something I didn't want you to hear," she said. "I just wasn't
ready to let you go yet."

Daddy intervened on my behalf. He drew Momma into the last
family huddle I remember seeing, and when they emerged, I had her
halfhearted endorsement to work at Webster's. I started the next day

and began to experience a life beyond the protected universe of school and home. It was wonderful and I immediately fell in love with going to work.

Beyond the sliding glass doors and front showcases where mannequins beckoned were wooden gondolas holding neckties, socks, underwear, belts, handkerchiefs and jewelry. On the side walls were stacks of dress shirts; and in the back, the big-ticket items: polyester suits and leather coats. The store's cramped interior was made even tighter by a tableload of sweaters and shirts brought in for a special sale that weekend.

The store always reeked of cola, cigarette smoke and window cleaner, scents that seemed ingrained in the shaggy reddish orange–and–brown carpet that, despite repeated vacuuming, never appeared clean. The soft sounds of easy-listening music played all day from a small radio, all the better to put customers in a tranquil and docile mood for the aggressive salesmen.

At almost sixteen, I was a few months shy of the legal age for a work permit and a North Carolina driver's license. So I had to lie to Dave about my age to get that job. I scribbled sixteen, trying to make it hard to read, on the one-page application form. Since I was reasonably large for my age, with the beginnings of a beard, Dave never asked any questions and hired me. Later in the summer, when I had to sign my W-2 tax forms and other work papers, I was terrified of being fired when confessing my true age.

"That's no big deal," Dave said. "You're doing so well I don't care how old you are. Just don't make a big issue of it." His lack of concern was an affirmation of my work ethic, or at least that's how I opted to view it at the time.

For me, Webster's was a new, different kind of school, where I anxiously learned new lessons in life, beginning with a crash course in sizing up people by how they dressed.

"Nobody dresses for themselves," Dave told me that first day. "I don't care what a customer says, everybody dresses to impress someone other than themselves." This was Salesmanship 101, my introduction to the business world. "A wife, a boss, somebody," he continued. "But not just because they like this suit or that tie. Most people don't know what they like. It's your job to tell them what to like."

I nodded. "Do I tell them to like what I like or what I think they want?"

"That depends," Dave said. "If you think they will like what you like, by all means. But your style may not be the same as someone else's."

At some level, I guess I had always been aware of this, knowing for example that dressing up was important to the black people around me. It was their way of asserting and defining themselves in a world that rarely acknowledged their humanity.

Dave was the first white man I had met who admitted to taking clothes seriously. Dressing up other people, after all, had been his only job for nearly twenty years, starting in Asheville, North Carolina, where he was a clerk in a hometown clothing store. He married early and left college to support his docile wife and young daughter. Dave had spent most of his working life studying how and why people bought clothes. He was a crackerjack salesman, the silent type who put customers at ease and spoke only when necessary—say, to convince a recalcitrant shopper that a rep tie and white shirt were all he needed to make a petroleum-based, fiberless pinstriped blue suit complete.

Was it my imagination? Did Dave wince as he looked over my outfit? Were his eyes now trained on my feet, size $10^1/_2$, shod in scuffed knock-arounds in that Hush Puppy material? From the moment I was hired, I became self-conscious about the way I dressed for the job.

My usual wardrobe consisted mainly of blue jeans, T-shirts and high-top Converse basketball shoes with Chuck Taylor's all-star autograph on the ankles. The suedelike shoes drawing Dave's disdain were my Sunday best. I decided then to make a new pair of working shoes my first purchase with my new earnings. I scanned Webster's to see what kind of shoes my colleagues were wearing. Black wing tips flapped over that dirty carpet.

"Let me put it this way," Dave continued with Salesmanship 101. "Do you like every item in this store?"

This was a trick question. I paused before answering, to consider the possible responses. Should I tell the truth and say "No" and then be required to point out which item—this pair of socks or that belt or that glove-and-scarf set—I absolutely hated, and risk insulting this white store manager, who obviously prided himself on his wares? Or should I simply tell a little fib and say I liked it all?

Dave rescued me from the dilemma. "Of course you don't," he said. "Nobody likes everything in here. But somebody ought to like something. That's where you come in. Your job is to find out what they like and sell it to them."

He smiled and looked me over. There was no mistaking it this time. "Who knows, you might find that you will learn to like something that you didn't care for when you first saw it. Like brussels sprouts or cauliflower. Nobody likes those vegetables the first time. But after you get used to them, you develop an appreciation for them."

Brussels sprouts and cauliflower. God, he really doesn't like my clothes, I thought at the time.

Dave paused for a moment to find a prop. He grabbed a cellophane-wrapped package of grape-colored Jockey briefs with his right hand and a pair of white boxers with his left. "After all, what is more personal than the underwear you put on every day?" he resumed. "If a good salesman presents the options correctly to the customer—'Sir, would you prefer the purple ones or the white ones?'—he can sell more of these." Dave thrust out his left hand as he offered the choice. "It's all in the way you ask the question.

"Remember, the sale is the most important thing. What you like or what I like isn't as important as what the customer likes well enough to buy. Got that?"

"Got it," I said.

What he was saying rubbed a raw nerve. Not once had he criticized me personally, yet his message rang out clearly. Superficially, he was talking about approaching the store's customers. But there was another, subtle—but unmistakable—message in what he was not saying: *Get some new clothes if you are going to work here.* I understood. *Clothes make the man. You should go along to get along.*

I made a mental note to buy myself a pair of those thick-soled wing-tip shoes, the ones with heavy welt stitching and covered by a glossy skin perforated on the toes and along the sides. They were the ugliest things I had ever seen, but I figured they were a workplace necessity, like fake smiles, to be worn daily. To do otherwise risked angering someone more important than myself: the boss or, worse, a paying customer. Working at Webster's, learning how to dress and to negotiate with white people, rounded out the lessons I got in class and from my family.

It was as though I had unlocked a secret that those closest to me, my parents and teachers especially, had kept to themselves. In the workplace, however, everything seemed so clear. Once I understood how to please white people, I had a new set of rules to follow, whether I liked them or not. I could work around the personal, unpleasant feelings. I would buy those wing tips, wear them only at work and put them back in the box each night when I returned home.

The only black salesman at Webster's, I quickly learned that black customers insisted on my service and that white women often requested my advice, assuming I had a natural talent for picking the right color combinations of shirts and ties for their husbands' ubiquitous blue suits. I never failed them—and sometimes would pick the most garish combinations, knowing they would be back to exchange them "for something more conservative." Then, I was happy to show them something much more subdued—and more expensive. I basked with pride every time this ruse, which became known as "Sam's shuffle," worked, earning me a few cents more in weekly commissions.

Commissions were the way we ranked ourselves, and were closely monitored by all in the store. I received an hourly wage, a few cents above minimum, and commissions that amounted to 1 percent on the first $1,500 of weekly sales, then 1.5 percent on all subsequent sales. As a part-timer, I worked about twenty to twenty-five hours a week, rarely pocketing more than $50. The money wasn't important to me; I loved the competition of selling. Working in that clothing store became a personal challenge, a way to prove I could compete, dollar for dollar, with white people. Often I won.

Webster's was a world apart from my neighborhood, home and school. Every day that I entered that store, I was learning more and more about the ways of white folks. This was an education not found in any of the classes I attended or the hundreds of books I read. This was the real world, I concluded.

Chapter Four

CAROLINA BLUE

"I don't understand why you have to go to school two days earlier than you're supposed to," Momma said.

I was packing the remainder of my clothing in a footlocker. The next morning, we would travel to Chapel Hill, North Carolina, where I would enter the state's flagship university. My life would then spin out of Momma's orbit. She knew that I was slipping away, but I had no clue.

I expected that my family relations would continue unchanged, except I would no longer be living at home. Momma is more disturbed about my going away than she should be, I thought at the time. I know now that I was failing to read her anxieties about my no longer being her protected child. I understand now that she wanted only what she imagined was best for me, to keep me safely inside the world she knew.

"Momma, I've explained it all before." I was exasperated at her stubborn refusal to accept what I had told her several times over the last month. "The BSM has invited all the black freshmen to come early for preorientation, before all the other students arrive," I repeated. "That's why."

"What's this BSM? Who's in charge of it?"

"The Black Student Movement is a student organization," I said with a sigh. "A *university-approved* student organization for black students. They're putting on the preorientation."

"Well, why can't the blacks go when everyone else goes? It doesn't make much sense to me. We didn't have any of that foolishness when I went to college. They just told us when to arrive and that was that. Not black this or white that."

"When you went to college, blacks didn't go to Chapel Hill," I said, thinking that might end this unnecessary discussion.

"I don't know about this," she said, finally resigned to my early departure. "It just doesn't seem right to me. But I can't tell you anything, so go on. One day, you'll recognize what I'm trying to tell you. I just hope it's not too late for you by then."

Momma had never been in favor of my attending the University of North Carolina, or of my decision to major in journalism. It was no secret that she preferred Johnson C. Smith University, where I could live at home and walk to classes. It had been good enough for a long line of Fulwoods and Masseys before me, and it was good enough for me. She never said anything about Smith being better for me because it was a black institution, but I figured that had a lot to do with it.

She also feared I was hardheaded, thinking myself way smarter than I should. How else could she explain my refusal to take her advice? "Get your teaching certificate," she said. "You never know when you'll need something to fall back on."

But I had long ago decided against attending Johnson C. Smith, which was too familiar and too close to home. I was opposed to the idea of becoming a preacher or a teacher. A newspaper career was on my mind.

During the summer, I had lucked into a part-time job as a copy boy at the *Charlotte Observer*. I had applied for a summer reporting job right after high school graduation, but was told that all the internships were filled and the paper did not hire high school students as reporters.

But several weeks later, the executive editor, James Batten, called me, saying that my earnestness had so impressed him that he wanted to invite me to work in the newsroom as a copy boy for the last few weeks of the summer. "We can't pay you very much," he said, "but you can get an insider's look at how we put a newspaper together before you go off to Chapel Hill."

I agreed, silently calculating that I could work at Webster's from ten in the morning till about four in the afternoon, then race uptown to the *Observer*, where from 5 P.M. to midnight I would answer phones, fetch coffee for editors and rip stories from the teletype machines.

Momma thought I was nuts. "Lord have mercy. In all my life, I've never seen a boy so eager to be around white men," I heard her say to Daddy.

On August 8, 1974, as I walked into the newsroom, another clerk was carrying in a large coffee urn and a tray of sandwiches. "It's going to be a long night," he said. "They've ordered in sandwiches because no one can leave for dinner."

I ambled over to the editors' conference room, where Batten and his lieutenants were huddled over a mock-up of the next morning's paper. The headline in large type read NIXON RESIGNS.

"Is that tomorrow's headline?" I asked one of the editors.

"Yes, but don't tell anyone until it is printed," he said in a voice suggesting conspiracy.

The world of ink and presses was so unlike anything I had ever known, and its reporters and editors had such power, that I just had to be part of it. I decided then and there I would become a reporter, no matter what it took.

It was precisely that kind of foolishness that worried Momma. She feared I was going off half-cocked. I was being inflexible by not considering alternatives. I was being too easily influenced by other people.

She was even more concerned when she saw me select courses from the university catalog based on what I needed for a journalism degree.

Momma was convinced that a journalism degree would be worthless. She tried to warn me that white people had the luxury of going into risky fields like newspapers but I should play it safe. "You don't know a single black person who has ever worked on a newspaper. What makes you think they will let you?"

"The world is changing," I said. "Things are going to be different and better for me than they were for you or other black people."

"Different, maybe," she countered. "But not better."

Momma had often lectured me on how well-schooled black boys of her generation became school principals and preachers, and till then, I had always believed in her infallible judgment. But it seemed to me that she was failing to recognize how circumstance and fate had placed opportunities in my path that she had never dreamed about. Well, I would seize those opportunities and show her how well I could do. I knew I could not explain any of this to her satisfaction, so I didn't try. A better course was to let my deeds speak for themselves. I would work hard, become successful and make my skeptical momma proud of me.

The Carolina campus first impressed me with its comforting colors. The landscape was mostly greens and blues, just like home. The expansive lawns of perfectly manicured grounds were an even and seamless green. Here and there, huge oaks, spreading hickories and leafy poplars dotted the quad, separated by ribbons of blood-red bricks and veined with ivy. Carolina blue, the school color, recalled the cloudless skies that canopied the campus. This blue was reproduced everywhere, on banners and T-shirts in the streets, on automobile decals and even in the decor of the local McDonald's.

Not only did the campus have the familiar colors of home, but Larry was there too. After attending a recruitment weekend at Chapel Hill as a high school junior, I had persuaded him to apply to Carolina so we could room together. "It will be a continuation of high school," I told him.

He agreed, preferring Carolina to my alternative choice, Morehouse

College in Atlanta. "Too many faggots," he said, refusing to consider the black campus because it was all-male. That was just as well, I thought. Momma wasn't inclined toward Morehouse either: Atlanta was a bigger city than Charlotte, and how she hated big cities!

So it was that I ended up steering the blue Deuce and a Quarter into Chapel Hill in late August 1974. The trunk was loaded with my favorite possessions to help ward off homesickness and fear of the unknown. Like thousands of other freshmen in the class of 1978, I was melding the essential artifacts of my past and present with all my optimism for the future. Larry and I had agreed on the communal property each of us would contribute. The small yellow refrigerator and the stereo were my responsibilities; his were the nine-inch black-and-white television and a prized record collection. Later, I became aware of how simple our tastes were compared to those of other black students, who unpacked their expensive stereo components and color televisions. More than a few hauled in microwave ovens, then relatively new innovations; the father of one girl exhibited Herculean strength wrestling a full-sized refrigerator into her room.

Larry and I had been assigned to Hinton James dorm on the southern tip of the lower campus. Two of the four residential towers, Morrison and Hinton James, were ten stories high and housed a thousand students each; two smaller, six-story dorms, Craige and Erhinghaus, contained six hundred students each. These four redbrick X-shaped dormitories were the first on campus to go coed in the early 1970s.

I knew I was moving into a coed dorm, but decided not to tell my parents until it was too late—just as we crossed the Chapel Hill town limits. I had applied for this dorm because I had been told that it was the unofficial headquarters for black student life. When I arrived on campus, five hundred of Carolina's eleven hundred black students lived in Hinton James, which we affectionately dubbed "The Ghetto." I never heard a white person use that nickname.

Our room was on the sixth floor, not requiring too long an elevator ride, but high enough to afford us a view. In fact, our window faced a panoramic northern sweep over South Campus, giving us the perfect vantage point to track all the comings and goings through the front doors of Hinton James.

Every floor in the dorm had a student lounge and kitchen, located directly across from the elevator bank. Male students lived to the left of the elevators, past a heavy metal door, and female students lived to the right. The door to the women's side, however, was locked promptly at midnight. It struck me as more of a display to appease parents than a real barrier to protect any of our virtues.

Not long after my parents left, a BSM representative who called herself my "Big Sister" showed up to take me and other new arrivals for a walk across campus to dinner. She was a chubby, cheerful junior who promised to help with any problems during my first semester. I wished my parents had stayed to meet her. I knew that if Momma had met a black upperclass student like my Big Sister, she might have felt a little less anxious about leaving me behind. Big Sister said the BSM offered their programs because they felt black freshmen might find Carolina intimidating. In her experience, she said, white students rarely went out of their way to make black students feel comfortable on this overwhelmingly white campus.

Though white students at Carolina outnumbered blacks by 20 to 1, I am stunned that I remember so few names or faces of whites who took classes with me. Black students carved out a community—separate and apart from our white classmates—and I easily settled into our communal routines. We ate together in the dining halls, studied late into the night in our cinder-block dormitories, partied at weekend "sweatbox jams" and cheered the black athletes on the school's football and basketball teams. (Once, in my junior year, Larry and I expressed doubts over whether to root for the Carolina basketball team during a home game against all-black Howard University; we resolved the dilemma by going to the game with a large contingent of black students, who loudly applauded both teams.)

The white students seemed indifferent to us as individuals, and we blacks stuck together because no one else would acknowledge us. Class projects, or occasionally an extracurricular activity, brought about some interracial collaborations, but rarely were such relationships continued out of any sense of genuine affection. These attitudes spilled over into dating patterns. I was not aware of many mixed-race couples, though I knew some black students who had clandestine sexual relationships with whites.

White students at Carolina were a largely transparent backdrop to whatever was going on in our world as black students on campus and, when it suited us, in the town of Chapel Hill. The university was a microcosm of the outside world, a tiny black college within a larger white one. Everybody—black and white alike—seemed to prefer it that way and worked at maintaining racial harmony by avoiding uncomfortable and unfamiliar interactions. It took me a while to adapt to all this, but adapt I did. And I found comfort in it.

By midterm of my first year, I began to imagine that I might flunk out. My terror of failure was heightened by the example of a handful of black students who, after spending a semester engaged in a neverending, loud and profane bid whist tournament in the Student Union, were never seen again. Their fate propelled me to take extra precautions. In most of the huge lecture halls, I made it a point to claim a seat dead center in the front row, where I could hear every word clearly and, more important, be seen by the professor.

I was having no academic problems, yet I sometimes dreamed of missing class for an entire semester. A form of this dream replayed itself in a looping and unwanted reprise, always ending with my bolting upright in bed to chase it away. So I decided to study harder, setting my alarm clock so I would be on time for each day's first class and made sure I would never miss an exam.

I took one additional precaution. I made out a budget for my time. I figured I should spend fourteen hours a week in class, twenty-eight hours studying in the dorm or library, fifty-six (off-chart) hours sleeping, with a balance of seventy hours for anything else that might crop up. No problem, I thought. I tacked the chart over my desk, a reminder of my twin penchants for making order out of chaos and engaging fear with military-like precision and discipline. The chart stayed on the wall for a whole semester. I took it down after hearing a classmate—a bottle blonde who made certain everyone in our freshman English seminar realized she had been valedictorian of her high school class in some small North Carolina town—argue with the graduate teaching assistant over whether Canada was a state. This convinced me, finally, not only that I was *not* the dumbest kid in the class of 1978, but also that the dumbest one was not necessarily black.

In the same way that dogs mark their territories, I looked for opportunities to leave silent markers of my presence on campus. I wanted to create tangible proof that this black boy had been at Carolina. I told no one, especially not Larry, about this plan, but from what he could observe, my behavior must have seemed senseless and totally outside the norm of black life on campus.

One of my early moves was arranging to have my picture taken for publication in *Yackety Yack*, the two-inch-thick yearbook that hardly anyone I knew purchased. For me, it became an annual ritual for providing documentary proof, in black and white, that I was still on track for graduation in the class of 1978. I did this for me, and for anyone real or imagined who would question whether I had been a student at Carolina.

I also applied for a staff reporter's job at *The Daily Tar Heel*, the campus newspaper. I got the job, which was no great feat, since nearly anyone willing to contribute the time could become a reporter at the *DTH*. Black students interested in journalism tended to work for the BSM's publication, *Black Ink*, so I was the lone black on the entire *DTH* staff. But my fears of flunking out prevented me from taking the student paper as seriously as the white kids, who spent far more time working on it. Some forgot about classes or, at least, relegated them to a subordinate role while working around the clock to put out the equivalent of a morning daily.

Although classwork was my priority, I went to work at the *DTH* because it served two purposes—it got me involved in a campus activity and it helped advance my career in journalism. If I was going to be a reporter, I would need experience. I knew that many of the former

DTH staffers now held important jobs in newsrooms across the state—the *Charlotte Observer*'s publisher was a former *DTH* editor, for example—and I figured the credential could only help when I went looking for that all-important first job.

I spent three years on the paper's staff, first as a reporter and later as a staff photographer, but developed no important friendships with other *DTH* staffers. I maintained a cool distance from the white students who were so absorbed by the paper. Ironically, my participation on the *DTH* represented my greatest interaction with white classmates.

As in the outside world, dealing with white folks at Carolina could be an ordeal that sapped your spirit. In my sophomore year, for example, I was assigned to interview residents of the all-female Spencer dorm, some of whom had complained of a foul odor, like rotten eggs, being emitted from a nearby stream. My editor, suspecting that something may have been dumped in the water, sent me off too find out.

"I'm from the *DTH*," I said as I knocked on doors in Spencer. "I'm working on a story about the creek in the arboretum. Have you smelled anything bad from that creek?"

None of the women responded affirmatively and some seemed peeved at my intrusion. I knocked on at least a dozen doors to no avail before returning to the *DTH* offices with an empty notebook.

On my way back, I was stopped by a pair of campus police officers. "Have you been knocking on doors in Spencer?" one of them asked.

"Yes, why?"

"We received several calls from students in there. Would you mind getting in the car?"

I did as instructed.

"Can we see some identification, please?" the officer said. I handed him my student ID card, with the color photograph of me laminated into the lower left corner.

I explained to the campus cops why I had been asking the questions. They remained expressionless as they scribbled on their report forms.

"Do you mind if we call the newspaper?"

"No, if you have to. But I would like to know if I'm being charged with some crime. Why are you detaining me?"

Then the officer who had so far said nothing spoke up. "Did you know your fly was unzipped?"

I looked down. He was right. My anger at being stopped by the campus cops faded into embarrassment at how absentmindedly foolish I had been. And slowly, as I thought more about it, I became angry all over again.

The officer continued, "Do you have any idea how you came off knocking on doors in a girls dorm and asking people if they smelled anything bad?"

I was now furious with myself for being reckless, for not thinking about how dangerous it could be to overlook the details of my presence around white people. I knew they weren't overlooking them—a lesson I hated to learn in so humiliating a fashion.

I continued to work for the school newspaper and even allowed myself to be a candidate for editor in my junior year. While nearly everyone on campus watched *Roots* on television, I knocked on dorm doors asking students to vote for me in the upcoming campus-wide election for *DTH* editor. As was the case with nearly every student-run organization, the *DTH* was a hotbed of political intrigue and games-manship. The editor, through manipulation of daily editorials and choice of targets for us reporters, wielded more influence over student opinion than anyone else on campus.

Whatever it was that convinced me to run escapes me now. I was not well connected politically across the campus. I had virtually no support and no chance of winning, but I campaigned hard and finished second in a three-way race. My campaign garnered enough attention that the Journalism School awarded me a $500 scholarship for my senior year.

The campaign also taught me a lesson about what happens, even in the protected environment of a college campus, to overachieving black students. About the time I started lobbying for votes, I began receiving a series of threatening typewritten notes. They were always slipped under my dorm door and warned me against accepting the position if elected. The notes were signed by "the K.K.K. of U.N.C." I never figured out for sure who sent the notes, but doubted that any of my black friends would consider such a prank funny. I've always suspected the notes came from the only white boy in our suite; he was from rural eastern North Carolina and had boldly tacked a Confederate flag to his wall. All semester, he never spoke to the rest of us, all blacks, who shared the suite with him. I reported the notes to the campus police. As more letters appeared under my door, I considered confronting the boy across the hall. But I didn't, and tossed the letters in the hall trash can.

Nevertheless, the experience frightened me. I felt as though I were being watched, maybe even followed. The police were ineffective, but what could they do? The whole incident made me feel vulnerable and served as an example of how aggressive and resistant some whites could be to a black presence on the UNC campus. It also drove me closer to the other black students, who were not deceived about how scary the white folks could be even if we played their game, and made me want to excel all the more to demonstrate I could make it at Carolina.

Larry and I were more than roommates, we were fast friends. Prowling Franklin Street, we were often accompanied by a skinny guy from Raleigh named Spurgeon Fields. The three of us hung together and rarely noticed the many white faces we passed along our way. This was how the real world operated, whites and blacks sharing the same spaces but living parallel lives that ran on different tracks. I say that even today when white people complain about the so-called "resegregation" of black students on white campuses. Reflecting on my college experience at Carolina, I find such complaints from white students and administrators very hollow. No white student ever expressed any concern over the absence of blacks in their clubs or gatherings. The contemporary complaints more likely reflect the growing tensions between black and white people that extend beyond college campuses and into the open competition for jobs. These tensions are palpable to me when I visit Carolina now, years after my graduation, and hear white students argue about affirmative action taking away their rights and scholarships. I hear frustrated black students say that white students make them feel unwelcome on campus.

For all the time I was a student at Carolina, hardly anyone, least of all any white student I met, seemed concerned enough about race relations to try to build bridges. Nearly all of us had attended racially desegregated high schools. We knew how to coexist without stepping on one another's toes.

Some politically aggressive black students, mostly leaders and activists within the BSM, relished the opportunity to confront white students as they struggled to keep alive the 1960s tradition of campus protests; the BSM, in fact, owed its existence to that protest spirit. In October 1967, Phil Clay, a black student leader who had served as president of the campus's NAACP chapter, founded a student-government-supported program, which he called Carolina Talent Search, to recruit black undergraduate students. In November, other black students grew frustrated by the conservative tilt of the NAACP chapter and wanted more than Carolina Talent Search promised. They founded a new, more aggressive organization—the BSM. Its demands included a full-credit black history course, student government funding of its activities, representation in the Student Legislature and the hiring of more black faculty.

By the early 1970s, some of these concerns were being addressed— but rarely to the full satisfaction of, or with the serious intent demanded by, the black student leaders. By the time I arrived, many BSM leaders felt they were being pacified and that their organization was not wanted on the Carolina campus. Their attitudes, as rigid as their blown-out Afros, made me uneasy. The BSM activists were effective at invoking guilt among white administrators, and sometimes even among black students who declined to follow them.

"They don't care if you're here or not," one BSM leader proclaimed. "The chancellor knows the federal funds will be cut off if there aren't enough niggers getting their precious Carolina degrees. But

don't be fooled by all their smiling faces. They don't want you here.
But we are here anyway."

On occasion, the BSM mustered a rousing protest such as the one,
during my freshman year, that coincided with David Duke's appearance on campus shortly after the Christmas break. The Union Forum,
a student-run speakers panel, had invited Duke, then the national information director for the Knights of the Ku Klux Klan, to deliver a
lecture at Memorial Hall on January 16, 1975. The idea that campus
funds, to which black students contributed, would be used to bring in
an avowed racist so outraged black students that BSM met to plot a
counterattack.

As a card-carrying BSM member, I attended the skull session held
in Upendo Lounge, the BSM activity center. There must have been two
hundred angry black students present, all trying to talk at once, all
willing to march in protest. But where? On the chancellor's office in
South Building, someone suggested. On the Student Union, where the
Union Forum was headquartered, said another. When? Before the
speech or during or after? As the meeting wore on into its second hour,
a consensus took shape. The group would march on Memorial Hall just
before the speech and line the walls on all sides; then, as the Klansman
took the podium, the BSM members would sing and shout to prevent
him from being heard. As this plan evolved, a tiny minority of those
attending (with whom I identified but lacked the courage to support
openly) tried to dissuade the group from disrupting Duke's speech. One
among this group was Mae Isreal, the editor of *Black Ink*, who argued
that even a Klansman had freedom of speech.

But the BSM president, Algernon Marbley, labeled that kind of
thinking foolish. "Coloring this as a free speech episode is a journalistic
invention," he said. "We're protesting the insensitivity of the invitation
and, additionally, the fact that student fees are going to pay a spokes-
man for a group that advocates the systematic killing of blacks."

I was troubled. I would have preferred that my portion of student
fees be spent to bring in people more to my liking than David Duke,

but I rarely attended the Union Forum's lectures anyway. I failed to understand why this one man, who appeared to have no support on campus but had generated a degree of curiosity as an oddity, posed a danger to me. As long as he was contained in Memorial Hall and I was elsewhere, live and let live, I thought. After all, what if the BSM wanted to bring Stokley Carmichael or Huey P. Newton on campus. Fair is fair, I argued with Larry and some other freshmen later in the privacy of our room. I would not participate in any protest, I told them as they argued for racial solidarity and support for the BSM.

While I truly believed what I had said, there was more to it. I was also afraid. The black students at that meeting seemed out of control with rage. Remembering the disturbances of my high school years, I expected the scene in Memorial Hall to deteriorate from heckling to physical assault. I suspected that many of the BSM leaders, eyes blazing and tempers rising, wanted as much confrontation as they could summon. So what if it came to blows? "If I go to jail, I'll have my checkbook and bail myself out," one BSM leader shouted at the suggestion that things might get violent. This fool seemed unaware that his check would be no good in jail. I wanted no part of that scene.

My fears were unrealized. Duke tried and failed to speak. The black students—joined by a white group calling itself the Coalition to End Racism—began chants of "Power to the people" and "Go to hell, Duke" each of the five times he approached the Memorial Hall podium.

Seventeen years later, Duke has resculpted his face, disavowed his membership in the hate group, come within a razor's edge of winning a Louisiana gubernatorial campaign tainted with racist symbolism, and, like Dracula, risen from the land of the forgotten dead to make an unsuccessful run for the White House as a Republican. But back on that freezing night in January 1975, the BSM boosted its stock with many black students with its defiance of and victory over the Klansman.

While the majority of black students were impressed with this victory, few did more than pay lip service to the BSM. Like most students, the bulk of the black population was focused on earning academic credentials that could be cashed in for good, high-paying jobs in the outside world.

After the Duke incident, Carolina seemed different to me. I began to see limits, boundaries chalked all over the campus defining where black students belonged or should feel welcome. We black students, myself included, drew in among ourselves. We went through each day with pained expressions whenever we faced white students, and relaxed only when we were back in Hinton James or in off-campus apartments that functioned as safe havens. These patterns of behavior kept us sane, I thought, and kept white students—and more than a few white professors—at bay.

Nonetheless, I felt a heaviness at Carolina, like the downy comforter Momma used to drape over my childhood bed in winter. It was both reassuring and stuffy, warming and stultifying. Why had I not noticed this feeling before the Duke disturbance? Maybe it had been there all the time, waiting for a spark to jolt me into sensing it.

My insular life on campus changed completely after I fell in love. Doris Jefferson entered my life in my sophomore year. I had volunteered to serve as a counselor for incoming black freshmen and she was one of a half dozen in my cluster. Just as my Big Sister had done for me, I invited my charges to dinner their first evening on campus, and she caught my eye. I couldn't avoid staring, drawn as I was to the fullness of her body straining against worn denim jeans and a white tube top. I was lured into those clear twinkling eyes of burnished mahogany and amazed by the perfection of her round, curly Afro. More than a decade hence, I still find it impossible to visualize my college days without fleeting memories of her face and form. This is involuntary. I can't help myself, because she was my first love.

I pursued her awkwardly at first with invitations to show her around or introduce her to my friends. Later, as we shared a meal together or simply strolled the campus, I resolved that Doris would be my girl. I never paused to consider whether she desired this, partly because I was elated that she accepted most of my invitations and partly because I assumed she wanted my company as much as I wanted hers.

Past dating fiascoes no longer preoccupied me once I met Doris. This relationship was special. We cheered together at football games, cruised the shopping mall, hurried across campus in the rain for classes, studied past midnight in dorm rooms or at the library. We even went to parties together, which was quite a big deal given my insecurity in such settings.

Before meeting Doris, I had drifted into and out of the black students' party scene with a practiced enthusiasm. My self-righteous indignation over excessive drinking and public drunkenness, the smoking of tobacco or herb, and, of course, all forms of drugs, didn't make me a party animal. I'll admit I was too uptight to get loose and enjoy a good time, but that was fine with me. Just as I accepted the fact that some of my friends considered me a downer in social outings.

The truth was I hated dancing, the most important skill needed to make it on the black social scene. I never mastered all those intricate steps that had to be coordinated with hand, head, shoulder and even eye movements. I much preferred slow dances that required less energy and virtually no effort.

After meeting Doris, I became more of a fixture at those parties where a good time seemed directly related to the ear-splitting volume of a Funkadelic platter leading guttural voices in rhythmic chanting: "We-e-e want the FUNK! Give up the FUNK!" I still don't remember ever having a good time at one of those parties, but I relished the chance to be out with Doris. She loved dancing and would plead with me to join her so we could "shake a booty," and I would go and dance with her.

It still surprises me that I cannot remember the first time Doris and I slept together. I know it must have been blissfully traumatic, having to push aside years of church-steeped guilt and visions of hellfire melting my everlasting soul. All I remember is that somehow I worked up enough courage to do it, and I was overjoyed that God did not strike me dead afterward. I lived to repeat the pleasure Doris gave me over and over, and given the frequency with which we spent subsequent nights together, I questioned why I hadn't done this long before.

Doris once said my forceful personality dictated the nature of our relationship, and I must admit she was right about that. From the moment I set my sights on her, the time we spent together followed my design. But that was the male-female pattern I believed all relationships followed. I assumed that my leadership was the natural, normal course in all romances. I thought I was benevolent and sincere, though admittedly pushy. Since she never complained, I assumed all was well between us.

"I'm thinking about pledging," Larry said one evening as we were studying. This came out of nowhere. While black fraternities and sororities like the Deltas, the AKAs and the Ques had a presence in campus life, they remained on the fringes, where they had been consigned by the more rebellious black students during the civil rights and anti-war movements. I knew Larry wouldn't join a white fraternity. That would have been the kiss of social death among black students, an act of self-hatred that only confused, crazy niggers would commit.

"There is talk of a line forming for Alpha Phi Alpha," he said. "I thought I would check out their group meeting, a smoker they call it."

I had only vague and negative impressions of fraternity life. It seemed to me like the depths of zombie-like stupidity to march about campus in lockstep, dressed like a bunch of robotic morons who derived their status from a collective identity—an identity based on dead white Greeks no less. Nope. Not my style. I quickly rushed to knock the idea down before it settled in Larry's mind. "Why on earth would you want to do that?"

"Damn, Sam," Larry said. He resented my doing the thinking for the both of us. "I didn't say I was going to join. But you shouldn't be so rigid. You ought to at least examine something before you rush to condemn it. You don't know what you're talking about."

He was right. So I decided to attend the smoker, to look into this fraternity thing, never expecting it would take root but wanting to be well enough informed so I could have a reason for rejecting it. One more college experience, I thought, nothing more.

The smoker was organized by a group of graduate students who had pledged Alpha at a variety of all-black colleges. At Carolina, they were shocked to discover other black fraternities and sororities, but not an Alpha chapter. They invited the Alpha Phi Alpha state director to speak at this first meeting.

Gus Witherspoon, chairman of the chemistry department at North Carolina State University at Raleigh, was an impressive man. He had pledged the fraternity as a student at Fort Valley State College in rural Georgia and had remained a faithful fraternity man ever since. "The tonic effect of Alpha will stay with you forever," I remember him saying. "Wherever you go, whatever you do, you will be an Alpha for the rest of your life."

Witherspoon, whose college and early professional life had been marked by strict segregation and Jim Crow laws, told us about how his Alpha brothers boarded him whenever he traveled with his family across the South. Hotels and restaurants refused to serve them, even though he had the money to pay and more education than many in the small-minded cracker towns of rural Georgia, Alabama and Mississippi. "All I needed do was call ahead to an Alpha man," he said. "Sight unseen, one of my brothers would take care of me and my family. That's what brotherhood is all about. That's what Alpha Phi Alpha has meant to me. And, my potential brothers, that is what I want you to mean to Alpha."

I was impressed by his talk, but not enough to give up my individuality. It sounded suspiciously like a surrogate religion. How, I thought, can I ever explain joining a fraternity to my folks back home?

At the reception following Witherspoon's talk, I browsed through a display of Alpha paraphernalia on a corner table in the meeting room. The array of artifacts included shields carved from solid blocks of balsa and trimmed in black and gold enamel, scrapbooks with photographs of bushy-headed men wearing medallions around their necks, embossed matchbooks and napkins commemorating Black-and-Gold Balls. I picked up a book.

"That's the Alpha bible you've got in your hand," one of the Alpha men said with all the seriousness of a deacon. Like most of his brothers, he wore a black sweatshirt with an ΑΦΑ making him look somewhat like a comic-book superhero Alphaman, ready to do battle against the forces of discrimination, repression and racial injustice.

"Handle it with care," he said.

"Gimme a break," I muttered under my breath. I focused on the book and ignored Alphaman, who was obviously someone who took himself and his club way too seriously.

The book's title page read *The History of Alpha Phi Alpha: A Development in College Life*, first published in 1929 by someone named Charles H. Wesley. The copy I held was from the twelfth printing, in 1975. I thumbed through a few pages and discovered, purely by accident, a picture of black men studying together in what looked like a library. The scene was something I could embrace. I read a couple of chapters, curious to know more about the men who founded Alpha Phi Alpha.

The original Alphas, or "jewels," as they called themselves, were enrolled at Cornell University in Ithaca, New York, in 1905. As black students, isolated by race and class from social activities on their campus, they sought a bond among themselves that reminded me of my experience at Carolina.

At Cornell, the white students had study clubs and fraternities to provide mutual support. These black students—nearly all of them strapped for cash and working to pay tuition and other fees—wanted something similar but couldn't agree on what. Some wanted to form a fraternity, patterned after the Greek-letter organizations popular among the white undergraduates. Others wanted a literary society that would address social concerns, particularly those affecting black college students and, later, black graduates.

The question of whether to mimic a white organization proved contentious. The students argued over whether "the Negro in America had . . . cultural background upon which to build the framework of a college fraternity," according to Wesley's history.

After a year of debate, the Greek-letter proponents won out, with seven founders styling the organization—Alpha Phi Alpha—after the white fraternities operating in secret on the Cornell campus.

Wesley, who served as the fraternity's general president from 1932 to 1940, wrote: "As black college students, they desired that the fraternity should have some racial significance. This attitude called for an acquaintance with the history and background of black life for which none of the reading and study of the classroom had prepared them."

After reading that, I wanted to know more. Witherspoon obliged by ticking off the names of some of the fraternity's most prestigious members, including the Reverend Martin Luther King, Jr., Thurgood Marshall and W. E. B. Du Bois. "Whenever the first black man is elected President of the United States," Witherspoon said, concluding his remarks, "he will be an Alpha man—or I'm not going to vote for him." That comment drew cheers and applause from the row of Alphamen lining the room.

What finally persuaded me to pledge was an offhand comment by Witherspoon: that if I joined the Alphas, I would be one of the founding brothers of the University of North Carolina chapter.

I figured out the rest. I would, in a small but very black way, make history on campus. Alpha Phi Alpha, the oldest black Greek-letter fraternity in America, did not exist at UNC, which touted itself as the oldest state university in the nation. My name would thus be linked to something—even if that something was a fraternity—which would give me immortality at Carolina. That was an opportunity I could not allow to pass.

So, along with Larry and fourteen other black male students, I went along with the six-week pledge program. For most of that time, the sixteen of us dressed in black and gold, and behaved as though we were in a military boot camp. The pledge process molded a diverse group into a unit. We emerged as a group of overachievers, all of whom believed it our destiny to one day become the Negro Community Guardians for future generations of black youth.

I reveled in my circle of new friends. This was the world I had always wanted to be part of. My identity as a black college student was defined by belonging to this fraternity of careerist brothers. I was convinced, much as I had been after Mrs. Cunningham's pep talk years before, that the world was waiting for our conquest.

My world at Carolina now seemed perfectly ordered. My grades soared during the pledge period because the graduate brothers who guided us into Alpha stressed studying and high grades over all else— even partying, the prime activity of other fraternities. I ended that term with near-perfect grades and made the Dean's List for the first of many times to follow.

Moreover, I had peer approval and social acceptance within this federation of like-minded black brothers. I was sleeping with one of the prettiest girls on campus. There was no way I could have planned college life any better. My spirit floated as free as those cotton-candy clouds that skimmed the silent breezes in the Carolina blue sky.

Bliss never lasts.

"I'm pregnant," Doris announced without preamble. It was late, after our usual evening study session and midnight snack of cheesecake and cola. We were lying naked in her bed, nestled like silver spoons in a drawer. My body pressed against her back as she faced the cinder-block wall. The light from the parking lot outside her dorm room window cast silhouettes of the Ziggy cards and love notes I had sent her and she had taped to the milky pink wall beside her bed.

"What? You *think* you're pregnant? Or are you telling me you *are* pregnant?"

I knew she was not kidding. Doris was no prankster, and I knew she would never joke about anything like this. But I could not, under the circumstances, come up with anything else to say. Maybe, dear God, I have misunderstood her, I thought.

"You heard me. I'm pregnant. I visited a doctor today. He told me I'm about six weeks along now."

The air in that tiny room became heavy and then disappeared. I put my arm around her shoulders. My chest heaved as I tried to breathe in through my nose. I forced my mouth not to gape open and willed myself to stay conscious. I had heard her correctly the first time. The movie projector in my brain flickered the scenes from my life so far on a tiny screen between my ears. School is over. FLASH. Momma's voice was on the soundtrack: *"I told you so. Nothing good will come of that school."* FLASH. No career in journalism. *"You should have had something to fall back on."* FLASH. What am I going to do? FLASH. My future is gone. FLASH. Damn. I am dead.

"Birth control. I thought you were on the pill or something," I said. I was wishing there was some way to erase this whole episode or, better, change the channel to a cheerier show.

"I was, but you remember I stopped."

Slowly, painfully, the memory came back to haunt me now. Two months before, we had had this discussion. She was concerned about the possible long-term health consequences of taking the pill and wanted to stop. I did not object, but I did not ask any follow-up questions, nor did I assume any responsibilities for birth control. Damn, I thought. Is she saying this is all my fault? *Is* it all my fault? Why is this happening to her, to me? Damn, Sam. Damn.

Warm tears dropped off her cheeks and onto my arm. I had not noticed them until that moment. I pulled her tighter, so tight she had to feel my gulping breaths, so tight she could not turn to look into my face and see my tears. Crying made me feel better—and gave me time to make computer-like calculations of my options, our options.

"Well, okay," I said after a long silence. I still wanted to calm my nerves, be reasonable before revealing how pitiful I truly felt. "So what are *we* going to do?"

"I don't know. What are you thinking?"

"I'm not thinking anything. I mean, I'm just trying to absorb this. I mean, do you want to have a baby?" I did not want her to answer before I finished saying what was on my mind. "If you do, then I'm all for it. If you don't, then I'll go along with that too. But I want you to decide. You tell me what we should do."

"I don't know," Doris said.

For more than two weeks, we spoke sparingly of our predicament. The deed was done and talk would not change the facts. Ignoring problems had never been my way, but this was different. I did not know what to say. In that immature silence, I suppose we were both licking our own private wounds. I feared offending her with any utterance on the subject of birth or abortion, so I did not bring it up. More important, I wanted to be rocklike in my support of whatever Doris chose to do. But I insisted it be her choice. I did not want to impose my will on hers in a decision that I knew would impact her more dramatically than it would me. I never wanted to hear her say, *"You made me do this."* I couldn't live with the prospect of her being able to throw that phrase in my face. Whatever happened would be her choice; whatever she decided I would agree with.

I also had decided something that I wouldn't reveal until after this baby matter was resolved. I would ask Doris to marry me. But not under these circumstances, not out of guilt or pity or sense of sin. Now more than ever, I was certain that I loved her. I wanted her, but I wanted something else too. Whether she had the baby or not, I just had to finish school. This was my junior year. Just one more year to go. I could make it. We could be together come what may. But first, let me get that degree. But I said nothing, nothing to anyone, least of all to Doris.

It was her decision to have an abortion. It was my decision to accompany her and to pay for it. After it was over, I came away from the campus clinic with the feeling a condemned man must experience after the governor has placed the pardoning phone call. *I had ducked the bullet.* No one ever needed to know of our sin, save whomever we trusted enough to share these intimate details with. For me, that meant no one.

Our life together returned to its normal pattern: the semester ended with her making plans for summer school and me setting my sights on an internship at the *Charlotte Observer*, where I hoped to convince the editors to hire me as a regular reporter after I graduated the next summer. All will be well again, I thought.

I was wrong. Again.

When the fall term of my senior year began, Doris was somewhat changed. True to my self-absorbed nature, I did not notice it until just before the Christmas break. Weary of dropping ignored hints, Doris decided to state her feelings explicitly. This time we were dressed. This time she was looking flush into my face. This time she said good-bye. "I don't want to date you anymore. I want to see other people."

"Who? Have you picked someone out to replace me already?"

"That's none of your business."

"Like hell. I think I deserve to know."

"I think that is the problem exactly," she said. "You think you deserve everything. But you don't. I've made up my mind."

I couldn't believe that Doris was actually making this decision. For the entire course of our relationship, I had told her to be her own person, make decisions and stick to them. Now, she was doing what I had counseled. She had made a firm decision and it was to dump me.

"I'm not happy with you anymore," I heard Doris say. "I want to be with someone who makes me happy, someone who is more fun and not so serious. I'm sorry it is over. But we can always be friends, can't we?"

Shit. I did not want to be friends. I wanted more. I had it all planned. Just let me get out of college. I can make this work. C'mon, Doris, you don't know what you're doing to me . . . to us . . . to the future I have planned.

It did not matter. Nothing—late-night phone calls, dozens of roses, promises, tears—nothing was going to change her mind. Her decision was final. The love of my life was leaving, and there was nothing I could do to stop it.

At a time when all had seemed so perfect, so complete, this was the sourest end I could have imagined to my college career. Summer at the *Observer* had gone even better than expected. The editors had virtually promised to hire me when I graduated, a promise they made good in early February with an offer to start as a night police reporter as soon as the term ended in May.

I had beaten the odds, proved that Momma had been wrong to say I needed education classes to have something to fall back on. And I had achieved my life's ambition—to be a reporter for the *Charlotte Observer*.

Nothing could stop me from conquering the world. My grades and class standing assured me of on-time graduation, even if I slept through one more perfunctory semester. I was twenty-one years old, black and a Carolina graduate. This was what I had wanted for so long, and now, at last, it was within my reach.

But without the person I loved. Without Doris.

What the hell was wrong with her? Why was she spoiling everything, making my final semester the most miserable period of my life? Why did it have to end like this? Why was it happening to me?

The day before graduation was one long and lusty bacchanal for me and my Alpha brothers and some of our closest friends. After sixteen years of elementary school, high school and college, we felt we had earned a final frenetic flurry of drinking, picnicking, dancing and lovemaking—sort of a ritualized communal exclamation point to mark our achievement.

Doris was long gone, hanging out with my replacement, a bad chap I referred to only as "the drug dealer." Amy took her place. I had met Amy back home in February, had sought her out after seeing her photo in the black weekly newspaper to which Daddy had been subscribing. Tall, with delicate features that inspired her part-time modeling career,

Amy was an understanding friend who quickly became the recipient of ardent letters, boxed roses and Ziggy cards—like those I had formerly sent to Doris. By graduation time, Amy had visited me several times at Chapel Hill and we were hot-blooded lovers, making her the perfect date for my last weekend on campus.

But my revelry was laced with dejection. Carolina, I realized amid the congratulations and best wishes of that June weekend in 1978, had been a bittersweet experience, and one last night of debauchery couldn't wipe that away. So, as my parents beamed within the stuffy confines of Carmichael Auditorium the next day, I received my diploma with tears in my eyes.

Chapter Five

DIVING INTO THE MAINSTREAM

A week and a day after graduating from Carolina, I bounded into the *Charlotte Observer*'s fifth-floor newsroom at precisely 10 A.M. to meet my long-awaited future.

I have arrived, I thought.

In 1978, the *Observer*'s newsroom resembled hundreds of others across the nation. Bright fluorescent lights glowed above the heads of some hundred people engaged in writing, editing and designing the morning paper. From midmorning to well past midnight, reporters, photographers, editors, copy readers, printers, truckers and route-carriers worked in relays to deliver the newspaper before daybreak. By nightfall, that day's pages would have fluttered into trash bins across the Carolinas as the next news cycle began.

If I live to be a hundred, the thing I will never forget about that newsroom was its smell. The ink, in those days hot-pressed to the low-grade paper favored by publishers, reeked acrid and musky even after it dried. Not only did the black stuff smear off on my fingertips and clothes, it seeped into my being. I acquired a near-chemical dependence on these daily fixes of printer's ink. From the moment I reported for my first day, I began a love-hate relationship with newspapering, its great opportunities and its preoccupation with trivia.

There was more to my being a reporter than an infatuation with the environment. I thought of my job as a calling, akin to the one that drew Daddy to the pulpit. Just ten years earlier, Martin Luther King and Bobby Kennedy were blown away, the last of my era's heroes to fall. Four years later, the Vietnam War lurched to a tired conclusion, after which the nation plummeted into self-doubt and social upheaval. Overseas oil embargoes led to domestic shortages and hourlong waits at the gas pumps, a choking reminder of the nation's economic downturn. Alternating spasms of recession and inflation made Americans feel uncertain about their financial futures and less willing to spend tax dollars on domestic social experiments, which had begun during the more affluent 1960s. Four years before I went to work at the *Observer*, Richard Nixon left Washington in disgrace. A peanut farmer from Georgia then entered the White House. The media duly recorded each of these watershed events. I had lived through them all and reflected on each in journalism classes at Carolina.

I was a Watergate baby, a member of the first graduating class to enter journalism school in the aftermath of the *Washington Post*'s Pulitzer Prize–winning reporting that exposed Nixon as a crook and led to his fall. The media's role as public watchdog and social critic saturated nearly every journalism class I took at Carolina. Most of us came out of school hoping to win our own Pulitzer.

My favorite television show then was *Lou Grant*, Hollywood's depiction of the contemporary newsroom. I watched the show religiously, hoping for insights that I could use in my daily life. But there were few black characters in Lou Grant's newsroom, so I had to look elsewhere for professional tips. I doubted that white reporters scanned the show, which glamorized newspaper life, for role models; they seemed comfortable with their actual experience. But I wasn't, and the characters on *Lou Grant* failed to ease my real-life anxieties as a black rookie striving to be a professional in an all-white environment.

I believed that black people and their often unique perspectives on current events deserved a voice in every newsroom in the nation. My own evolving awareness of how white people viewed me and other black Americans was grounded more in intellectual and media-driven images than in real interaction with them. I earnestly believed that newspapers needed and wanted my black perspective in their pages.

Black-run publications had long been a fixture in my parents' home. The *Charlotte Post*, a local black weekly, along with *Ebony* and *Jet* magazines, had shared coffee table space with the *Observer* and *Time* magazine for as long as I could remember. Daddy bought and read them, then passed them along to me. I noted the clear differences in the publications. The *Observer* rarely carried the full range of stories about black people that could often be found in the black press. I attributed the mainstream print media's shortcomings to the narrowness of the white people who ran their newsrooms. They lacked awareness of black people; therefore, they had no desire to include them in the regular flow of news.

My purpose was to broaden the *Observer*'s reach with my stories about people who looked like me. I envisioned myself as a latter-day John Russwurm or Samuel Cornish, my journalistic heroes, who in 1827 published *Freedom's Journal*, the nation's first black-owned and -operated newspaper, with the pledge "to plead our own cause." I had learned about them in my "Minorities in the Media" class at Carolina and was immediately drawn to their story. I adopted their slogan as my own. My quest, a century and a half later, would be as noble as theirs had been. I believed, as Russwurm and Cornish had argued, "too long has the public been deceived by misrepresentations which concern us dearly."

I was now standing in the center of my hometown paper's newsroom. How profoundly the world had changed since Russwurm and Cornish's time, I thought. I had the opportunity to inscribe the story of black America in the white folks' journal. I would do this for posterity's sake. And for my own.

"You'll sit here." Joe Distelheim, the city editor, broke into my reverie. "That's John York's desk next to you. He's out chasing an ambulance or something. You'll get to know him well. He's been covering cops since long before you were born."

He pointed out the newsroom necessities: coffee, men's room, coat closet and such. "This is your typewriter," he continued. "Don't get too used to it. Before long we'll be using CRTs. We don't have enough of them to go around yet, so you'll start out on a typewriter."

"CRTs, what's that?" I asked.

"Computers. CRTs stand for cathode ray tubes. They're like a typewriter that works without paper. Makes the work go faster, or so they say. We'll see soon enough."

Damn, computers, I said to myself. I really *am* in the big time. At Carolina, the Journalism School did not yet have the money to purchase computers, although the business school and some other departments had them. I could not recall ever seeing a desktop station CRT, and the thought that I would soon be writing newspaper articles on one was intimidating. But, what the hell, bring it on. I can deal with anything.

Instead of turning out my first Pulitzer Prize–winning story on that virgin day, I spent most of my time scribbling my name on an array of employment forms. I also wandered around the newsroom to reacquaint myself with the staff, now my colleagues and bosses. I had interned there for the past two summers and recognized many faces. I have never been good at remembering names, especially those of white people who only casually cross my path. I remembered those of the editors because I considered them important, but I had to re-index many of the reporters' names with their facial characteristics and refile them into my long-term memory. All those faces—much more lined, mature and pale than mine—made this mental task difficult. I chuckled to myself as I went around the room on my own, introducing myself and repeating whatever name was offered up in exchange. They all look alike, don't they? I thought.

Not everyone in the newsroom or in the building was white. Peppering the fifth floor were fewer than a dozen black reporters and clerks. Among them were Charles Hardy, a slightly built chain-smoker who came to the *Observer* from *The Evening Star* to cover education and later left to do the same for the *San Francisco Examiner*; Lafleur Paysour, a stylish Vassar graduate with a bohemian air; Vanessa Gallman, who had graduated from Carolina two years ahead of me and who was now raising her small daughter alone; Al Johnson, who had come to the *Observer* after eight years at the *Richmond News Leader*, where he had won several national awards; and Patrice Gaines-Carter, a flower child who worked as a clerk in the features section and wanted desperately to break into the writing ranks at the paper. In the photo department, there was Jim Wilson, a sharpshooter who left the paper for the *New York Times*.

But it was Milton Jordan who made the biggest impact on me. Milton was a prolific writer and an engaging personality. Tall and dark-skinned, with a nose shaped like a lightbulb, Milton strutted about the newsroom as though he owned it, forcing others to yield ground to his presence. If not the most talented, he was the oldest, blackest and most outspoken of the black reporters. I thought of him as our Godfather.

One day, after reading an aggressively edited version of a story he had just written, Milton blew a gasket. "Gawd dammitt!" he roared at Mark Etheridge, one of the up-and-coming young assistant city editors, "why is it that every time we refer to black neighborhoods, it's a gawd-damn ghetto. It's a neighborhood. Black people live in neighborhoods, just like fucking white people."

Those kinds of outbursts were rare. The *Observer* was a civil, collegial place. My friend Al Johnson, who went on to become vice president/executive editor of Georgia's *Columbus Ledger-Enquirer*, recalled the atmosphere in the newsroom "as very healthy . . . There never was a time when someone said or behaved in a way that suggested 'I dislike you because you're black.' There was mutual respect, a healthy professional respect, among a bunch of people who were all very good journalists."

Sometime that summer, I decided to grow a beard, thinking that it would make me look older, more mature. Along with my fully sprouted facial hair came a fresh air of swagger. The combination—beard and bravado worn like an aegis and visor—made me feel better in the newsroom and on assignments. With any personal setback, I could retreat behind the hirsute cockiness as I learned and grew more confident. Over time, my dread of being issued a pink slip diminished.

The night police reporter is the cub reporter's traditional entry point to the newsroom. My day began about 3 P.M., when I arrived at the office. I picked up the keys to the paper's staff car and a two-way radio and drove over to the Charlotte-Mecklenburg County Law Enforcement Center, which housed the city and county police departments, a morgue and the municipal jail. There I read the police blotter of crimes and officer calls from the most recently completed shift. (I struggled through enough fractured grammar and made-up words to marvel at the fact that these police officers had graduated from high school; it was beyond my comprehension that they had passed through anything that called itself an academy.)

Next, I would make a series of rounds to the various duty officers to see if anything had happened—as though they would actually reveal anything of importance to me. Then, if nothing turned up that I thought worthy of a ten-inch notice in the morning paper, I cruised the city, listening to the police scanner for some newsy incident and attempting to make friends with any police officer I saw on patrol. My day ended around midnight, after the final edition had gone to the back shop.

It did not take me very long to realize that I had a lot to learn about being a reporter and writer. As I recognized this, I became intimidated by how easily the newsroom veterans seemed to do their work. While my editors were fastidiously correcting my copy, I struggled to get the hang of what actually went into a story, and often my concept of what the story should be failed to come alive once I committed words to paper. My early elation at having arrived at the *Observer* melted under summer's heat. It frustrated me that I was not contributing more to the paper from the start.

My few successes stemmed from lots of trials and even more errors. Every day I arrived at work ready to conquer, only to have my confidence flag after discovering I had missed a story or an angle to our major competitor, the *Charlotte News*, or *The Snooze*, as we called it. Their crime reporter, Ted DeAdwyler, a black man no older than I, frequently had a story stripped across the front page of their more sensational afternoon paper—reporting a development that I had completely missed the night before. This happened regularly enough to worry my editors.

My mistakes were politely and discreetly brought to my attention, but I lacked a mentor to help pilot me through these turbulent waters. I sensed my editors were unhappy with the quality of my work, though they never actually said so. I hung in there, gallantly trying.

One day as I stood in the back of an elevator at the Law Enforcement Center, two detectives entered—they were wearing suits and rubber-soled patent leather shoes. They seemed to ignore me as they continued their conversation.

"—with an axe. I never seen so much blood in all my life," said the taller of the two men.

My ears perked up in anticipation of an excellent story.

"Joe ain't going to be happy with having to write up a report on that," said the other, a flattop-wearing butterball. "You know, when you have those axe murders, you have to fill out Form No. 2495. In triplicate. Should take him the better part of the night to get that correctly done."

"Maybe. But if there had only been one body, it wouldn't be so difficult to write up. But two bodies. I had a case like that once when—"

"Excuse me." I just had to interrupt to find out more. Murders, relatively rare in Charlotte during those days, were a sure-fire front-pager. I whipped out my skinny reporter's notebook. "Excuse me. I couldn't help overhearing. What happened? Where—?"

The elevator doors opened on the fourth floor, near the offices of the homicide detectives, which required a pass for reporters. Flattop rushed off the elevator without looking in my direction. The tall one looked at me, said nothing and disappeared behind a set of frosted-glass doors. The elevator doors closed.

I called the office, only to discover my editor was in a meeting, so I told a clerk that I had stumbled upon a double axe murder and would write a story about it for the early editions. But first, I said, I needed to pin down a few details. I didn't want to say too much because I feared the editors would take the story away from me and give it to a more seasoned reporter. That wouldn't do. I wanted this one on the front page under my name. I spent the next three hours on the phone tracking down that story, to no avail. I called police duty officers and the area hospitals and funeral homes. No luck.

In desperation, I called Art Norman, an experienced black reporter who also covered the cops for WSOC-TV. He was probably working on the story as a competitor. If not, he would be alerted to it by my call. But I felt it was worth the risk. I needed help. Art had been friendly and helpful to me on the frequent nights when both of us arrived at some bad automobile accident or house fire. So if I have to share the story with anyone, I thought, might as well be a black guy at a television station.

Art burst into laughter after I explained my predicament. "You didn't fall for that old double axe murder trick, did you?" he said, choking between guffaws. "That's the oldest trick in the book. They always pull that one on youngbloods. Detectives would never discuss a case in an elevator in front of a stranger, especially one that looks like a rookie reporter. Bet you had your notebook and pen out before they finished talking. Those two jokers probably are cracking up over how you got suckered."

I felt a knot balling up in the pit of my stomach. I swallowed hard to keep the tears from flowing.

"You didn't promise your editors a story," Art said, suddenly turning serious.

"Yep. They're expecting something about now. That's why I was calling to see if you heard—"

"Ohmigod!" Art wasn't laughing any longer. He suggested we meet for dinner at a greasy spoon diner near our respective offices. "But first, call your office and tell them you got duped."

I did so. I was certain I heard the editors chortling as I hung up the phone. I went to meet Art. After we had ordered burgers and Cokes, Art—always jovial and informal—suddenly turned deadly serious.

"Sam, you've got to be more careful," he said. "I hope you've learned a little lesson here, because nothing is going to teach you like experience. The white folks in your office and the cops—they're worse—they don't give a shit how well you do or whether you screw up even worse in the future. You've got to be more careful.

"Let me tell you something else," he continued, drawing closer over the formica tabletop. "Try not to be too excited about any one story. You're going to write a million stories in your career. One is not going to make or break you. It's not brain surgery. It's only a newspaper and tomorrow somebody will wrap fish in your story. So don't go running off half-cocked, announcing stories before they're reported and written. Let the editors be surprised when you deliver, not when you fail to give them what you promised to deliver."

I wanted to reach across my burger and kiss him. Never before had I received that kind of useful advice, and I felt grateful he took time to offer it. To this day, I hold a warm spot in my heart for Art Norman, the first person to kick me in the ass and tell me to grow up as a reporter. I would hear it again, but never so affectionately. Norman went on to become an anchor-reporter in Chicago. We often toast a glass or two at our shared Charlotte roots whenever we run into each other, usually at professional meetings.

One of those gatherings is the annual convention of the National Association of Black Journalists. The NABJ is one of a myriad of black organizations formed shortly after legal segregation eased and a fresh crop of black professionals began seeking admission to the clannish white establishment. When I started at the *Observer*, the NABJ was still in its infancy, having been organized in 1975. It was founded by a dozen black reporters who worked in virtual isolation in white newsrooms and bumped into each other repeatedly as they covered an NAACP convention, an Urban League dinner or some other black political function.

In the days when Momma and Daddy began their careers, upwardly mobile black teachers and ministers offered modest financial contributions to their local branch of the NAACP, which addressed the political and social needs of middle-class black Americans. By the time I entered the workforce, much of the NAACP's heavy lifting had been done and it was losing out to the appeal of more radical and charismatic street activists. What remained of the once-proud NAACP was a hollow shell, as college-educated black professionals turned increasingly toward job-specific associations, which dealt more with workplace issues and less with racial politics. "For the most part, we were the first generation [of black Americans] to enter corporate America," Derryl L. Reed, a forty-four-year-old president of the National Black MBA Association, told me in 1991, explaining why he had dropped his NAACP membership and how he had risen in the ranks of the black MBA group. "One of the things that drew us together as black MBAs was the fact that there were no organizations or persons who could share our common experience of being isolated in our jobs and careers."

I felt the same way when I decided to attend my first NABJ convention at the Galt House Hotel in Louisville, Kentucky, during late August 1981. On a hot day in June, I had received the convention brochure, a mimeographed and stapled document that listed two days' worth of workshops ("How to Get Ahead in the Newsroom" and "So, You Want to Be an Editor" and "Freelancing for Fun and Profit"), a luncheon speech by *Ebony* senior editor and author Lerone Bennett, cocktail parties and other social gatherings. I had been told that most reporters who attended the convention had their way subsidized by their employers. So I studied the program for hours before approaching the corner office of Mark Etheridge, who was by now the managing editor at the *Observer*.

I checked on the costs of transportation and lodging, figuring all together I would need about $300 to $350. I had never asked for anything like this before and had no idea how to make the case for the paper's sending me. There was no standard written policy about employer-paid conferences and seminars. I knew that some people had attended gatherings for investigative reporters, religion writers and other specialized beats. Of course, everyone in the newsroom knew when the top editors attended the annual meetings of publishers and managing editors; we knew because our immediate bosses rushed to get their work approved before temporary supervisors, who were no more than ordinary colleagues when the big cheeses were in town, took over.

Etheridge scanned the NABJ program. His eyes paused on the second page. "I'm not paying for you to party while cruising on the *Belle of Louisville* down the Ohio River," he said. He thrust the papers back at me.

"But that's just one social activity," I protested. I was angry that he would void the entire convention over a two-hour cocktail party. How petty, I thought, swallowing all traces of hostility that might spill from my lips.

Instead, I forced a tight smile. "What about all of the other stuff?" I said. "There are some interesting workshops I would like to attend. Don't you attend cocktail parties at the managing editors' convention? I don't see the difference."

"Okay. You've made your point," he said. This was obviously a trifling matter and he wanted me out of his office so he could attend to other, more pressing business, like changing into his shorts for an afternoon jog around downtown. "I'll authorize $100 for you. You don't have to fly up there. You can drive. That will cut down on your expenses."

I flew anyway, paying the difference out of my own pocket. Once in Louisville, surrounded by all those black faces—more black reporters (and a few editors) than I had ever seen in any one place in my life—I fell in love with the NABJ. There were 218 delegates officially registered at the convention. Everyone seemed to know everyone else. I knew no one, but it did not matter. People were friendly, eager to welcome a newcomer into their midst.

I returned from my first NABJ convention determined that I would attend every year—even if I had to take vacation and pay for the trip myself. To me, so anxious to move up in an industry I did not fully comprehend, this fellowship of other black journalists fortified my spirit against the loneliness I felt in the newsroom.

Not long after the double axe murder hoax, and about five months after I had started at the paper, the phone on my desk rang. Editor Dave Lawrence's secretary, who sat no more than ten feet away, summoned me to a meeting in Lawrence's office. My head jerked toward the large glass panel that gave us grunts in the newsroom a spectacular view of the goings-on in his large rectangular office. Waiting there was a phalanx of editors, among them Lawrence himself; Managing Editor Stu Dim, a cerebral New Yorker with the demeanor of a professor and a wickedly sharp editing pencil; my immediate supervisor, City Editor Gil Thelen, a stern-faced, athletically built man who had recently come to the paper from Chicago, where he had had both an aggressive career and a messy divorce; and Dale Bye, the young sports editor for whom I had interned during the summer after my junior year at Carolina. It looked as if their afternoon budget meeting had just broken up and they were waiting for the next order of business—me.

"Okay," I said, putting the phone down. As I walked those ten feet to Lawrence's door, I wondered what story I had missed this time.

"Come on in, Sam," said Lawrence. He was being friendly, and so a bit of my apprehension evaporated. I peered into each face for clues as to why I was the only reporter invited to this meeting. My apprehension flooded back as I sat down.

"Don't worry, you're in no trouble," he said, reading my face. "In fact, we're here to celebrate. Your probation period has passed."

I smiled weakly and offered a feeble joke. "Does that mean I get to keep my job?" Everybody chuckled. "Do I get more money?" What the hell, why not keep the joke going, I thought.

"No, you don't get more money," Lawrence deadpanned. Everyone in the room continued to laugh.

"Sam," Lawrence said as the chuckles subsided, "who's your favorite editor?"

Wake up, Sam. Think fast for the politic answer. I decided to pick someone outside the room—that way, no feelings would be hurt and I'd avoid future recriminations. Truth was, I had no favorites. None of them had involved themselves in counseling or working closely with me. With the exception, perhaps, of Thelen, who politely admonished me for my most egregious errors, they were all negligible influences in my working life.

"W-e-l-l-l-l," I said. "I get along quite well with Stan Brennan." As the night city editor, Brennan edited my deadline copy. He had been at the paper since Gutenberg invented movable type and everybody liked him. I thought I had picked cleverly. "I think he likes me too," I added.

"That wasn't exactly the answer I was looking for," Lawrence said. "I thought you might have selected someone in this room—Dale, for example."

I liked Dale Bye. At twenty-seven, he was not that much older than I. He had a profane sense of humor and never took himself too seriously.

"Okay. What's the point?" I said.

"The point is we are reassigning you to the sports department," Lawrence said.

Dale's skinny face split into a toothy grin. "Welcome back, Sam," he said.

The deal had been done before I entered the room.

Effective immediately, my new job was to cover high school sports in the ten rural counties outside Charlotte. The high school football season was nearing completion; the basketball season was approaching. I would cover my first football game that Friday night—and I knew next to nothing about sports writing.

In fact, the previous summer I had displayed the absolute depth of my ignorance about sports. For a number of years, the Kemper Open, played at an all-white suburban Charlotte country club, was an annual stop for many of the big names on the PGA Tour. Among the feature stories the *Observer* published that summer was a brief article, assigned to me, explaining how spectators tracked scores by watching a leader board located near the clubhouse. I had never before set foot on a golf course. My reporter's credentials protected me from worrying about an ugly racial incident, but I still did not know how to comport myself at a country club. What on earth would I wear?

I reasoned that rich white people were regulars at country clubs, and a blue suit was always acceptable in the presence of the affluent. What a fool I must have seemed, trudging across the fairways in ninety-degree weather in my navy polyester suit from Webster's. By the time I finished reporting that story, I had spent a good five hours on the golf course and felt like a tomcat that had escaped drowning in a croker sack hurled into a river.

Bye was undaunted by these minor misadventures. "I welcomed having you back in the department," he said when I asked him last year why he had hired someone as ignorant as I was. "You tried hard and paid attention. And there are some nonjournalistic reasons a person gets hired. You got along with everyone in the department and that was important to me.

"Even I was naive about what it took to be a good sports reporter," he added. "I just figured a journalist was a journalist, a reporter could report about anything. I didn't give a shit that you didn't know much about sports."

In the late 1970s and early '80s, Charlotte was a striver's town. Major firms—regional banks, airlines, Fortune 500 branch offices and light manufacturers—were attracted to this booming city in the New South. Corporate executives groomed their promising recruits, freshly minted from colleges around the country, in Charlotte. Many of these companies were trying to diversify their executive ranks. I was one among many black professionals with an impressive entry-level job in Charlotte.

The bulk of those transplanted to the city were there almost exclusively because of their jobs, having no expectations of sinking roots. They labored during the week in their white-collar professions, then fled on weekends to Atlanta, Washington or New York for hearty partying with their real friends.

My situation was slightly different, since I was homegrown. I had expected Momma to resist my renting an apartment when I graduated from college. "I wondered how long it would take for you to do that," she said, not really putting up a fight. But Momma was not releasing me totally from any guilt she could inspire about my determined independence. "I just don't understand what you need to live there for unless there are things you want to do there that you can't do at home."

My two-bedroom apartment was located in a complex across town from McCrorey Heights, in a neighborhood that had been suburban and predominantly white until busing integrated the schools. Almost overnight, the white families moved elsewhere and black families rushed to replace them. I liked living in that apartment because it was mine. I decorated it in Spartan, recent-graduate-poverty style. I bought a new bed and a dining room table with vinyl chairs. I hung a framed poster from the 1972 Olympics by black artist Jacob Lawrence, who portrayed five black track stars in vivid primary colors. I also mounted some of my original photographs from college on the walls. My most expensive and prized possessions were my stereo and my record album collection.

I had tried to persuade Larry to take the IBM job in Charlotte he had been offered. But he wanted to get away from our hometown more than I did, so he took a first-rung management job with Union Carbide in the eastern part of the state. He would never again claim Charlotte as his home address.

I had to develop friendships from scratch, without the social links I had relied on in the recent past. To make matters worse, my weekend work schedule left me with leisure hours that were not conducive to making new friends. Typically, my days off were Sunday and one random weekday. Friday nights, prime time for dating in Charlotte circa 1980, were, nine months out of the year, claimed by high school or college football, basketball and baseball games. On many Saturdays, I had office duties or covered some small-town sporting activity, such as a softball team or a bowling league. Once in a while, I could persuade a date to accompany me on these working excursions, but the overwhelming majority of weekends I spent working alone.

Since there were a handful of black reporters in the newsroom, I decided to cling to them as much as possible in after-hours settings. In particular, Al Johnson and I would prowl some of Charlotte's tacky discos or late-night diners after getting off work in the early morning hours. More often, however, I would spend much of my free time alone in my apartment reading paperback novels and popular magazines.

One afternoon, not long after I had been transferred to the sports desk, I was rushing out of the *Observer* building for an assignment when I noticed Milton Jordan holding court with two women. I had witnessed this scene before and thought briefly about turning on my heels, since I knew Milton would want to include me in an extended conversation with his friends.

Milton, who thought himself a ladies' man, noticed every black woman who entered and exited the building. He made it a point of personal pride to introduce himself and to detain her in pointless conversation for as long as possible. If any other male acquaintance was in the vicinity, he would summon the unlucky victim into his web for an introduction to his "new friend."

"Sam, my man!" he shouted. I had nowhere to run for cover and decided to meet the matter head-on and make a break at the first pause in the conversation. "Come over here. I want to introduce you to two of my new friends."

I exchanged halfhearted pleasantries with the women and continued on my way.

"What did you rush off for?" said Milton when I returned to the newsroom several hours later. "One of them, Cynthia, really wanted to get to know you."

"Yeah, yeah, Milton. I'll let you handle both of them."

"No, Sam, I'm serious. That Cynthia—she's the one that works across the hall at the *News*—she asked me a lot of questions about you. You ought to go over and talk to her."

"I'll do that," I said, never intending to do any such thing.

Cynthia Bell, a chocolate-skinned woman with a perfect smile, had come to Charlotte to attend Johnson C. Smith University from her home outside Columbia, South Carolina. She had just graduated with a degree in marketing and was fumbling around Charlotte looking for what she called "a good job." Whatever it turned out to be, she was certain she would not find it back home in Columbia. She was restless, lacking a clear idea of her own potential as well as a network of professional contacts who could help her exploit it. But she planned to remain in Charlotte for as long as it took to find her way professionally.

While attending Smith, she had worked at a succession of part-time retail jobs to earn tuition money and maintain an off-campus apartment. She drove a battered yellow Volkswagen bug. When Milton served up his introduction, she was the receptionist at the front desk guarding the *Charlotte News*'s entrance, just across a common hall on the fifth floor of the newspaper building.

Cynthia was not the shy, reticent type. Although I had not said a word to her since our first meeting, the next time I saw her—about a month later, on the elevator—she struck up a conversation. "So what do you do over there?"

I told her I was a sports reporter. I was looking past her, scanning the newsroom for one of the evening paper's reporters.

"Oh, really?" Her voice was commanding me to stay awhile and chat. "I like sports a lot. I'm a big Dallas Cowboys fan," she added.

"Dallas? Why Dallas?" I wanted to test her, see if she was shamming me.

"They're good. They played all those championship games against Green Bay. I used to watch them play with my daddy. Also, one of my seventh-grade teachers was Mike Ditka's sister-in-law."

My face must have revealed my confusion.

"You know who Mike Ditka is, don't you?" she went on, talking nonstop. "He was a receiver for Dallas. But that was before he became a coach, an assistant coach for the offense, I think."

Not quite convinced she was telling the truth, I broke off the conversation. I went to the sports department's library and looked up the Dallas Cowboys media guide. There was Mike Ditka. She had it all correct. I was impressed. I had never heard of the man before, but she knew a good bit of his professional history. Maybe there was more to this woman than I had suspected. I wanted to find out more. If nothing else, she liked football.

"Would you like to go to see Maiden High play on Friday?" I was standing over the same receptionist's desk I had hurried from fifteen minutes before.

"Sure, what time?" Cynthia Bell said.

Our relationship started slowly, like a marathon race where runners pace themselves to avoid hitting the wall too early and burning themselves out before completing the course. During the high school football season, she accompanied me to many games in the rural outback of North Carolina. We delighted in the rides, especially the return trips along tree-shrouded country roads in total darkness, listening to old radio mysteries in mock terror.

Cynthia really did like football, understanding the nuances of the game as well as any guy I had met and able to keep up with the statistics better than I could. She laughed a lot, at herself and at me, and her sense of humor was a quality that sneaked up on me. It made her good company on those Friday night rides to prep ball games.

Though I liked Cynthia best, I dated other women, often asking them to join me on working dates too. One of these dates taught me a lesson in how important finding the right mate was to young middle-class black professionals in Charlotte. Cheryl, a naturally straight-haired, copper-hued black woman, surprised me by asking me to go out with her. She joined me at a couple of high school games, which she freely admitted were boring.

Like almost everyone else I associated with, Cheryl was new to Charlotte and did not know very many people, least of all, she said, unmarried black men she could date. We had met several months earlier, introduced by a mutual friend, who described her as "just your type. You know what I mean—she's preppy, like you." I bristled at her description of me as preppy, but had to admit that it fit Cheryl perfectly. Our subsequent phone conversations tended to be brief and unrevealing, leading me to think she considered me date-eligible only because I was unmarried.

Cheryl was a workaholic whose only recreation was a daily hour and a half of rigorous calisthenics to preserve her narrow waist and flat hips. She said she feared getting fat because it detracted from the "executive look" favored among the heavy hitters in her firm, a major national corporation with extensive satellite operations in Charlotte.

One day, she suggested I might find it fun to be her date for the Wake Forest/Carolina basketball game. Her employer, a middle-aged white man who had graduated from Wake Forest, was hosting some people at his suburban Charlotte home to watch the game on his new big-screen television. I agreed, fully aware it would be less fun than whooping and yelling in front of my eighteen-inch screen.

The basketball watching went exactly as I had expected—a white-folks party with lots of expensive booze, little rib-sticking food and plenty of banal chitchat. Carolina won; I smiled, but resisted gloating. Cheryl introduced me as her friend to all the executives and wannabes along with their significant others. We were the only two black people in the house, perhaps the only two black people for miles around, judging by the neighborhood. My date was in her element the entire night, smiling broadly even after we left the party at a respectable hour.

"You were a big hit." She reached over to give me a tight-lipped kiss on the cheek as I waited for her to unlock her apartment door.

"How could you tell?"

"My boss told me so. He pulled me aside just before we left and he said, 'That young fellow is quite a catch. I like him. He's articulate, smart and very presentable.' "

I felt violated, and flushed with resentment. What was I, a Mandingo on the auction block? Had her massa looked into my mouth and felt my balls to make sure I was worthy of her purchase?

"Did he say anything else?" I was curious to know just how perfect Massa found me.

"Well, he did say you had one negative, but I didn't understand whether he was joking or not. He said you were a near-perfect corporate husband. He said you lost a point because you did not have a Phi Beta Kappa key."

I was livid now, understanding the true reason Cheryl had invited me to her boss's home. I was on display as an example of her taste and judgment in the men she dated. I assume I passed the test for her because I knew exactly how to strike the proper pose around white folks. She knew that I would wear my blue blazer with gold buttons, that I would laugh sociably (not guffaw) and that I could hold my own in any discussion without being obnoxious.

In short, I would fit in and, most important, I would not embarrass her in front of the white boss who was eyeing her for promotions and perks. I was a proper trophy date and potential husband who would fit in with her white employer's program.

"Aren't you coming in for a nightcap?" she asked with a wink that promised more than a snifter of brandy.

"No, I think I'd better pass," I said. We never dated again.

By 1981, covering high school sports had taught me how to write on deadline, build a network of sources and, most important, deliver the story my editors wanted. I also realized sports writing would serve me as a journalistic way station to a more meaningful destination. I began to cast about for the next step.

I needed to look no further than the front page of the *Observer*. Like most American newspapers, it was no longer dismissing economic issues as something indecipherable and uninteresting to most readers. Rather, there was increasing consumer demand for more sophisticated knowledge about business and personal finance. The *Observer* was aggressively moving beyond the occasional Chamber of Commerce flackery that once pawned itself off as news. More often, it gave over part of its front page to stories about interest rates, international trade, economic trends and the stock market.

As these stories crept into more prominent positions, I approached Henry Scott, the *Observer*'s business editor, about the prospect of my joining his staff. He humored me with a serious conversation about his plans for expanding the business section. Talks were in progress to begin publishing a tabloid section every Monday morning and new staffers would be needed.

"Do you know anything about business news?" he asked.

"No. But I didn't know anything about sports before I started writing about them," I said.

He liked that response and said he would see what he could do. I wrote the sample business story he requested, but I never heard anything more from him.

A year later, on a rainy February day in 1982, I returned to the office after spending most of the day interviewing high school track coaches. I could not help noticing how the lobby of the building had been prepared for a giant cocktail party to kick off the *Observer*'s new "Business Monday" section, which had been the buzz of the newsroom for weeks. Other departments were envious of the resources being diverted to this new project.

I had given up hope of landing a job in the section and had tried to ignore all the editorial meetings and planning sessions because they did not involve me. I had jumped through a series of hoops demonstrating my eagerness to become a business writer, but had concluded that the editors had no intention of adding me to this high-profile department.

But that afternoon, Mark Etheridge, now the paper's managing editor, approached me and asked me into his office. Motioning for me to close the door and take a seat, he told me I was being reassigned to the business desk immediately. He said he wanted me to attend the cocktail party that evening for Charlotte's business leaders and other movers and shakers.

"Congratulations on your promotion," he said. "I'm glad you wore a suit to work today. But before you go down to the party, you had better clean the mud off your shoes."

Once again, it seemed to me a swift and arbitrary decision. I was qualified for this "promotion" simply because he said I was, not because of any measurable expertise. I was overjoyed nonetheless. It was an assignment I wanted and I looked forward to learning about business. But as I went into the men's room and cleaned up my shoes, I wondered what had caused this sudden and unexpected change in my career.

I had been at the *Observer* for almost four years and should not have been as shocked as I was to be surrounded by so many white people at that cocktail party. What jumped out at me for the first of many times to come was the fact that not very many people in the city's business community were black. I counted the black faces, a habit I had picked up long before and exercised whenever I entered an unfamiliar room. I stopped counting after two—mine and Dr. Mildred Baxter Davis's.

Davis was a long-time friend of my family's and another of those Negro Community Guardians from my grade school days. Her title was honorific, a tribute to her influence in Charlotte's well-educated black circles. She had served as an elementary school principal and had developed a supportive following among some Westside blacks with her impassioned advocacy of her students before the school board and other municipal administrative bodies.

We saw each other at the same time, exchanged knowing glances and rushed to embrace.

"I must say, Samuel, I did not expect to see you here."

I winced at hearing my proper name. Old school teachers never change. "Well, I didn't know I was going to be here myself until about thirty minutes ago. I was just assigned to the paper's business desk."

Dr. Davis's face broadened into a smile, revealing nearly every one of her mint-fresh dentures. "Well, they listened," she said. "When they invited me to this party, I asked them if any blacks were going to work on this new business section. I told them they needed to have some black reporters on it. Samuel, I got you that job."

She grinned with pride at her achievement. The aging civil rights veteran savored her victory and beamed with enormous pride. "Well, go on, mix and mingle with the white folks," she said, shooing me away with a chuckle. "It will never do for them to think we're plotting the overthrow of the paper, will it, Samuel?"

I did not have the stomach to discuss Dr. Davis's comments with any of the *Observer*'s editors. Could this be why I was hired, plucked from the sports department on such short notice for this new, high-profile assignment? It seemed difficult to believe that the editors would have hired me in response to Dr. Davis's suggestion, but I had no doubt she had raised the issue just as she had described. That's exactly how the Negro Community Guardians operated; in private consultations with white power brokers, they pressed for whatever issue or cause they wanted white people to support. Whether she had indeed gotten me my job was something I figured I would never know and I dared not pry. If I had, I might have discovered something I was not prepared to understand. At that moment, believing my own myths seemed far more palatable anyway.

I was convinced that I deserved to be a business reporter simply because I wanted it. I refused to listen to any inner voices calling my attention to the advantages or disadvantages of being black and getting ahead in the world.

The year I spent as a business reporter at the *Observer* was my best— and my last. My tenure at the paper probably would not have ended when it did except for a well-connected friend who helped deliver a story that launched me into big-time, national journalism and away from Charlotte and the *Observer*.

In late spring of 1983, an old childhood friend, Kelly Alexander, Jr., called me at the *Observer* to ask who from the paper would cover the NAACP's annual convention in New Orleans in July. Alexander was the son of Kelly Alexander, Sr., who was one of the most enduringly prominent leaders of Charlotte's black communities. The elder Alexander, I was informed by his proud son, was about to be named national board chairman of the NAACP, as acknowledgment of his near lifelong crusade for the civil rights organization.

Kelly Sr. was the youngest of five overachieving sons born to Zachariah Alexander, who built a successful business burying colored people in Charlotte after the turn of the century. To be black and successful in that mean-spirited time presented an ironic predicament: though slavery was still a fresh memory, the political liberties delivered after the war were quickly snatched away. But Zach Alexander taught his boys they were no man's niggers, a lesson Kelly Alexander, Sr., never forgot and spent all his life proving.

Along with his brother Fred, who was elected Charlotte's mayor pro tem when I was a high school student, Kelly and the other Alexander boys continued their father's funeral home business, which eventually was passed along to Kelly Jr. and his brother, Alfred. The Alexanders also dominated the NAACP in North Carolina, founding the Charlotte branch in 1940 and rabble-rousing for the organization and on behalf of civil rights for blacks across the South. Kelly Sr. led the delegation that tapped Dorothy Counts to integrate Harding High and negotiated with the school boards in Charlotte, Greensboro and Winston-Salem to submit to the Brown decision.

I had known Kelly Jr. since I was a student at Garinger, and he was a recent graduate of the University of North Carolina, returning home to organize NAACP youth branches in the public schools. A born politician, but not quite so gifted in the give-and-take with white folks as his father or uncle, Kelly Jr. in 1983 was an ambitious young buck seeking to strap on the big shoes worn by two generations of men in his family.

During our phone conversation, Kelly Jr. made me swear to keep the news about his father's impending elevation to myself. He suggested that if I persuaded the *Observer* editors to allow me to cover the national convention, he would guarantee my getting the inside story along with exclusive interviews with his father and other NAACP officials.

It seemed like a real opportunity. I set out to persuade the editors to give me this assignment. They agreed, with one caveat: I could stay only one night in New Orleans. If I did not get the exclusive story after twenty-four hours, they would pull the financial plug and I would have to return home. Kelly had not assured me of a one-day turnaround, and knowing that board decisions at NAACP conventions never occur on schedule, I feared I could not get the story in a single day. The editors were adamant. One night in New Orleans. No more. I nervously submitted to their terms, worried that I might fail on my first national reporting assignment.

New Orleans in July is an oppressively humid place. But as the Piedmont Airlines jet landed in the Big Easy on a hellish Monday afternoon, I started sweating even before I left the air-conditioned plane. I had a day to chase recalcitrant NAACPers, nearly all of whom had far more important things to do than escort me through their Byzantine political machinations.

My anxiety only increased when I arrived at the room set aside to register the various media types covering the convention. "There's a big turnout for this one," someone said. By the size of her badge and the number of colored ribbons attached to it, I judged her to be an NAACP dignitary. "I guess the white press loves a juicy nigger-mess story. We don't usually get this kind of turnout from the big papers at our convention unless there is some kind of controversy."

There was indeed a controversy afoot. Earlier in that year, NAACP Executive Director Benjamin Hooks and Board Chairwoman Margaret Bush Wilson had been engaged in a series of internal power struggles. In May, Wilson suspended Hooks from his duties, setting up a dispute over which official—the board chairman or the executive director—spoke for the organization and wielded the power. Misreading the support she had on a board composed mostly of men who were more loyal to one of their own than to a female attorney from St. Louis, Wilson lost.

Virtually none of this made the big-city newspapers as it unfolded. During the month before the convention, the NAACP's internal strife roiled the organization in much the same way that a feud between the choir director and a deacon board member had once upset Daddy's church. The big-city editors began to pay attention when it was announced that Kelly Alexander, Sr., a steady, loyal NAACP warhorse and the organization's board vice chairman, was being tapped to give the chairman's keynote address on Monday night. This was a sign that the men on the NAACP board were waxing the skis under Wilson.

The ribbon-wearing dignitary handed me my press package and the credentials granting me admittance to many of the convention functions. I scanned the registration list. There were indeed reporters from all the big newspapers: Dorothy Gilliam from the *Washington Post*, Acel Moore from the *Philadelphia Inquirer*, Sheila Rule of the *New York Times*, Vernon Jarrett from the *Chicago Tribune*, and Jerilyn Eddings from Baltimore's *Sun*, as well as Jack White from *Time* and Carol Simpson from ABC News.

This was a high-powered bunch of black reporters, who were better known and certainly had more sources than I did with my one insider. They were going to blow me out of the water in pursuit of the same story. How in the world was I going to get my exclusive competing against such a formidable group?

I was right to be worried. I did not score any major scoop at the NAACP convention. But, as luck or fate would have it, the *Observer* editors revised my terms for covering the convention. Since we were in the run-up to an election year, they decided they wanted a daily story and I should make national politics the main angle of my reporting instead of the NAACP squabbles.

The paper published my first story of the week under the headline NAACP IN NO HURRY TO ENDORSE CANDIDATE, a curtain-raiser that prominently featured Charlotte's Kelly Alexander, Sr., and the fact that "a parade of presidential hopefuls" would address the convention's four thousand delegates during the week. Before the week ended, I wrote a story about Hooks challenging the Reagan Administration's economic policies and another piece on how the NAACP leaders were old black men, "veterans of the civil rights struggles of the '40s, '50s and '60s."

My editors, shocked at first that I delivered such good stories, were overjoyed. Each article ran on the front page. One excitable editor went so far as to compliment me upon my return. "I had no idea you could do political reporting," he said.

I was bitterly disappointed that I had not done the job I set for myself in going to New Orleans. I wanted to pursue the black angle of the story, the one about the internal struggles of the nation's oldest civil rights organization. That would have to wait for another day. The *Observer* editors were satisfied with what they got.

Unbeknownst to me, my work at the NAACP convention attracted attention beyond the *Observer* newsroom. The business editor of *The Sun* in Baltimore called me a few days after I returned from New Orleans.

"I heard about you from Jerilyn Eddings, who was in New Orleans," the voice, that of a white man, said on the other end of the phone line. "I'd like to talk to you about coming to work at the Baltimore *Sun*. Can you send me some samples of your work and come here for an interview?"

Of course I could. And since no one had told me otherwise, I assumed I should inform my present editors that I was going to talk to the man from Baltimore. Silly me, I thought that was the way it was done, getting permission from my present owners to trade up to a new team. I rushed into Mark Etheridge's office and told him I would be interviewing at *The Sun*.

"I knew if we let you out of town, someone would try and steal you away," Etheridge said. Although he meant it as a compliment, I believed it as a fact.

By now, I was spending most of my free time with Cynthia, either at her apartment or at the house I now shared with an old college buddy. I told her about the job interview and she had the same reaction as my family: she did not like the idea that I might move away.

I knew she wanted to get married, but I avoided that discussion, thinking that if I did not talk about it, it would not come up. But it did come up. On one occasion, her mother, who reminded me for all the world of my own, suggested to Cynthia, loud enough for me to hear, "You two ought to play house, get married or do something other than mark time with each other." Knowing Mrs. Bell to be a deeply religious woman and sensitive to what the neighbors might say about her daughter's shacking up in Charlotte with some man, I dismissed her suggestion that we play house as hyperbolic rhetoric. I knew she felt that I was wasting her daughter's time by not bending my knee, proffering a diamond and popping the question. I suspected Cynthia felt the same way.

My moving to Baltimore, if the job materialized, threatened our relationship, Cynthia said. She volunteered no more, allowing me to draw what conclusions I would from her statement of fact.

"I'm only going on the interview," I said. "Let's see what happens after that."

Chapter Six

DAZED BY *The Sun*

My decision to move to Baltimore was equal parts careerism and serendipity.

I wasn't looking for a new job, but I was ready for a change. Charlotte was the only place I knew and I longed for an opportunity to test myself somewhere else. I had talked with editors about assignments at newspapers elsewhere in North Carolina, but moving within the state seemed a backward step. Unsolicited inquiries from editors at newspapers in New Orleans and Louisville didn't excite me enough to move to one of those places. I wanted to work in a big city like New York or Washington. Those were the only places I imagined the best journalists would consider.

Part of my facination with big-city journalism stemmed from having met black reporters who worked for the *Washington Post*, the *New York Times* and other "national" newspapers at NABJ conferences. They were an attractive crew, swaggering about in packs and spinning great stories about their travels to cover political campaigns and overseas assignments. They had expense accounts and would treat several of us "rookies" from poorer newspapers to dinners at expensive restaurants. When the waiter arrived with the bill, they all made big productions of reaching for their wallets, flashing corporate credit cards and scrambling for the honor of picking up the tab.

I listened to them talk about themselves and heard only what I wanted to hear: if I worked hard and long enough at my job, one day I might be like them. That wasn't a hard sell. I was turning out business stories about farm reports and corporate annual meetings that nobody outside of rural North Carolina read. My job at the *Observer* was a far cry from the one I craved. I imagined myself covering national and international stories. Politics. Wars. Riots. I wanted to travel to far away places and send back reports that put my analysis of current events on the front page. I wanted to be an important and powerful journalist.

My few attempts to get hired at a national newspaper had always been rebuffed. I sent letters, with photocopied clippings of my favorite stories, to the *New York Times,* the *Washington Post* and the *Chicago Tribune.* Typically, nothing came of my applications, except a form letter saying the newspaper had no openings available that fit my qualifications and they would keep my letter on file.

Sometimes I got the letdown after flying in for an interview that went nowhere. I squandered a day in 1982 visiting with the editors at the *Philadelphia Inquirer* and the *Philadelphia Daily News,* only to be told by a senior editor of the *Daily News* that they had nothing to offer and weren't really sure why they had asked me to come to Philadelphia in the first place. "It was really a waste of your time and our money to bring you up here," he said, ushering me to the door with a check for my travel expenses.

My experience with the *Washington Post* was worse: I arrived on the morning of my scheduled interview to find that Milton Coleman, the editor who had invited me, had no time to talk with me.

"Can you come in tomorrow?" Coleman, then Metro editor at the

Post, said when I called to confirm my afternoon appointment. "I'm sorry. I'm going to be in meetings all day that I can't put off."

The next day, I met Coleman and learned that those meetings had involved his mop-up operations in the wake of Janet Cooke's "Jimmy's World," a fantastic story about an eight-year-old who had injected himself with heroin. Before the story was disclosed as a fabrication of Cooke's creative mind, it won the Pulitzer Prize for feature writing.

The next day, when I finally got my interview at the *Post*, the editors were in no mood to take another chance and hire a reporter like me without a pedigree endorsed by someone from within their organization. The Cooke episode did more than drive one misguided black writer out of journalism and tarnish the *Post*'s reputation—it also stigmatized black journalists. Cooke's ambition was interpreted as an endemic character flaw. By her example, all of us were accidents waiting to happen unless newspaper editors selected their black reporters carefully.

"Are you a black first or a reporter first," one white editor asked me during my interviews at the *Post*. The assumption, a racist one at that, was that, as a black reporter, one must choose sides; I suspect no white male applicant would have had such an option presented to him. Les Payne, an outspoken editor and columnist for *Newsday*, offered the most perfect answer to such a question that I have ever heard, a simple and direct response that would settle anyone's confusion. "I have never seen a black woman give birth to a little baby reporter," he said.

I didn't have the presence of mind to give Les Payne's more appropriate answer, so I gave the editor the one I thought he wanted. "I'm a reporter who happens to be black," I said. I didn't get hired at the *Post*, but I continued to want a job there because it was the big time.

The one side benefit of these unsuccessful efforts was my discovery that the protocols of a job interview involve a series of well-coordinated steps between the applicant and the hiring editor. Any experienced job seeker knows that the rules favor the person who looks the least needy during the interview. Many white applicants and employers play this game without the racial rules interfering, thus starting out with less cultural distance to cover before the interview gets serious.

If you add expectations about race and class to the interview interaction, then the chemistry changes entirely. A white person, whether applicant or employer, will assume the offensive, superior pose, while it is assumed that the black person will naturally—as gravity pulls objects to the center of the earth—settle for the subordinate position. For his place, so to speak.

During an interview in a city where I did not particularly want to relocate, I experimented with role reversals by interviewing the white employer. After all, I assumed, it was as important for me to know all I could about the job as it was for my prospective boss to learn all he could about me. The interview went along swimmingly, with me dutifully—and in a modest and unassuming fashion—responding to his questions about my life and background and work experience, until I leaned forward to signal that I had a question.

I asked the hardest one I could imagine: "Are you interviewing me because I'm black?"

"Well, er, uh, no," he replied from behind a beet-colored face. "That's not a requirement for this job. Frankly, I hadn't noticed whether—what I mean to say is I don't care whether you are black or not."

As I was told later by friendly spies within that newsroom, the editor considered me "arrogant," a catch-all word for black folks who don't play the game according to the rules.

So by August 1983, when I landed in Baltimore for my job interview with *The Sun*, I was an accomplished buppie careerist and trying hard to shift gears to a faster track in journalism. Philip Moeller, *The Sun*'s business editor, had suggested that I arrive on a Sunday, a day early, to have dinner at his home.

A pleasant, round-faced woman with blond hair answered the door to the brick-front row house and identified herself as Cheryl, Phil's wife. She ushered me through a darkened living room, sparsely decorated, and past an even more modestly appointed dining room into the kitchen. Judging by the looks of the place, I assumed they were renovating or planned to live there only temporarily. I made a mental note to ask discreetly if they intended to stay in Baltimore. Moving here would not be wise if the guy hiring me was not committed to sticking around. And if he sounded dubious about staying in Baltimore, maybe I would have my excuse to reject the job offer, if one was made.

The man sitting on a director's chair in the middle of the kitchen had to be Phil Moeller, the editor I had come to see. He was a pudgy, balding man in a T-shirt, white shorts and sneakers. He sweated profusely and sucked hard on a can of beer. He looked as though he had just finished plowing his backyard.

I smiled. It was a struggle to suppress the surprise I felt, but I knew better than to expose an inch of myself. Everything was informal. He was not playing by the rules. He was not imposing his superiority over me. How could he strike a lofty pose if he was sitting there in a sweat-soaked T-shirt and shorts? I liked the fact that he was treating me like a Sunday visitor in his home, not a job applicant he had to impress.

Later, in the more formal job interview, conducted on Monday morning in his newsroom office, I felt compelled to put him to my guilt-o-meter test: "Are you hiring me because I'm black?" I watched closely to record his every reaction, feeling certain he had already decided to offer me the job.

Moeller's eyes narrowed. "Yeah, partly," he said in a clear, firm voice. "If I were hiring the best person I could find, I would probably hire someone I already know. That would be somebody white. You're not the best business reporter I know. You're probably a B, B-plus. But we don't have a black reporter in this department and I think we should. You're what I want and what this department needs."

Bingo. An honest, if unflattering, answer. As I mulled over his comment for the rest of the day, I thought that maybe I had heard a compliment, that maybe Moeller had honored me by speaking truthfully, revealing a form of self-disclosure I had never heard before.

Despite the impertinence of my question, it hadn't unnerved him.

He said exactly what he believed. His words were unsanitized by the smiley-faced deceit so common in these interview situations. He didn't serve up the compliments he might have imagined I wanted to hear. I could take what he said or leave it, but I would know where I stood in his opinion. I felt flattered that he would take me so seriously, something I felt no potential newsroom boss had done till then.

So when he called me at home in Charlotte a few days later, formally asking me to accept a business writer's job, I went through the motions of bargaining for a few extra dollars and additional vacation benefits. Pro forma stuff, just for the sake of employer-employee protocol, and to avoid appearing too eager. But I had already decided to accept the job back in Phil Moeller's Baltimore row house kitchen.

In a sense, my life as a self-aware middle-class black American debuted with my relocation to Baltimore. The process, of course, was gradual. The first step commenced with my packing all my possessions into the back of an eighteen-foot orange-and-white U-Haul truck.

I remember thinking, as I arrived for my first day at *The Sun*, how life repeated itself. This was going to be like college and like the *Observer* all over again. I would have to prove myself anew. I promised myself to work hard and to avoid the kinds of early mistakes that had dogged me at the *Observer*. This was a new opportunity, I thought, a fresh start where no one knew my history and there would be no comparisons to the past. I could re-create myself in any fashion I chose and the only pressures on me would be those I put on myself.

I realized that the new challenge of living in Baltimore would nudge me into rethinking who I was. But I was thinking solely in professional and career terms; I had no idea how profoundly personal those changes would be.

It became quickly apparent to me that *The Sun* was radically different from the *Observer*. Most obvious was the fact that its stories were longer and its reporters had the luxury of more time to gather information, as well as greater independence. In Charlotte, I had grown accustomed to editors who dictated the contents of stories and waited like huge beasts to consume the large quantities of short articles we reporters shoveled into their gaping maws. But in Baltimore, story production was more leisurely. The pace was so laid-back that some reporters seemed outright lazy, writing stories when, how and if it suited their fancy.

This greater freedom allowed me to explore various parts of Baltimore's black communities, even though my job at *The Sun* kept me busy. Both Baltimores—the newsroom and the city surrounding it— were new and exciting to me. In Charlotte, I had been plugged into the black community because I had grown up in it, and I felt more comfortable in the *Observer*'s newsroom because it had been the only one I knew.

But Baltimore was different. I knew no one and needed to develop contacts and sources inside and outside the newsroom. Navigating the newsroom was the easier of the two because my time there was more structured than my off-duty hours.

I quickly settled into a routine of reporting to work, writing stories as they were assigned and returning to the apartment I rented six blocks away.

My weekends and evenings were another matter. There were only a handful of places in which I found easy acceptance as a professional in this strange city, all of them in a black community. In making my rounds of middle-class black Baltimore—from the upscale Gatsby's nightclub on Charles Street to the homespun Five Mile House on Reisterstown Road, from worship services at politically charged churches like Bethel AME to fraternity meetings at the Alpha Phi Alpha alumni chapter to business organizations like the President's Roundtable, composed of the chief executives of the city's black-owned firms—I listened to the voices of black Baltimore that went unheard in the more powerful white establishment. Though the city's black population had nearly doubled between 1950 and 1980, turning Baltimore into yet another

Chocolate City surrounded by Vanilla Suburbs, one twenty-seven-year-old black attorney told *Baltimore* magazine in 1984, "We're the new 'silent majority.'"

My responsibilities as a business reporter, however, required that I move into the white world of corporate board rooms, stockholders' meetings and security analysts' briefings that no other black reporter at *The Sun* had previously entered. Once I was inside that world, my editors took for granted that I would see the same story angles as any good white reporter and write my articles accordingly.

But the windows of my world as a black professional newcomer in Baltimore opened out on a place extremely different from that witnessed by many of the white reporters in the newsroom. For me, the racial disparities apparent on Baltimore's streets affected me in emotional and intimate ways, but judging by the comments I heard from many white colleagues, the same sights could be discussed dispassionately in terms of sociology, politics or behavioral psychology—anything but personal identification. People living and begging for money on the streets came as a shock to me because the homeless problem had never seemed as acute or visible back in North Carolina.

"Why don't they get a job?" a white reporter muttered under his breath as we waved off a cluster of aggressive panhandlers blocking our way back to the office from a Harbor Place lunch.

"I guess they would if someone would hire them," I said.

My response slipped out as a reflex, triggering a voluble discussion that changed nothing for the homeless and neither of our respective opinions. But it did leave me feeling depressed, as though I had failed to acquit those poor, nameless people of the collective scorn of white people.

I credit the city with my becoming more aware of the curious differences in attitude between me and my white colleagues, because Baltimore was the most socially diverse and at the same time racially stratified place I had ever experienced. In both Charlotte and Chapel Hill, the two towns where I had lived, cultural diversity was little more than male and female, black and white, Christian and heathen.

But after I had been in Baltimore several months, the city stopped surprising me. I delighted in learning how it had enclaves of ethnic Europeans, Jews, WASPs, black underclass and a tiny minority of buppies. All of this provided a constant source of ideas that I shaped into business news stories. My stories were novel to *The Sun*'s readers and I could always find a place for them in the paper, often on the front page. To my way of thinking, this was the kind of journalism I was born to write.

After I had been in Baltimore a year, I fully realized how much I missed Cynthia. My longing for her confirmed what I had often promised but failed so far to do: end our long-distance courting and get married. When I left Charlotte, Cynthia had been adamant about not moving to Baltimore on her own. If and when we got married, she said, she would relocate. But not before. Since then, we had talked about getting married in ambiguous terms, but I had resisted making any long-term commitments to her or to myself.

For Christmas, my first in Baltimore, I gave Cynthia a pair of diamond earrings—and was taken aback when she was angered by the gift. She wanted an engagement ring. "I don't see the difference," she said. "If you can afford earrings, you could afford a ring."

"Yes, I guess that's right," I said. "But they mean totally different things. I'm not ready for what the ring means."

By spring, my convictions had changed. Living alone in Baltimore seemed to alter my attitudes about many things, including having Cynthia in my life on a permanent basis. I was making a new life for myself and it seemed right that I complete the process by getting married. For all the delays, Cynthia had stuck with me. She was the first woman I had met who truly knew me and still loved me. Once I realized that, I knew it was time to marry her. There wasn't any doubt. I could never find anyone else that special and I would love her for a lifetime.

During a weekend visit to Charlotte in mid-spring 1984, I gave

Cynthia the engagement ring. She immediately made plans for a September wedding and to resettle in Baltimore. I remain convinced, even now, that asking Cynthia to marry me was the best decision I've made as an adult. It forced me to become less selfish, because I knew she deserved and would tolerate nothing less. I also became more deeply grounded in Baltimore, where I expected to be for a long, long time but as yet had only professional roots.

Our plans for a future together seemed to catch the attention of some *Sun* newsroom managers. After I announced our engagement, one of the editors with whom I had had little previous contact told me how happy he was that I was getting married. He said it was a good idea for me to settle down because a family would make me a more reliable employee. He also said that he liked "what I have seen of" Cynthia because she seemed "like a good woman who will enjoy married life with you."

Though I thought it impolitic to tell him, his comments never sat well with me. First, he had never met Cynthia, only seen a framed photograph of her on my desk, and had no clue about whom I dated. Perhaps he was operating on the erroneous assumption that I was involved with a colleague, a white woman who often ate lunch with me. He might not have been aware of it, but I had noticed his ogling look and the curious way he bit his lip whenever he saw the two of us together in the cafeteria. I hadn't thought much of it until he made a special point of congratulating me on my impending wedding. I wasn't being paranoid; rather, I think he was.

About the same time, I began widening my circle of acquaintances in the city to develop new contacts among white business executives. This was not as hard as I had imagined it would be. I represented *The Sun,* an institution that the business leaders respected as a part of their own constellation. I was acutely aware, however, that it was the institution they honored, and not necessarily its ambassador—me.

But every now and then, when their guards slipped and they honestly revealed themselves, I got the impression that some white people considered me special or unique for circulating easily in their midst.

On one occasion in early 1985, I was invited to a black-tie dinner honoring some of the heavy hitters in Baltimore's advertising and public relations industry. I attended because it was a professional function, just the sort of place where, along with the chewy chicken, reporters might get served some bit of gossip that could be worked into a news article.

During the cocktail hour preceding dinner, I wandered through the room listening in on conversations and planting myself in others with hopes of learning something newsworthy. As I worked the large room, I looked for black faces among the hundreds of white ones.

I was alone.

I wasn't surprised by it. In fact, I had expected it, having recently written a story about how few blacks were included in Baltimore's social-business circles. Part of that story relied heavily on research compiled by Baltimoreans United in Leadership Development, a church-based coalition, which had found that only 3 of the 121 directors of the city's largest banks and none of partners in the major law firms were black.

I found my place at a large round table, next to a chatty white woman who identified herself as "a fallen attorney" who now wrote part-time for a legal newspaper. She waxed enthusiastic when I told her I was a reporter for *The Sun*.

"I don't think I would be here otherwise," I said.

"Why not? This is a lovely party. I'm just thrilled to be surrounded by so many talented and important people," she said. "I would think you would enjoy this too."

"Nope. Not my crowd. This is work, nothing more." I could see she was baffled by my comment, so, against my better judgment, I decided to lecture her on how a black professional feels in a white world. I told her that my job at the paper was to write about the city's business community and that the overwhelming bulk of my work involved issues related to the travails of white men who wore monotonous gray, pin-striped suits and—yes—wing-tip shoes.

I identified much more with the black people in Baltimore, I said, noting that I tried to include their affairs in my work. As often as possible, I sought out black people as sources, many of whom had never figured in a story that did not specifically deal with racial issues.

I rarely saw a similar effort by white reporters to include ordinary black people in the pages of *The Sun*. This is a point of distinction between black and white reporters, and has been a constant sore point for nearly every black professional I have ever known. We all complain about our shared frustration at having to master the complexities of the white world without a corresponding urgency on the part of white people to understand the black world.

"I'm here to meet people and to find out information for the paper," I concluded. "These are not my friends. They are people who might be helpful, but I don't confuse them with buddies."

"Oh-h-h," the woman said. "But you seem to be having a grand time. That's why I thought you enjoyed parties like these."

She fell silent for a long time. After the dinner plates were removed and as coffee was being served, she faced me squarely. "Excuse me," she began. "I've been thinking about what you just said. Let me ask you something?"

"Sure," I said. "Ask me anything."

"Is your wife white?" she said.

When I granted her permission to ask me anything, I never imagined she would ask me that. No one had ever asked me a question so off the wall, so irrelevant to what had preceded it. I was speechless, unable to think of what to say. The best I could do was blink my eyes hard and croak, "No."

I do not remember either of us saying another word until we parted with polite "Nice to have met you"'s, which to this day is one of the big regrets of my life. I remain haunted by the fact that I did not pursue the matter. I wish I had had presence of mind to ask her just what made her think Cynthia might be a white woman. (I can only speculate that my shiny new wedding band tipped the woman off that I was in fact married; I had not mentioned it during our conversation.)

I have replayed our table talk over and over from memory, and can only conclude that she saw my ability to project a semblance of ease around white people—at the same time that I hid any frustrations at being perpetually surrounded by them—as having roots that reached deep into my home life. Ergo: he has a white wife, for surely no black man could achieve such a state on his own. But her question still leaves me baffled.

Toward the end of my first year at *The Sun,* a racial controversy erupted over a series of stories by a white reporter in our sister publication, *The Evening Sun.* The five-part series, which ran during the first week in December, depicted in vivid detail the lifestyles of an unprecedented number of poor black families headed by young women. Among the statistical underpinnings of the articles was a 1982 National Urban League study revealing that 76 percent of all black births in Baltimore were to unmarried mothers, a higher percentage than in any other U.S. city. The series also highlighted the Urban League's finding that 53 percent of all black families with children under eighteen were headed by women.

Within hours of the papers' hitting doorsteps across the city, telephone operators at the newspaper building fielded angry calls from readers canceling their subscriptions. The series touched the raw nerves of many black Baltimoreans, no longer willing to suffer silently from what they felt was deliberate negative coverage of their communities.

While the angry voices outshouted all others, the series did prompt mixed reactions from across the city. Between seventy-five and one hundred people telephoned *The Evening Sun* in the first three days following publication of the articles, about half praising them. Among the callers were a group of workers at the Westinghouse plant in suburban Linthicum, a housewife living in a bedroom community between Baltimore and Washington, and a black minister—all of whom told the paper they wanted to donate clothing and furniture to the families cited in the stories, but wanted to remain anonymous.

But outrage dominated the black communities' discussion of the *Evening Sun* articles. "I don't understand why [the series] was done," said Arnett Brown, Jr., principal of Cherry Hill Junior High School, in the impoverished black community south of downtown. "These problems are known in the black community. We are all aware of the problem. It should have been left where it is." Samuel L. Banks, president of the National Association for the Study of Afro-American Life and History, spoke on behalf of the Baltimore branch of the NAACP. "The series, in toto, constituted a flagrant, mean-spirited, superficial, and monumental affront [to] and impugning of Baltimore's majority black community," he said at an NAACP meeting called to organize a protest against the newspaper's treatment of blacks in the city.

Before too long, the NAACP's anger over the series escalated into demands from Samuel Banks and other black leaders for the newspaper to disown the series and to initiate extensive minority hiring and positive coverage of the black community. The paper's management agreed to hear the NAACP's demands but refused to buckle under to them, further outraging the black leaders.

From our perch inside the *Sunpapers* building on Calvert Street, we black reporters were divided regarding the paper's difficulties. Some thought the series was well done, others felt it should have been written by a black reporter, and still others were just as angry as the protesters. The series was accurate and told an unpleasant truth, but the anger of blacks seemed reasonable to me as well. Newspapers tend to tell one side of the truth about black communities and usually it's the negative side.

On the other hand, marching in protest outside the newspaper building seemed to me a stupid, futile and self-aggrandizing waste of the NAACP leaders' time. Editors will report whatever they choose. Loud protests are little more than great sport for the people participating in them, and give newspapers the opportunity to publish more stories while generating letters to the editor and subscription-boosting publicity. In other words, the NAACP protest was a marketing opportunity for *The Evening Sun.*

This view was borne out as the management hit upon a stalling strategy to defuse the community's sense of outrage. The black community leaders set up a series of closed-door meetings with *Sunpapers* publisher Reg Murphy and other executives. These talks dragged on for weeks with no resolution of the tensions between the NAACP leaders and the papers' management.

Shortly after the New Year, the publisher decided to go directly to the black community by hosting a series of community gatherings in black churches and community centers. It was an excellent opportunity for angry black folks to let off steam and air their grievances, while making the paper appear accessible and interested in their views. To publicize these meetings, the marketing department promoted them on black radio stations and ran advertisements in the newspaper itself that ostensibly informed concerned citizens when and where they could "meet the editors" of their hometown newspapers.

I attended the first of these meetings at the insistence of ranking editor at *The Sun*. I am certain he wanted to have a few of its black reporters present to prevent the paper from appearing as white as it actually was.

The meeting began pleasantly enough when a newspaper spokeswoman stepped to the microphone in the basement fellowship hall of a neighborhood church. She explained that *The Sun* cared about the community and had tried to portray all segments of Baltimore with fairness. That was the reason for this meeting, to clear the lines of communication between the paper and its readers, she said. A number of the editors then took turns introducing themselves and describing their jobs. Later, the protesters marched to the microphone, this one decrying the paper's insensitivity to the black community, that one threatening an economic boycott that would ruin the paper's financial base.

I finally reached my limit when one of the NAACP leaders launched into a thundering oration about how Baltimore's black community was a sleeping giant that would soon wake from its slumber and stomp out all the city's racist institutions. "We will not stand for such abuse and disrespect from *The Sunpapers* any longer," he said to rousing applause and shouts.

None of the speakers before him had ignited the audience the way he did. Until this point, the meeting had proceeded like a well-rehearsed play performed by third graders, the actors mouthing their lines with some exuberance but none of the participants giving any hint of really caring about what the others were saying. But now the mood was changing and I was convinced that from this point on attitudes would harden, making it difficult for anyone to emerge from the church with a renewed spirit of cooperation.

I had come to this meeting with no intention of speaking. But all of a sudden, I felt the need to say something. So, with butterflies as huge as bats flapping in my gut, I waited for a turn at the microphone.

"I've been listening to you all talk for more than an hour and I think everyone is missing the point here," I said after I had identified myself as a new reporter for *The Sun*. I looked at the NAACP leaders, sitting in a front-row corner with their arms and legs crossed. "You don't change a newspaper with protests. If you must protest, why not direct that at advertisers, not the newspaper building. Advertisers might be more sensitive to the adverse publicity, but a newspaper can't appear to buckle under to community pressure. Especially pressure from interest groups that feel they have been mistreated by the paper. When that happens, it only gives the paper more reasons to write about the interest groups."

The NAACP shifted in their seats. It was clear to me they felt umbrage at my criticism. I turned away from them and toward my newspaper bosses.

"However"—I cleared my throat—"I don't think the editors from the newspapers understand how upset black people feel when they only see themselves as something pathological in the paper. I don't think any of you have heard what the community is saying here tonight. I also think it is rather hypocritical to pretend you're just practicing good journalism when you hold one segment of the community up for ridicule and never see anything of value in it."

I tried to read the reaction of the editors, who were sitting down front and center, but their faces revealed nothing.

"I think if you really wanted to be a part of the whole community, this entire episode would never have occurred, because there would have been black reporters and editors involved in the decisions that went into producing the stories," I continued. "I know—because I work there—that there are no black editors at the paper who make decisions or could stop the paper from making a mistake that would be embarrassing to black people or to the paper itself.

"Many of the black reporters at the paper are like me, basically new to the community and not well grounded in what's going on among black people anyway. If *The Sunpapers* cared as much as you are saying, you would know the people in the room and wouldn't have needed this threat of a protest to get you to talk to them."

One of the community leaders, a bear of a black man whom I had not seen before, grabbed me by the arm after I stepped away from the microphone. He gently pulled me aside and launched into a whispered lecture. "I understood what you said up there," he said. "But you're too young to understand what we're doing here. You can't appreciate the importance of street protests because you didn't see the civil rights marches. I did. I marched with Martin and I saw how that changes things."

I should have anticipated his lecture, but I was caught off guard. If this had happened in Charlotte, I would have known better than to sass one of my elders from the Negro Community Guardians. This man was a Baltimore NAACP official and I hadn't respected the conventions of my adopted home. If I had been more perceptive, I would have realized that he was a member of Baltimore's Negro Community Guardians.

Actually, every city with a distinct black middle class has a subset of black folks who assume the self-appointed responsibility for monitoring white folks' behavior and for governing the welfare of the entire black community. Although there is no formal or official organization, they may belong to or lead groups like the NAACP or black business associations. They can most easily be identified as black leaders, through the news media, because influential white people turn to them for advice and as negotiators for the entire black community. In fact, their status as middle-class stems more often from their ability to talk rationally with white people than from any economic-based or income-indexed definition.

Influential whites don't know anyone else in the black communities to help them access the masses of black people living out of sight in their midst, and so they turn to these self-appointed leaders to perform the task. The Negro Community Guardians participate in this arrangement because they derive great authority among their black supporters for dealing with "the man." Sometimes they receive money, jobs or other instruments of power from whites to broker within the black community, which in turn increases their influence over their black followers. Most often, they just receive media exposure and public attention, which is enough to ensure they will have higher status than the quiet majority of black people in any city.

The Guardians also exist because within black communities, where class and economic stratification among black people are often overlooked by white elites, there is a collective sense that community integrity is forged primarily by sharing a racial identity.

As a child, I had accepted the counsel of the Guardians—Mrs. Cunningham, Mrs. Wheeler and "Pop" Moreland—because they were the elders and authorities in my community. I didn't dare question them or their motives. If I had grown up in Baltimore, I would have been more deferential to the leaders of the NAACP. I would have recognized them as this city's Negro Community Guardians and treated them accordingly.

"How could you, a black man, stand up there and berate the NAACP for organizing a protest against that white paper?" the NAACP leader said as the meeting continued without us. "Unless you were grandstanding to curry favor with your editors." He then told me I should have been ashamed of myself because had it not been for activists like himself "who had marched in Selma with Martin Luther King, Jr., you wouldn't have had your job at *The Sunpapers.*"

There was nothing I could say to this man. He hadn't listened to everything I had said. My editors were not pleased by my lecturing them either. He continued his verbal barrage until one of his friends shushed him. He then quickly turned on his heels and walked away. The whole scene must have lasted about three minutes, during which I said absolutely nothing.

While I knew clearly I was not a part of Baltimore's white business community (I only wrote about it), and knew with equal assurance I was not a member of the black underclass in the inner city, I was perplexed because I didn't feel right following the city's old civil rights warhorses. I came from the black middle class, but not from Baltimore's black middle class. I realized I had broken the local rules by berating this respected NAACP leader in the basement of a black church. I had breached the solidarity of our race—and in front of white folks no less. I am convinced that was what angered him most and prompted him to pull me aside for that lecture. His talk taught me plenty about Baltimore, its black leaders and where I stood with them.

By February, the NAACP leaders broke off their negotiations with the paper and called on readers to cancel their subscriptions. Samuel Banks, as leader of the protesters, said the terms for removing the boycott included reopening a foreign reporting bureau in South Africa, hiring more blacks as reporters and editors and improving coverage of the black community. After a few weeks, the protesters grew weary of trudging around the building and called off their demonstration. They declared victory, but could not point to any of their demands having been met. Further, as far as I could tell, no one ever held them accountable for failing to do so.

The day after I made my speech at the community meeting, Barry Rascovar, assistant editor of the editorial pages, called me down to his office on the third floor. I had never met him and was unaware that he knew me. "I noticed your comments at the meeting last night," he said. "We're looking for another editorial writer and thought you might be interested."

Rascovar said Jerilyn Eddings, the only black editorial writer for

The Sun, would soon leave for a Nieman Fellowship at Harvard and they wanted a replacement. After hearing what I had said at the town meeting, it dawned on him that I might be a good choice for the position.

It was obvious to me he wanted to replace a black with a black. With all the racial tensions swirling around the paper, they would not want to lose a black editorial writer without having another take her place. This had less to do with me than with the newspaper's needs. But after thinking about it briefly, I decided that it was also an excellent career move. Editorial writing is one of the last provinces of white men in journalism. I agreed to move to the paper's editorial board, thinking this would be a great place to assert my opinions.

As it turned out, I was being rewarded by being silenced. No one ever said this to me. All I ever heard was praise for my work and resourcefulness. Everyone was gracious, solicitous and supportive. Joe Stern, the editor of the editorial pages, treated me with great respect. But it was clear that the pages belonged to him and not the individual voices of the editorial writers, which were to be subordinated to his imperial and moderate-to-conservative opinions.

I wasn't particularly happy as an editorial writer. I had an office, a bookcase filled with important documents, and business cards identifying me as an editorial writer. On occasion, by praising a congressman for voting this way or condemning another for voting that way, I caught the attention of someone outside the paper and would be invited to speak before a gathering of important and well-read white people. I had the status and prestige that went with being the only black who had leapfrogged over all the others in *The Sunpapers'* newsroom to get that glass-fronted office.

But I was uneasy because I was not saying all that I wanted to say. The words were my own, but the ideas belonged to the institution. And I was discovering more and more that offended me. This was not the newspaper business I had been attracted to.

I had plenty of opportunities as an editorial writer to think about such things, like the time an advertising executive for *The Sun* explained to me in all candor that the newspaper sold ads by marketing to its white suburban readers and not to the black residents in the inner city. He described this sales pitch as selling the "meat of the doughnut, not the hole." He was right, of course. In a city where more than 50 percent of the residents were black, a great percentage of whom were poor and working class, the daily newspaper of record most concerned itself with attracting readers from the outlying suburban areas of Hunt Valley, as well as rural Howard and Anne Arundel counties. I took the advertising executive's comment to heart, believing it supported the fact that black reporters and editorial writers fit in a newroom only to service the status quo, not challenge it.

Chapter Seven

SOJOURN TO SOUTH AFRICA

By 1985, I had made a strange sort of peace between myself and *The Sun*. My job was comfortable, even if I was uncomfortable in it. But I assumed everybody chafed in their jobs (that's the nature of work, I often said to myself) and I tried to make the best of it, which wasn't hard to do. I was a careerist who had a cushy life. Cynthia was happy with her job at Johns Hopkins University Hospital, where she worked in an office that sent family planning materials to Third World countries. We had a two-bedroom apartment in a quiet suburban Jewish neighborhood just outside the Baltimore city limits and we were saving money to buy a house.

From time to time, I discussed my growing sense of racial frustration and isolation at work with Cynthia, but neither of us knew how to make any sense of these strange feelings. We had no mentors or reference points. Our parents had worked in segregated environments and could offer no guidance.

When Cynthia and I talked about how different our life was from that of our parents, we concurred—as my best friend, Larry, and I once had done in a late-night conversation back at Carolina—that we were trailblazers. Cynthia was now my closest confidant, having displaced Larry, who by this time was a suburban Chicago homeowner, married and father of a young son. While some other college friends had gone on to do as well or better, I considered Larry the most tangible success story among my peers from the old days. We made time for phone conversations and compared notes about our salaries, the personalities in our workplaces and our family lives. Based on what he told me, I considered him better established and further along in his career. He was an example of all I wished for myself. If anyone, Larry would have been the person to call for advice about career moves or dealing with the white folks at work.

But I didn't because that would have been admitting my second-class status. I would have been embarrassed to let on that I had fallen behind him, so I kept up the pretense with a stiff posture and cocky attitude. Keeping my fears secret from Larry made it easier to avoid discussing my worries with anyone else. Heaven forbid my colleagues at *The Sun* should ever know how queasy I felt about my job.

The swirling confusion I felt at work pulled me all the closer to Cynthia at home. I held on to her as my link to the security and optimism I remembered feeling back when I lived in Charlotte, back when I believed anything was possible, when it all seemed so easy for me. I felt closer to her than anyone else I knew and assumed she shared the same feelings toward me. We drew strength from each other's fear, binding us in a mutually dependent and supportive way from the very start of our marriage. Alone at work, we protected ourselves as best we could during the day; together at home, we comforted each other through the night. Whatever the stresses, we offset them for each other because we were determined to advance in our careers.

In late April 1985, Richard O'Mara, foreign editor at *The Sun*, called me at home to ask if I would consider going to South Africa for a temporary assignment. I was shocked because I hardly knew O'Mara and had never worked with him. His call came totally out of the blue. I was elated because foreign jobs were about as high in the pecking order as a reporter could aspire. But until I answered O'Mara's phone call, I had taken little professional interest over events going on in South Africa.

So, I asked myself, why me? Why South Africa? Why now?

Of course I knew the answers to all the whys without putting them into words: the editors wanted a black reporter in Africa. Sending a black reporter there had been one of the demands of the NAACP protesters. Now, it seemed, the editors were asking me once again to be The All-Purpose Black.

The Sun had closed its Johannesburg bureau in 1983, shortly before I was hired at the paper, relocating its white correspondent to Moscow. The editors' thinking at the time was that the slow-moving story of black resistence to apartheid in South Africa failed to warrant the continuing expense of a full-time correspondent, one who in addition covered the entire fifty-four-country African continent.

Their opinion must have begun to change on November 21, 1984. On that Thanksgiving Day, the Free South Africa movement went public in the United States as a trio of civil rights leaders—Randall Robinson of TransAfrica, Mary Francis Berry of the U.S. Commission on Civil Rights and Delegate Walter Fauntroy, the Democratic congressional representative for the District of Columbia—launched a series of protests outside the South African embassy in Washington, D.C. Robinson, Berry and Fauntroy were mediagenic veterans of the 1960s. They knew their demonstrations would gain maximum coverage on Thanksgiving, a slow news day that offers newspaper readers and television viewers little but football games, parades and banal features on do-good volunteers doing their once-a-year charity work of feeding the homeless turkey dinners.

It was a brilliant stroke of news manipulation—but by no means a spur-of-the-moment event. The antiapartheid movement had been organized and carefully choreographed to arouse public attention and focus opinion against South Africa and the Reagan Administration's wink-and-nod opposition to the apartheid regime. The protesters' well-covered arrests had been peaceful and were coordinated with the D.C. police, leading to further demonstrations at the embassy. A week later, some more protesters—mostly black leaders and celebrities—had been arrested in Washington, plus more than a dozen in New York City. All of them were released after being booked; the federal authorities refused to prosecute them because the Reagan Administration feared giving the activists a platform to further embarrass the government's relationship with South Africa. Meanwhile, a disinvestment movement swept the nation's college campuses and corporate board rooms; eventually, it made South Africa and its imprisoned martyr, Nelson Mandela, household words across the United States.

The Free South Africa movement captured my imagination, conjuring up the images and symbolism of the Civil Rights Movement that I knew only from old people's tales and televised news specials. For black folks of my generation, especially middle-class careerists like me, South Africa was our Civil Rights Movement. "Free South Africa" became our battle cry, complete with clenched and upraised fists. It had all the elements needed for our participation: white supremacist Boers as the oppressor bad guys and the too tolerant and long-suffering black majority population. But there was more to it than that. We could challenge South Africa's apartheid and not worry a whit about risking our station on the corporate treadmill in the United States. South Africa, for many buppies, was the safest and most comfortable means of protesting our pain and suffering in America.

Before the embassy protests, I knew next to nothing about what was happening in South Africa or, for that matter, how racist the country was. Steve Biko's death, the Soweto uprisings, Sharpeville—all occurred well before I began to pay attention. Few people I knew made an issue of these events, so South Africa easily escaped my notice. I was remotely aware of the horrors of apartheid, but in an academic and dispassionate way. That was way over there in Africa, someplace I had never imagined living or even visiting. As South African atrocities began to rule the daily newspapers, I began to pay more and more attention.

By the time O'Mara called, I could only regurgitate the skimpy facts I had gobbled up from the media. I knew the country was a sensational media story, but the finer details of who, why, how and what were missing.

No one in either my family or Cynthia's had ever been outside the United States. I was elated at being asked, but questioned whether I should accept the offer, since I knew so little about international politics—especially those on the African continent.

Cynthia was all for it from the start. "It will be a great career move," she said. "You can learn as you go. White people don't know much about Africa, but they go over there all the time. Why not you?"

Another of Cynthia's arguments carried the day. She said she would be willing to move in with a friend who had just had a baby and needed some help. "We can save money," she explained. "So by the time you get back, we will be able to afford to buy a house." That bit of logic settled it for me. I left the United States for South Africa thinking that when I returned our life as good, home-owning, middle-class buppies would be set.

Black Americans who arrive in Africa for the first time report varying first impressions. The truly ignorant say something foolish about their surprise at not seeing tigers or Tarzan, while other, more sensitive types report vaguely familiar sensations of homecoming and ancestral ties. In all honesty, I felt neither of these extremes upon arriving at Johannesburg's Jan Smuts International Airport. Instead, I felt shocking disappointment: South Africa didn't live up to the level of racial oppression and hostility that I expected. I was primed for a scene out of *In the Heat of the Night*, where all the white people would stare and be rude. Arriving at Jan Smuts was no more traumatic or stressful than arriving at Hartsfield International Airport in Atlanta.

The airport terminal buzzed like a giant beehive, passengers arriving and departing with little regard for anything other than making their connections. The place was awash with black faces—my first big surprise. From all I had read, I expected only whites at the airport. I guess I felt that way because I remembered my folks saying they had never taken plane trips before the 1960s; no doubt I projected that attitude onto blacks here. But some of the people carrying suitcases and overnight bags—many more than I expected—were obviously black Africans, who looked to me like business executives or tourists. As I had expected, the overwhelming majority of the passengers were whites speaking in harsh, guttural voices. And I was not surprised to see that nearly all the custodians and baggage handlers and taxi drivers were black men wearing dour and depressed expressions.

I saw black and white people sitting alongside each other on the airport bus. I knew that Johannesburg's municipal buses were segregated, so I did not know what to do. After studying the situation for a few minutes, I decided to hire a taxi. I passed up one driven by a white man for one driven by a black man.

I later learned I could have taken the airport bus, which held a special dispensation allowing it to transport fares of all races to certain hotels. Racism will always yield to commerce. I also learned in short order that so-called "international hotels and retaurants" had government-sanctioned clearance allowing them to serve all races, as long as guests could afford their steep rates. There was even a special twenty-four-hour telephone number to a government office in Pretoria, the nation's administrative capital, where a hotel or restaurant manager could get immediate approval to admit a wealthy-looking black person or group to his establishment. It made no sense to me.

Apartheid laws, designed to divide the races and keep them from mingling, never fully operated as their creators had envisioned. Little wonder. It was impossible to keep the races totally apart because the society depended on black labor and economic resources. Blacks, though discriminated against by government laws that limited where they lived or moved throughout the country, were welcomed by urban businesses that depended on them for a significant share of their sales and profits. The shifting sense of what was acceptable and what was forbidden in daily life under apartheid allowed black and white South Africans to behave in what seemed to me illogical and capricious ways.

Outside the airport, whites were not readily visible, but black folks were everywhere. I saw them on the flatbeds of pickup trucks. I saw them driving vans packed with domestics leaving work at the end of the day. Here and there, I saw corpulent women wrapped in dull blankets, groaning under the weight of bulky parcels balanced on their heads and mute babies strapped to the smalls of their backs. I saw men trudging with slow gaits on well-worn shoes along city streets. I saw other men hunched over in groups tilling manicured lawns. I saw all this black humanity but few white people as I rode in the backseat of the cab from the airport to downtown Johannesburg's Carlton Hotel.

The airport is located several miles outside the city limits, off a huge six-lane highway. As with Atlanta or Baltimore or most other U.S. cities, the route into Johannesburg is a magnet for industrial and commercial development. I was surprised by the warehouses, chain hotels and glass office towers that I saw. That's where the white people are, I thought. Hidden and in control. This was no different from the United States, where First World overdevelopment and impersonal consumerism ruled the day. I had expected to find the exact opposite in South Africa. I had pictured—in my ignorance—a sleepier, more pastoral and more overtly mean society where whites stood everywhere with pistols strapped to their hips and shotguns at the ready, where black folks worked in the shadows as if they were the invisible ones.

The first person to initiate a conversation with me in South Africa was my black cabdriver. "What do you think of it here?" he asked. The ride from the airport to downtown Johannesburg took fifteen minutes and he wanted to know all my thoughts in that brief time. "When do you think we'll get our freedom?"

"I dunno," I said.

How could I know? I was a visitor in his country, confused, uncomfortable and frightened. If all I had read and heard was true, and I believed it to be, I was walking on the dark side of the moon. I didn't want to pontificate, because I didn't know enough, so I asked the cab-driver to tell me what he thought about his homeland. He was eager to oblige me. I caught only snippets as he droned on about his family's struggle to make a living and how the "white man" oppressed him. I heard some of his words floating in the warm air, but they failed to sink in. I wasn't ready for his reality. Not yet, at least.

With him providing a running commentary, I glanced out the cab window to witness an orange sun drop out of the sky and disappear behind a ragged ridge. Out of the opposite window, I noticed that the sky was dark, as if an eclipse shrouded only half the landscape. All I saw on that side was an enormous black cloud. I would soon learn that it was coal smoke, rising from thousands of kitchen stoves, mixing with the dusky atmosphere to blot out the twilight like an ugly, chipped and peeling awning. It had muted even the brilliance of the setting sun.

During the entire ride from the airport to the city center, the cab driver lectured. Once, he paused long enough to turn up the volume on the dashboard radio as Michael Jackson crooned "We Are the World." He sniffed and wiped away a tear as the song ended. "That tune always makes me cry," he said. I said nothing and stared at the glass office towers and black serpentine highway and the most spectacular red-orange sunset I had ever seen.

From the time I arrived in Johannesburg on June 1, 1985, to the time I returned to Baltimore on August 30, nearly everyone I met asked me the same question: "What do you think is going to happen in South Africa?" No doubt their curiosity stemmed from the massive amount of world attention being focused on the white-minority-controlled nation at the southernmost tip of an increasingly black-run continent. For sure, people seemed genuinely concerned about South Africa's future. But I suspect they were more curious about how I as an American journalist created images and shaped opinions about their country for readers thousands of miles away.

But in my case, I felt there was a second agenda within the question. Many of my interrogators were as fascinated with what I as a black man from America, given all the baggage that carried, thought about the South African experience. And if they scored points with an American, then somehow the situation in their country would come across as more credible to policymakers in the United States, Great Britain and points elsewhere where the antiapartheid pressures were mounting.

And, of course, since I am dark-skinned and nappy-headed, it seemed I was the personification of Mr. Black Everyman from America, an expert on racial caste systems both there and in South Africa. As I peeled back the layers of their questions, I also understood that my interrogators were asking how an American judged them. Here, being an American counted for something. I was a representative of the most favored nation, and even in racist South Africa, that privilege accounted for an extra dollop of respect. Thus the fascination with my personal experiences, which seemed more important—lending greater credibility to the travails of that nation—than the experiences of the people actually living there.

In that peculiar tabloid mentality of British and (increasingly) U.S. journalism, everyone seemed to want the up-close and inside account of what happened when a black American came to South Africa. How would he be treated? Where would he live? Was he an honorary white? So, for the in-depth story, people boldly asked: Did you go to the whites-only toilets or eat next to whites in restaurants? Could you travel freely? Did blacks in South Africa resent you? What did the government do to you? Were your phones tapped? Did you see the riots? Were you in danger? Did you meet Bishop Desmond Tutu or Winnie Mandela?

These questions, usually asked by other foreign correspondents from the United States and England, irritated the hell out of me. Once while drinking with a group of international reporters, a Canadian reporter let it slip he thought I had a triple unfair advantage over him. By his calculation, not only did American reporters get tips from the South African officials and antiapartheid groups, but, worse, he thought I could move freely in black townships while also "being afforded honorary white status and being able to attend the same news conferences as regular reporters."

"Fuck you," I said and left that group.

As I stalked away, he was gape-mouthed and sputtering. "Tell me, what did I say to offend you?"

That incident should have been an eye-opener. But it wasn't. I chalked it up to one man's narrow mind. I was an American, I thought, and what I saw and wrote about the effects of racism was as a visitor— a vicarious experience lived through the eyes of South African blacks. I didn't think it had anything to do with me. I was not a South African native. I was a trained, detached observer shielded by journalistic objectivity from feeling that country's inhumane treatment of its own natives. My experiences, therefore, were totally different from those of any South African, black or white.

Yet I did resent being questioned about South Africa's racism (as if the United States had solved its own race question) because I felt that people didn't necessarily want my opinions, but expected an answer that conformed to their predetermined attitudes about it. They wanted me to tell them how bad racism was there and that whatever was going on way across the ocean could never happen back home in the United States.

Early in my visit, I could more easily comply with such expectations because I did not know any better. I could move relatively freely between the two separate and unequal worlds, yet I was an American and belonged to neither. As an outsider and a reporter, my personal experiences in South Africa revealed only the crazy reasoning the ruling whites applied to justify their continued domination of their own black majority. It had nothing to do with me.

So I told anyone who asked that my situation in South Africa was materially cushy compared to how blacks there lived and died. I was a temporary worker, allowed to do my job, and for the most part, no one seemed to mind or bother me. I lived as well, perhaps better, than I lived in Baltimore. I had rented cars and a company American Express card and a suite in a luxury hotel with room service at my disposal. Though I was black and in a legally racist land, I was an American with the financial resources of a newspaper company only a phone call away. The South Africans—black and white, laborers and government officials—understood and adjusted their behavior toward me to reflect the very noticeable differences between my privileged life and what I assumed to be the hopeless existence of a black South African.

"If all our blacks were like you, we would have no problem sharing power with them," a conservative member of the South African parliament explained during the course of an extended and revealing interview. "You have benefited from the experience of three hundred years of interaction with whites in America. Blacks in South Africa are not as civilized as you have become."

On another occasion, a retailer in the shopping arcade adjacent to my hotel warned me against having a suit mended by a "native" tailor because "they're not used to dealing with expensive materials."

One Afrikaner told me she knew, before hearing my softly drawling North Carolina accent, that I was not South African because I looked into her eyes. She was one of many South Africans—white and black— quick to tell me, "You think and act like an American." They were right. And at first, absent critical scrutiny, I felt relieved by, if not proud of, the distinction. But that was only a fleeting impression.

In time, I would learn that, whether in South Africa or the United States, color tagged everyone, dividing human interactions into quick-scan categories that made associations and assumptions clear, without need of explanation or conversation. You just knew. Whites, who set up the system, fared better than blacks because they had created it. It was just that simple. And in South Africa, perhaps more so than anywhere else on the globe, the contrast was so vivid, so real and so brutal because the people in control did and said what they felt and thought. They just knew they were right—and had the mighty force and fire-power to back up their wrongness. Meanwhile, black South Africans suffered.

• • •

The best thing that happened to me in South Africa was meeting Nathaniel Shepard, Jr., a fellow black journalist working as Nairobi bureau chief of the *Chicago Tribune*. Larry and his wife, Jeanne, who was an editor at the *Tribune*, were friends of Nat's. Jeanne had suggested I call him for contacts in South Africa. I tried several times to reach him at his office in Kenya before I left the United States, but he was a man on the move and never received any of my messages. So when I arrived at the Carlton Hotel in Johannesburg, I was delighted to find out from the reception desk that he was registered there and I called him before I left the lobby.

"Well," I said on the house phone, "I finally caught up with you. When can we get together?" I introduced myself and offered Larry's and Jeanne's names as bona fides. He said I was unable to reach him in Nairobi because he had been in South Africa for several weeks. He also said he knew a great many black South Africans and would share some of his contacts with me. Great, I thought, and offered to drop by his room immediately to meet him face to face.

"Later," he said. "How about 7 P.M. in the hotel restaurant?"

That was about two hours later and I wondered why it would take so long. He had already said he was not on deadline or anything. I did not know a soul in South Africa and wanted desperately to see a friendly face, meet someone who might help ease my transition into what I expected to be hostile territory. Nat had been described as a good guy and savvy reporter. Since he was also black and knew Larry and Jeanne, he sounded just like the kind of person I wanted as a friend in South Africa.

At seven sharp, I was in the lobby, waiting. I paced the floor for about twenty minutes before I saw a tall, athletic chocolate-skinned man, unsmiling and with a cautiously deliberate air, approach me. Initially, I was startled, not sure whether this was the person I was expecting. The man walked closer. At first, I thought he might be a tall, dark African-looking Asian. He was wearing a black cotton suit that had no lapels and a Nehru-type collar; the suit was fastened down the front with embroidered hooks and eyes and had huge four-inch white cuffs. A Mao suit? Am I here in a South African hotel restaurant to meet a black American who appears out of the shadows in a Chinese suit?

I introduced myself. His somber expression evaporated, replaced by a dazzling smile that filled the bottom of his face. "Welcome to Africa," he said. Before I could respond, his outstretched arms encircled me in an exuberant clinch, the way football players embrace after a touchdown. From that moment on, Nat and I would never be strangers again.

We had dinner in the restaurant. A natural raconteur, Nat made marvelous company, the kind of man's man with stories and experiences to keep me laughing and awed. We talked a lot about South Africa that evening over the remains of giant prawns, bottles of blush wine and, later, champagne and Irish coffee. But more than that, we talked about growing up black in America in the South and about being black and working for large newspapers that have most of their circulation in white communities. We also talked about the Civil Rights Movement and riots and racial progress—and the lack of racial progress. Nat was a generation older than I, having witnessed the 1960s in his late teens from his home in Atlanta. Our experiences were as common as our shared skin color, yet we lived in separate times split by an enormous gulf of change.

Toward the end of the dinner, I felt comfortable with Nat, trusting him enough to ask if we could travel together on some assignments. He agreed immediately, saying it was wise and safer to travel with someone in unfamiliar places. Only after we agreed to this did he tell me that at first, when I called from the hotel lobby, he thought I might be a spy sent by the South African government.

"You can never be too sure," Nat said. "I have written a lot of things they don't like and I am sure they are always watching me. So when you called me and the first thing you said was that you 'finally caught up with me,' I wanted to make sure you were all right. I called back to the States to check you out. You're all right."

I was thunderstruck, not sure whether to be honored or insulted. Me, a spy? I decided to accept the comment as an honor, attributing his worries to the kind of paranoia that I was feeling in South Africa. As I later learned from friends within the hotel management, Nat's fears were well founded because official-looking people had on occasion inquired about our comings and goings, checking our hotel phone records and, at least once, surveying our rooms when we were away.

Nat and I were among a handful—no more than half a dozen at any one time—of black American newspaper reporters rotating in and out of South Africa that summer. Before I left in late August, I had been told some eighty foreign news correspondents had registered with the government to report in the country, but I saw few black Americans. Most of the black reporters got to know each other fairly well. We would run into each other at some news event, exchange knowing smiles and venture off on our respective assignments. I considered myself quite lucky to have a traveling buddy like Nat, especially after I discovered how likely it was that the government was watching what we did and where we went. Though many others did so, I was relieved not to have to go it alone. That would have been all the more frightening. Nat, too, I think, was relieved to have a colleague, one he could show the ropes to and bounce ideas off.

"Before we go anywhere else," Nat said, draining the last of his Irish coffee at that first dinner, "you have got to go to the location."

"Where's that?"

"The location," he said. He looked deeply into his coffee cup, saw it was empty and placed it sideways on the table, one more fallen soldier beside the discarded wine and champagne bottles. Nat thought I should make early and deep contacts with the black people of South Africa, and thought the first place I visited in their country should also be the most famous. "The location is where the cats live here," he said, realizing I still hadn't caught his slang. "The township. Soweto. It's called 'the location.'"

I liked the way he referred to black folks as "the cats" because it sounded so retro, like Nat himself, who struck me as a retro hipster, like cool Daddy-O.

"I heard some of the cats here refer to the township as their location. You can sometimes hear them singing"—Nat broke into the chanting rhythm of black South Africa—" 'Let's go to the lo-ca-tion. Let's go to the lo-ca-tion.' "

"When do you want to go?" I asked.

"Now. Let's go to the lo-ca-tion. Now."

I was tired from the day's travel, and the late-night meal didn't make it easier to stay alert, but I wasn't about to let this opportunity pass. "Okay," I said, down for my first glimpse of the place I had read so much about and was so anxious to see. "Let's go to the lo-o-cation," I chanted, smiling as a cover for my missing the rhythm of the place.

Nat and I drove along the one highway that leads out of Johannesburg and into Soweto. It was about midnight when we entered Soweto, and despite myself, I felt tense. I recall feeling as though I was being watched in the dark, even though there was no one on the streets. At the edge of the township, I had spied a fleet of armored vehicles— township dwellers called them Hippos, for the obvious reason—with flak-jacketed, jack-booted and visor-helmeted soldiers at the ready. Were they there expecting trouble or waiting to cause it?

"Wait and see," Nat said.

All my reading had failed to set the stage for my first visit to Soweto. I had missed seeing the impoverished black township, located ten miles south of Johannesburg, earlier when my jet plane descended toward the airport because it was hidden by the smoky sky. I knew that Soweto was a city of 1.5 million black people, though nobody viewed it as such. The city of Soweto had no economic hub or skyscrapers or any other hallmark associated with urban locations, but it had the one source of wealth required by every city: human labor, which provided the economic underpinnings for the entire Transkei region. In reality, Jo'burg—where less than a million whites lived—was a suburb, a smaller, richer and more powerful Edge City that fed off the human labor and suffering of black folks hidden away in Soweto. One vivid image, that of a large black city shrouded in smoky mist, sprawling out of view of a gleaming, modern white suburb, frames my most enduring impression of the place.

Nat drove into the township, past the police as they targeted a beam of light at our car when we sped by, past the giant Orlando soccer stadium that looked like a dinosaur silhouetted against the murky sky, past the tin shacks and cardboard structures that masqueraded as houses. He turned right and left and left and right as he pushed deeper into the blinding darkness. Good thing he is driving, I remember thinking. I would never have found my way, because every street—if those dusty, rutted paths deserved being called streets—looked identical in the glare of the headlights. There were no lights shining from poles above our heads, electricity having ended just as the freeway out of Johannesburg became rocks and caked mud. After a few wrong turns and some helpful directions, we finally arrived at the place Nat wanted to show me.

A shebeen can best be described as the South African equivalent of a Prohibition-era speakeasy. A meeting and drinking place for men and women to gather, to debate, to dance and to escape the reality surrounding them. At this location, the woman of the house (most shebeens I visited had a woman as the primary resident) met us at a side door and, after a brief moment to remember Nat's last visit, allowed us to enter her home. She demanded we address her as Tillie, a moniker she extracted from everyone else in the house. Tillie was a gracious, warm and hospitable woman who loved to smile, revealing a gummy grin and overflowing kindness. She seemed especially happy to see Nat, chiding him for being away so long that she had almost forgotten who he was.

"How could you forget my American accent?" he said, smiling through his mocking admonishment.

"No, no, no, I could never forget you," she said. "I never forget any Americans who come to my home."

Nat introduced me to Tillie, and judging by the bear hug and kisses

I received, I believed she would never forget me either; I was certain I would never forget her.

Inside the house, a dozen or more men were engaged in animated talk. The several women there took turns serving the men beers, for which they received a rand or two, or took time away from their bartending duties to dance to the cassette-taped music blaring from a small but powerful boom box in the front living room. Repeatedly, the group wanted to hear "We Are the World," which would cause the dancers on the floor to sway in rhythm as Lionel Richie, Diana Ross, Michael Jackson and the remainder of the ensemble crooned about brotherhood.

The zest of the people in that dismal place moved me. This was my first night in South Africa and the spirit of these dark, musty strangers seeped deep under my skin, bursting forth in our shared communion. In that brief time, we drank, we laughed, we shared unique identities that spanned continents and oceans and eons. All this happened involuntarily on my part. I had not expected this, but was open to whatever occurred among these proud and celebratory people. South Africa was thousands of miles away for them, just as America was a memory at that moment for me, because the immediate was all that mattered. I was totally at ease in their accepting company, so comfortable that I danced, synchronizing my body to the boom box beat and linking time to space to movement in the joyous expression of acknowledged and released oppression.

In a South African ghetto juke joint surrounded by the smiling black faces and warm eyes of coal miners and yard workers and domestics, my soul, my blackness, yawned and stretched at the cock-crow challenge to the vast differences between our lives. Where I sought job status, they sought dignity. I would not have been receptive—not yet fully open—to the black South Africans' inspiring pride and clarity of purpose as they celebrated life in the presence of surreal indignity. But this lesson awaited me later that summer in South Africa and would compel me to bear witness. I wonder whether my soul might otherwise have been roused if not for the experience of that Sowetean shebeen.

I returned to Soweto about two weeks later for a starkly different experience. On a crisp Sunday morning in June, the kind of South African winter day that begins with the sun bright and the air visible in your breath, I rode with Nat to Soweto to hear Anglican bishop Desmond Tutu at Regina Mundi Catholic Church. Tutu, the darling of the Western media and a fearless witness to the horrors of the apartheid system, headlined a long list of speakers gathered in the church for the annual observance of Soweto Day, an unofficial holiday among black South Africans commemorating the 1976 riots in the township that left 575 people, mostly young students, dead. The church service was organized by the United Democratic Front and the Azanian People's Organization, a pair of philosophically distinct black antiapartheid organizations. The two groups, often suspected of killing each other's supporters in what was labeled by the media as "black on black" crime and used by the government to justify its continued oppression of all its black citizens, joined forces this day in a show of unity and in an effort to patch up their differences.

Arriving well before the service, Nat and I drove around Soweto, taking in the sights and sounds of the township. Most of the shops were closed in observance of Soweto Day.

We chatted with some children alongside the road. One little boy, who could not have been more than eight or nine years old, rushed up to me. He wanted to know if I knew Michael Jackson. He thought I would, since I was from the United States and Jackson was from the United States and we were both black. I told him no. He then wanted to know if I had any guns in the trunk of the car that I would give him.

"Why do you want guns?" I asked, shocked at the request.

"To kill the white man who oppresses us," he said. His words were clear, unmistakable and matter-of-fact.

I shook my head. "No," I said softly.

And just as suddenly as he appeared, he turned on his heels and was gone.

I did not know Michael Jackson and had no guns; therefore, I was of no use to him. That thought saddened me. But more, it revealed that the children of apartheid, forced by the fate of circumstance and oppression, made the quantum leap from juvenile naivete to adult revolutionary with no intermediate stops along the way. Everywhere I went in South Africa, I would see that same young boy and imagine his future. That thought, on occasion, brought me to tears. He, in his way, and I, in mine, were fighting the same struggle to redefine ourselves in the context of another's rules, another's system. He had no more clues to solving his problems—with Michael Jackson or an AK-47—than I did to solving my own—with a ballpoint pen and wirebound notebook.

After our exchange with the township kids, Nat suggested we drop by the house of a friend of his, Sam Mabe, a journalist for the Sowetean newspaper, and ask him to ride with us to the church service. It was always a good idea to have a local in the car in case you needed someone to translate one of the many African languages or to introduce you to reluctant civilians. Nat had met Sam some time before while both were on an assignment in the township. He had been impressed with his courage as a reporter and the confidence the residents had placed in him.

Sam was glad to see us and invited us into his home. He lived with his wife and young child in Beverly Hills, a middle-class section of Soweto, recognizable as such by the brick facades, indoor plumbing and proximity to the large, gated houses belonging to Tutu and several other prominent township residents. He introduced us to his wife, a pleasant woman about whom I remember very little else, while he rushed to finish dressing.

The service was more of a political rally, with exhortations by a variety of church and political leaders and young street activists representing many legal and underground liberation organizations. There were freedom songs and more speeches. After about two hours of demands on the government and calls for unity, Tutu took to the pulpit. His clerical collar, flowing purple robe and avuncular manner quieted the congregation. He spoke for a long while, primarily urging the people to reject black-on-black violence in the townships.

Sensing the apprehension of the crowd inside the church and the apparent intentions of the soldiers outside, Tutu implored everyone to leave the church peacefully and ignore the white men with guns. "Let us not discredit our cause by some of the things that we are doing in some of our townships," Tutu said, noting the police would dishonor themselves by their brutal behavior. "It will use methods that we are about to witness, perhaps, with those gentlemen outside this building."

A cold, forbidding chill shivered along my spine. I knew then that something bad—heaven knew how horrible—would happen soon. Would the police shoot into the crowd? No doubt about it. I could sense it. It was coming. Tutu knew it, so he was warning those within the church to brace themselves for an attack, like lambs before crouching lions, with quiet, peaceful dignity.

I looked for Nat and Sam. Then, reflexively, I looked for the nearest exit, mentally preparing by marking a path for retreat from the front of the church by a side door. We had agreed that if something went down, Nat and I would take notes and Sam would dash for the car. Sam knew the territory better than we did and could negotiate our escape into the township. Once inside the car, we had planned to speed out of the line of fire and finish our reporting from a place of relative safety. If necessary, we had decided, we could return when the shooting stopped.

When Tutu began talking about the prospect of violence, Nat and I gave each other knowing glances. Sam then headed for the car as Nat and I inched past the crowd for the side exit. Other reporters, who were sitting at the foot of the pulpit with us, picked up the same sense of foreboding and began moving toward the side doors.

At the rear of the church, a commotion had begun. Some youths in T-shirts—bright yellow T-shirts the color of Easter candy—began jogging in place. The youths pumped their knotted fists skyward in unison. They chanted in tongues I didn't understand, their voices combining in a low rumble that grew louder and more demanding as they burst free of the church and into the sun outside. In time, I learned these youths were dancing the *toi-toi*, a defiant boogie against apartheid.

From the front of the church looking toward the rear, where the church's double doors were now flung wide open, those writhing, energetic bodies appeared as a single, giant canary breaking free of its egg to take flight into the South African sunlight and dust. From somewhere near, but outside the church, I heard the sharp crack of rifle fire. Screams bounced off the church walls, followed by the dull thudding and swishy scampering of hundreds of feet going in all directions at once. More rifle shots popped, popped, popped.

I made my way out of a side door, only to find I had lost sight of Nat, my eyes burning like fire. Though I couldn't see them, I felt people scattering in all directions in the small courtyard I had seen at the side of the church just off the pastor's study. The crowd surrounded me, forcing me to move where it moved. As I was swept along, I felt myself pushed toward a cyclone fence that enclosed the courtyard. If I wasn't to be shot by the police, who seemed to be shooting in all directions, I felt certain I would be crushed by the crowd against that fence.

I pushed against the body next to me and felt relieved when it gave way, allowing me to stumble from the crowd and back toward where I thought the church door would be. I wasn't sure where I was or where I was headed. I just wanted to escape the crowd, the fence and the bullets. A canister of tear gas whizzed over my head, trailing a plume of gray-white and foul-smelling smoke.

My eyes melted into tears. My nose and sinuses itched and felt raw. I coughed to clear my head. When I reached to rub my eyes, I felt a rough and callused palm push my hand away from my face.

"No, no," said a woman's voice, which I assumed belonged to the hand, since I could not see through the tears and smoke. The woman said something else in a comforting, but foreign, tone. "Come this way," I heard another woman's voice say.

I followed the sound of the second woman's voice, which led me back into the church sanctuary. Other women were sponging faces with water and paper towels. Another group of women lit scraps of paper and waved them under the noses and in front of the eyes of coughing and sputtering black faces. It was their way of burning off the immediately surrounding gas.

Nat was in the church too. He had apparently remained beside me the whole time, and must have been the person I pushed against in order to flee the crowd. "People in that church locked the door to avoid the crush of the crowd," Nat said years later as he conjured up the panic and confusion. "Someone, I believe it was that woman who led us back into the church, said the police weren't going to attack the church. She didn't believe what was happening, because the police had never fired into a church before."

The whole of the confrontation lasted no more than fifteen or twenty minutes. When the shooting finally stopped, the police, who never dismounted from their vehicles, rumbled away. We were safe now, nestled in the car, with Sam behind the wheel. We watched as the last of the police trucks cleared the area, with a young white police officer staring out the back. He raised his weapon and fired one final canister of tear gas, not at anybody but at a lone cow standing in a grassless field.

"Can you believe that?" Nat shouted, pointing to the scene of the last atrocity. "That's just sick. He tear-gassed a cow.

"Here we are on a Sunday, sitting in a church minding our business, and the police come along and spray us with tear gas," Nat continued. "This is one of those things you run across as a reporter and you know people aren't going to believe it happened. No one is going to believe any of it, not even the fact that the police tear-gassed a cow."

We were speeding through the location, where life had already reverted to what passed for normalcy, en route to Sam's house. We finished writing our stories on portable laptop computers. Later, back at the Carlton Hotel, we plugged them into the telephones and sent stories about the day's activities to our respective offices back home in Chicago and Baltimore.

But before I left Sam's place, I visited the bathroom to relieve my full bladder. Just as I closed the door behind me, I heard Sam's wife shout a warning of some kind. Too late. I had already unzipped my pants and begun to urinate when the most intense, searing pain I had ever felt detonated between my legs. I had transferred lingering traces of the tear gas from my hand to the most sensitive part of my body and the pain doubled me over as though someone had set fire to the tip of my penis. For more than an hour, as I gamely dispatched my account of the day, I ached in solidarity with the township residents.

That night, Nat and I attempted to retreat from confrontation by going to a jazz club in one of Johannesburg's northern suburban neighborhoods, a place called Quavers. Nat had been there before and had had a pleasant time and decent meal. "Sounds like just the right place after the day I've had," I said.

We arrived shortly after nightfall and were escorted to a table in front of the stage, where a colored singer belted out Otis Redding and Smokey Robinson tunes accompanied by a four-piece combo that was led by a white saxophone player who had studied in the United States.

After their set, the singer and saxophone player invited themselves to our table. "Why do you American journalists only report the bad things about our country?" the Afrikaner saxophone player said. "When I was in America, that was all I ever read about South Africa. Our situation is not as bad as you Yanks make it out to be. Why not report the good things, how we're trying to change our government?"

He spoke emotionally and with only partial accuracy, but with the crestfallen conviction of someone who felt terribly wronged by more powerful forces. I remembered hearing these arguments before—in Baltimore, most recently, among NAACPers who protested the media's bias toward dealing only with black America's pathologies and not its successes. It struck me as queer that at that moment, in South Africa, the tables had been turned on me, that a black reporter from the

United States was sitting in a restaurant at the southern tip of Africa listening to this argument from an Afrikaner.

On a Saturday morning early in my stay in Johannesburg, I noticed the billboard outside my hotel window for the first time. Sprawled across the hood of a red convertible was a ten-foot-tall Eddie Murphy in blue jeans, gray sweatshirt and sneakers. In his right hand was an automatic pistol and across his face was that toothsome grin. *Beverly Hills Cop.* Since the theater was in downtown, I assumed the authorities would have no problem with my buying a ticket to a movie starring a gun-toting black actor. I was both right and wrong. The hotel desk clerk told me the city's movie theaters were not "international," meaning blacks were not permitted to enter. But he said he had called ahead to tell them a black American, a resident of the hotel, was en route and I should have no problem. "They said it would be all right, but to be sure to bring your passport."

I was humbled. My mind raced to what might have happened. What if I had appeared at the theater without the clerk calling first? Would someone have said something to me? Would I have been turned away? Arrested? Shot? What had almost happened here? In the few seconds it took to imagine all the worst, my heart beat faster and, without forethought, I shouted at the hotel clerk, "Dammit, I'm not going now! And don't you ever arrange for me to go anywhere that questions about who I am are asked as condition of my admittance. Do you understand me?"

The clerk was caught short, apparently stunned by my sudden change of attitude. "Yes, sir," he stammered. "I understand."

I knew he could not have understood. I did not understand myself. Why was I reacting, overreacting, the way I was? Suddenly, I had a terrible headache and wanted to sit down. The incident with the desk clerk had unnerved me.

I found the house phone and called Nat, asking him to join me for a drink in the lobby bar. He ordered a bottle of champagne. As the bubbles washed into me, I told him about the incident. After I had finished, he and I agreed never to go anywhere in South Africa that black South Africans were not allowed. It would be a small, personal act of defiance that no one need know about save ourselves. Additionally, he suggested we include black South Africans in any social grouping outside our reporting duties. Funny thing, however, was that once we had decided on this course of action, I discovered we rarely needed to invoke it. For the balance of my stay, only on rare occasions was I turned away from any place for reasons related to apartheid.

Nat and I were denied entry into two nightclubs in downtown Johannesburg on a Saturday night. I suspected that it had less to do with either of us than with the company we were keeping—two colored, or mixed-race, women who looked white. At the first place, a gay club with young men and women dressed in high fashion standing outside, the doorman politely told us that our foursome could not enter.

"Why not?" Nat asked.

"Just because," the doorman responded. "It's just not done."

I had noticed the name of the place, scripted on neon above the entrance: HEAVEN.

"Is it just not done that blacks can't get into Heaven via South Africa?" I said sharply to the doorman as we turned to leave.

The second place was a popular nightspot called Q's. It was a favorite after-hours place among kitchen workers at the Carlton Hotel, who gathered there after their night shift for dancing and early-morning drinks. Some of the liberal white people at the hotel had suggested the place to Nat and me on numerous occasions. Behind the club's nondescript door were a narrow hall and a ticket collector in a glass booth. The man in the booth, again politely, asked us not to come in. Neither of us protested. But before I left, I grabbed a quick glimpse of the other side of the booth. Flashing strobe lights intermittently cast shadows across a dark dance floor and a huge platform where a black man (from Philadelphia, we were later informed) was playing the best of Motown. A placard behind the DJ announced TONIGHT—TINA TURNER LEGS LOOK ALIKE CONTEST.

"How can they have a Tina Turner legs contest and have not black legs in the place," Nat said. He and I laughed at the lunacy of it all, while our companions saw nothing funny about it.

One afternoon, I was denied lunch in a Chinese restaurant at a north Johannesburg suburban shopping mall. As before, on my night-club adventure, I was in the company of the same white-looking South African woman. But this time the rejection was different—for her it dredged up all the personal woes she associated with not belonging in her native land.

She had carefully picked this particular restaurant, having eaten there once previously as the business guest of a black South African woman. So the snub came as more of a personal shock, an affront to her inability to navigate the conventions of her own society in the presence of an American.

At the waiter's refusal to seat us, I lost my appetite and turned to leave the restaurant. My dining partner, however, girded herself for a noisy confrontation. She would not go quietly or, at least, not without a moral victory. I noticed the diners deep inside the place rubbernecking to see what was happening. I wanted to leave without an incident and whispered my feelings to her, thinking my hushed tones could avoid the noise I felt her capable of producing.

"I've eaten here before, so why can't my friend and I enter now," she said with the indignation of scorned black women everywhere. I could almost feel her tears welling up, but I knew she would never allow the waiter to see her cry.

"I'm sorry, madam," the waiter said. "I can't."

"I want to see the manager," she said. Her voice was now trembling with frustrated rage.

"Let's forget it," I said. "I don't want to eat here after all this."

Later, when I persuaded her to talk about why she had been so angry, the tears flowed freely. It was the unexpected, she explained, the not knowing when and why someone would treat her as though she did not belong. She was colored, by fiat of a government that she neither supported nor trusted. Her life in South Africa had been a mixed blessing, both unique and typical of the lives of people caught in circumstances they could neither control nor change. She was too dark to be white and too light to be black.

"We are all mongrels in this country," she said.

Her tears had dried by this time, as we sat in her studio apartment in a high-rise apartment building in the center of Johannesburg. She lived there with a wink and a nod from the landlord, who by law was forbidden to rent the place to anyone other than white South Africans. The apartment, reflecting the spirit of its occupant, was a study in contrasts with its blend of appointments collected from her travels to New York, Paris and Kinshasa, as well as her nomadic life across South Africa. Her ancestry was that of a colored person, from the Malayan slaves brought to South Africa in the nineteenth century. But her birth certificate and other identity papers registered her as Asian/Indian in recognition of her Muslim upbringing and her colored Methodist mother's choice of schooling for her.

By the time she was in sixth or seventh grade, she had decided she had no use for school, having been expelled for fighting or skipping classes more times than she could remember. Two unsuccessful marriages later, she had become educated by dint of mothering three children and traveling the world with her second husband, a successful but aloof Zairean businessman who commuted between Kinshasa and New York sans wife or children.

"I grew up being able to relate to blacks, whites and Indians," she told me. "I have many white friends and many black friends, but I don't belong with either community. I have always been able to move into and out of any situation that was put in front of me. I always felt I should have been born an American."

I am an American, I thought. There is not much difference between your life and mine. I wish I had asked her how much difference she thought it would make if she had been a black American. But I did not think of the question, not yet having posed it to myself, and so the opportunity passed for exploring just how different her life was from mine.

Judging by my view of South Africa, from the luxury suite at the Carlton Hotel, I could see how she got the false impression that I did indeed have it made. I was treated as an American VIP.

On the Fourth of July, Nat and I hosted a "birthday" party in the hotel bar. My friends in the hotel restaurant arranged a sheet cake with red, white and blue frosting to resemble the U.S. flag. I spent the morning making the arrangements. I invited all the American blacks registered in the hotel—there were about eight black businessmen from Washington there at the time—along with some press contacts from the South African government, friends from Soweto and fellow foreign journalists.

Most of the morning, I spent thumbing through the phone book for a flag shop. To give this celebration an authentic feel, I wanted to pass out miniature Old Glories as party favors. But finding a flag vendor proved to be more of a chore than I had expected. After a series of calls, I found a place that sold flags of the world, but jotted down its address incorrectly; so I wound up walking all over the central business district around the Carlton Hotel looking for this flag merchant.

At one point during my search, purely by accident and failing to consider the implications, I entered a gun shop. There were about eight or nine people inside, all men and all seeming to be the sporting/outdoors type so common among the white men I had met in South Africa. As I crossed the room, however, all conversation stopped and I felt eyes, many pairs of eyes, measuring my moves. A burly man with ruddy cheeks and a bushy auburn beard approached me. "What can I do for you?" he asked. He sounded neither helpful nor threatening.

"I'm looking for a place that sells American flags," I said.

"Oh, you're an American." The tension in his face melted and it seemed the entire room sighed at once. "We don't sell flags. You might want to go to the American Embassy."

As I left, I was vaguely aware that conversation stirred the temporarily silent air in the gun shop. I suspected they were talking about my cheeky nature, mistaking their sanctuary for a place to buy flags. Then, about three or four steps beyond the shop, it suddenly dawned on me. My knees buckled and I felt faint. Black people in South Africa cannot legally own guns! I bet no black person had ever entered that gun shop before me. What the hell was I thinking walking in there? All of a sudden I was breathing harder and could feel the pulsating beat-beat-beat inside my chest. I needed to sit down, but there was no place nearby. I looked back over my shoulder toward the gun shop, thinking for a brief moment that someone might have followed me. There was no one. Business proceeded as usual on the Johannesburg street as shoppers milled about and taxis honked and cash registers rang out in the normal course of a business day. No one paid any attention to me, a black man, crazy enough to walk into a gun shop in South Africa and expect generous and graceful service. I tried to will myself to calm down, mind over body. Easier said than done. My body refused to heed logic. My heart kept beating wildly, bombs exploded in my head, but only I felt their shrapnel, only I felt shell-shocked.

Just as quickly as this nightmare came, it dissolved into another vision—this one an out-of-body view of me going again into that gun store. But unlike before, I replayed the scene from another point of view, that of the white men. They were stunned when I suddenly appeared in the gun shop. Indeed, what must have crossed the minds of those Afrikaners as this kaffir strode cheekily into their sanctuary? Was I crazy? So, that was why the conversation stopped abruptly. Was he one of those black terrorists, come to kill them with a hidden bomb? Yes, that was it. They must have thought I was a terrorist. That was why they all watched me so closely, no movement on my part escaping their unified surveillance. They did not know what to expect. They were frightened. As far as I knew, they could be shaking in their boots now, slapping one another on the back in their relief at escaping a potentially dangerous encounter with a mad black terrorist bomber.

South Africa was a dangerous, insecure place with random bombings and occasional shootings. I had even noticed posters glued to rubbish bins warning people against terrorism, describing how an innocent-looking Coke can could be an explosive capable of destroying a city block. At any moment, there could be radical black activists taking aim or reactionary, neo-Nazi nuts trying to hold back the tides of change. I imagined everyone must have become numb to the idea of living in the crosshairs of a gunsight. And I had had the audacity to walk into a gun shop, of all places, where I truly did not belong. I felt weak and frightened all over again. I had forgotten who I was.

Such a mistake in a place like South Africa could be fatal. I should have known better—would have known better than to stop in a redneck bar or hangout if I had been passing through a small town in, say, Mississippi or Louisiana. How could I have let my guard down so completely here, where black folks accounted for even less in the view of whites.

Later, as I passed out cake and poured champagne at our Fourth of July celebration, I trembled when I thought about what I had done to purchase the two dozen Old Glories fluttering next to the sparklers in the air-conditioned lounge. I wished to be home in the United States. "To my country's birthday, in the hope that one day this country will know freedom," I said, raising my champagne glass in a toast. Everyone present cheered and clinked glasses.

Chapter Eight

EPIPHANY IN DUDUZA

One Saturday evening, with no story or deadline pending, I asked the concierge at the hotel to make dinner reservations for Nat and me at a Johannesburg cabaret called La Parisienne. We had seen the place advertised, noting in particular that it offered a buffet dinner with burlesque floor show. The place was booked solid and had no room for two more diners, the concierge reported back to me.

When I told Nat this, he called the concierge and demanded that she inform the cabaret owner that La Parisienne should make room for "the Prince Mkhonto Ovuthayo, royalty from the African protectorate of Kishamamu." The concierge dutifully complied, amid giggles from Nat and me.

"They found a table," the concierge announced, cupping the telephone receiver with her hand. "They want to know how many will be in the prince's entourage?"

"Tell them four," Nat said.

We were set with reservations for 7 P.M. But there were only two of us. "Well, Prince, how are you going to solve this?" I asked.

"Well, I saw in the paper that Charlayne Hunter-Gault is in Johannesburg doing some reporting for the MacNeil/Lehrer show. I know her from my days at the *New York Times* and I'll call and invite her to join us. You call Sheila and tell her to come along. Let's meet in the lobby at six-thirty and get our story together."

I had met Sheila Rule, then the Nairobi correspondent for the *New York Times*, years before at an NAACP convention in New Orleans. But I got to know her better during my travels in Africa.

We all met in the lobby of the hotel. Nat bedecked himself in a billowing African print gown and headwear that looked like a cross between a fez and a beanie, plus black canvas Chinese slippers with rubber soles. He looked convincing for his role as the prince. I played the prince's chargé d'affaires, Sam Matu, a Harvard-educated bodyguard, aide and advance man; I wore a conservative gray business suit and dark aviator glasses. Sheila, a beautiful woman with high cheeks, dark skin and enormous eyes, made the perfect fifth—and favored—wife of an African royal, complete with stylish purple dress. Charlayne's part was closest to reality in this absurd drama; she was an American journalist who had heard the prince was in town and had tagged along—tape recorder running—for an exclusive interview.

We arrived at the cabaret to discover there were no other black people in the joint, except the out-of-sight kitchen crew that peeked out from swinging doors for a glimpse of the prince. The hostess, a blond woman who was gracious and seemed honored, led us through a room with a floor that sloped down to a waiting table located next to the stage. Once we were seated, the hostess extended her hand to greet the prince. As Nat smiled broadly and reached to take her hand, I lunged across the table, upsetting a glass of water, to stop the woman from shaking hands with the prince.

"No! No! No!" I said with all the urgency and menace my caretaker character could summon. "You must not touch the prince."

The woman jerked her hand back and apologized profusely. The sides of her face were so crimson she looked as though I had slapped her with a quick back-and-forth motion. I softened my facial expression to reveal regret, leaned forward and whispered to her.

"I am so sorry," I said. "But you did not know. In my country, a woman never extends her hand in greeting to a member of the royal family unless she is inviting herself to spend the night with him. I know you did not wish that and I would have been bound to compel you to join us if you had touched His Highness."

"Oh, thank you. Thank you." She backed away, relieved at the narrow escape from a personal, and international, disaster. She never appeared at our table again, but did order one of the black South Africans in the kitchen to present our table with a bottle of delicious champagne. Compliments of the house, he said, pointing with his thumb toward the front of the room.

For a moment, this African stood face to face with the prince. He spoke in his native language to Nat, who quickly responded, in broken Swahili, with the only epigram he knew. Loosely translated, the prince's words were "The only thanks you get from a donkey is a kick in the ass."

After eating well and drinking even better, we watched as a procession of bare-breasted women danced and trolloped in a series of sexually suggestive skits and hokey routines. A comedian, who must have patterned himself after Don Rickles, told jokes at the audience's expense. The comedian had approached me privately before his performance and asked if the prince would mind being kidded.

"If you do," I warned him, "I will not be responsible for what happens. The prince is not one to play with, and his mission here is supposed to be secret. I think it best if you just ignore His Highness." All during his act, the comedian shot glances at Nat to see if he was enjoying the act. Nat was stoic, responding to some jokes with a sharp pat on the dining table.

The evening ended with the four of us deciding to get the hell out of that place before some snafu exposed us. I raced out of the restaurant, flung open the doors of our Mercedes-Benz and stood erect as the prince and his entourage climbed in. We laughed for days at the absurdity of how we had cheated the apartheid system and lived to chortle over it.

But daily life for black people in South Africa was no joking matter to me. I found it irrational and incongruous. Being there was like living within a Picasso, surreal and disjointed, yet exciting and colorful. Perspective was everything because nothing was really as it seemed. I witnessed the lives of black South Africans and reported on their living, struggling and dying under apartheid. All the while, I kept reminding myself how precious the freedom was that I enjoyed in the United States.

But my sense of place as an American was stripped away a few weeks before I left South Africa. I was raking for stories in the dusty streets of Duduza, about thirty miles west of Johannesburg, when I discovered that I could never escape race-based oppression—no matter how affluent or clever I thought I was.

"A black man is a black," declared Alexander Montoedi, my guide through his desolate township, "something to be despised and hated if you believe white is pure." He pointed out that every fifth house or so on one particular street had been torched, apparently by radical black activists opposed to the apartheid government. Montoedi, who was the founder of the Duduza Civic Association, a community self-improvement group, explained that the charred remains "were the houses of the briefcase toters," those middle-class blacks in the township who were set up by the authorities as role models for the disgruntled to emulate.

Some, but not very many, of the blacks who lived in the township were employed by major companies like IBM and Barclays Bank, which had offices in the big cities. A few of those workers drove BMWs, wore Pierre Cardin suits and carried polished leather briefcases. They patterned themselves after white businessmen.

"The government wants to create a black middle-class for us to look up to," Montoedi said, concluding his lecture. "Here in all this despair, they believe that those misguided blacks working for them in those city offices will serve as role models for the rest of us stuck here. It's crazy. All of us can't be middle-class."

This comment—"*All of us can't be middle-class*"—burst my bubble. I was black and middle-class in America. Had I been set up, framed like a pretty picture of upward mobility for other blacks to replicate? Montoedi shrugged.

"You live there, I don't," he said, his words softly fading into the South African twilight.

I wanted to scream. I had to come here for this. I no longer wanted to play the game. The trappings of my successful life mutated from badges of achievement to chains of oppression. Aspiring to be black and "middle-class" sounded like a curse that suggested the values of white people were more authentic than my own black American mainstream existence.

Sadly, I thought of David Bradley and his *Esquire* essay. He was right all along to say that it was impossible "to give a socially meaningful description of who I am and what I've done without using the word black." This was painful because it meant I had to accept his corollary: "Nothing I shall ever accomplish or discover or earn or inherit or buy or sell or give away—nothing I can ever do—will outweigh the fact of my race in determining my destiny."

I returned from South Africa with a new definition of American-style racism and classism, and how they acted like a pair of invisible hands molding the contours of my life. I wasn't in control of my destiny in the United States; I was living in Alice's Wonderland. The rules of life were always defined by someone white who decided whether what I did was acceptable, legal behavior. I knew more of the rules, so I played the game better than poorer blacks, who didn't know or didn't care to play the game at all. But I was still only a pawn in the white man's match. So why should I bother? The whole exercise was akin to my singing "Swing Low, Sweet Chariot" *en français;* the message came out garbled in my feeble attempt to chant the right words. What was the point of this professional black middle-class journalist's career? What was the point of selling my stories to upscale white suburbanites?

Did they care? Or did they only want to cluck their tongues as they turned up the volume on the nightly news, watching from the snugness of their homes and protected from ghetto violence? Was all this middle-class shit a waste of my time?

I began to fear that white people could never tolerate equality for black people unless it came on terms that made them happy. We would have to embrace their mistaken interpretation of reality as the only truth. That would never work. Even buppies, who wanted white people's approval more than any other black folks, would be ill at ease and silently hostile around white people under those conditions. Now that my blackness stood in opposition to their whiteness, what would I do with this knowledge? I vowed to find a more productive method of expending energy than proving myself, or anything else, to white people.

I withdrew into myself.

Returning to Baltimore was like going back to some place I had never been before. I was going home. But it would be different, or, more accurately, I would be changed. I held within my head a new perspective. But was it new only to me? I didn't know whether other black Americans knew what I had just discovered. Could I have been missing out all along on something as ancient as blackness in the New World—the dilemma of choosing between being black and American.

Now, I would stop running away from the questions that I had made a career of denying. I began to doubt whether America would ever be the race-blind haven that black people of my parents' generation had hoped it would become. It seemed, as I pondered this on the sixteen-hour TWA flight which ferried me across the Atlantic Ocean—across time, and across thought, from Johannesburg to New York City—that the twentieth century was dripping away and few cared enough to put a finger in the dike. W. E. B. Du Bois had called "the color line" the problem of my century. Those who remained alarmed by Du Bois's prophesy were accused of living in the past to bolster their own opportunism. The millennium would pass without my deliverance. Racism still stained the land, marking even me, a first-generation, post–civil rights era immigrant who had the liberty to live, learn, work and play alongside whites without legal restrictions. This color line would inevitably shade everything I did, perhaps not as virulently, but just as indelibly, as it had the lives of my parents, my grandparents and their parents and grandparents.

Living one summer in South Africa, of all places, roused me from my blind belief in the American Dream. I felt betrayed and isolated, marginalized in the society I thought should treat me as an equal citizen. I was angrier than I ever had been before.

I allowed no one in the office to know precisely how I felt. I did not discuss my thoughts with anyone, not even Cynthia. What could I say that she would have understood? These feelings were private. So, as far as I could tell, no one noticed any change in me as I went about my previous routines and duties. It suited me just fine to wear the mask of acquiescence, at least until I figured what to do with my new attitude. Inwardly, however, everything was distorted, as if I had just been awakened from a long slumber to experience life in a harsher light.

Chapter Nine

BLACK MECCA

Late one May afternoon in 1987, I received a phone call at work from a man I had never met.

"I'm John Maynard, assistant managing editor for business news at the *Atlanta Constitution.*" The voice was high-pitched, nasal and whiny, with a drawl invoking images of dusty pickup trucks, gun racks and floppy-eared dogs. A Southern white man, I thought. He didn't have to say another word. I knew what was coming because the only time I received calls from newspaper editors was when one of them was headhunting for a black scalp. As soon as he identified himself, I knew this Maynard person was calling to see if I would volunteer mine.

"I've heard enough about you and your work to be interested in knowing if we could persuade you to work down here in Atlanta?" Maynard continued, the flattery soft and sweet like his accent. I wanted to hear more: What had he heard about me? From whom? When did they say it? But I said nothing and his opening question hung out there on the telephone line, reverberating over the crackle of long-distance static and my silence.

"You there?" he asked. "Can you talk? Or should I call back later?"

I smiled at the thought of confusing him by not responding quickly enough. I was sizing up my options, thinking how I wanted to respond. I wasn't expecting this call. No need to agree to anything just yet. I remained silent, thinking, make him work to reveal more of himself. I could have sworn I heard gears grinding—the sound of his brain cranking up another question.

I had been a reporter at two good-sized newspapers for almost ten years and cold calls about job changes had become a regular component of my work life, coming at a clip of three or four per year. They were more frequent after I arrived at *The Sun*. So frequent that I had stopped being impressed by them. For the most part, the editors were ham-fisted, typically desperate in their efforts to hire a black staffer. I felt that few, if any, actually knew anything about me or cared how I might fit whatever job was being offered. Though I had never met Maynard, I suspected he was the latest in a long line of these editors.

My instinct about Maynard's call was a reflex, involuntarily triggered by previous experiences. I determined by little more than the inflections in his voice—a disembodied voice reaching out to someone unseen and unknown—that this call most likely would represent no progress over what I already had at *The Sun*. I wasn't paying attention to what Maynard was saying, only listening politely for the appropriate length of time before branding the call unworthy of bringing home to Cynthia for discussion.

He broke the silence with another question. "Do you know anything about our newspaper?"

"A little." I tried to be cool, indifferent and noncommittal.

"We're the largest newspaper in the Southeast and we're growing," Maynard went on. "We've got a new editor, you may have heard of him, Bill Kovach, who used to be with the *New York Times*. Well, he's interested in improving our business coverage and that's where you come into the picture. We have an opening for an assistant business editor and I'd like to know if you're interested in talking about it."

Kovach, I thought. He had dropped that name in rather smoothly. Bill Kovach had made a name for himself as an outstanding reporter for Nashville's *Tennessean* and as an excellent editor and a fine judge of newsroom talent when he was the Washington bureau chief of the *New York Times.* He had also created a media stir by moving to the Atlanta papers the previous year. His appointment as editor was heralded among some journalists nationwide as a sign that the New South was ready for the New Journalism. I had been impressed with him by what I read in *Newsweek, Time* and other publications. He had attracted several brand-name journalists to Atlanta, and the improved and aggressive reporting they produced was finding its way onto the pages of the newspaper. Everything I had read or heard about the dramatic progress in the Atlanta papers credited Kovach with a remarkable transformation.

By mentioning Kovach, Maynard coerced me into thinking about Atlanta. Now the gears were whirring in *my* head. Atlanta was Black Mecca for buppies, and had long held a magnetic attraction for me. It was the exemplary late-twentieth-century metropolis, combining what was best in Southern small-town sensibilities with big-city affluence for middle-class black people like me. I could sink roots there, raise my family without sacrificing too much of the hustle of urban living that I had come to enjoy.

My curiosity was genuinely piqued now, swaying me to listen a little more intently to what Maynard was offering. I began then to imagine what it might be like to move to Atlanta.

"Can you tell me about yourself?" Maynard interrupted my thoughts.

Now I had to talk. But what to say? Okay, I was interested in *talking* about the job. Should I say so or not? How aggressively should I pursue this inquiry? The hiring process is like a sales job. Maynard was leading with what seemed to me a hard-sell approach. That suggested he was eager to close the deal and implied that I, the buyer, had the upper hand. But that could be only for the moment. Once I surrendered control and wanted the job more than he wanted me to have it, the process would reverse itself.

He was the boss, a white man entitled to hire and fire whomever he chose. I had only the choice of whether or not to seek the job and I feared losing that little bit of control by seeming too eager to accept. I had to *not* want the job too much, then he *might* let me have it.

"I wouldn't mind living in Atlanta," I said, starting to tell him about myself, highlighting parts of my résumé. I tried to craft sentences so I would say precisely what I wanted him to hear me saying. This was a hard mental exercise because my mind was elsewhere. From the moment I heard Maynard's voice, all that tore through my mind was knowing that he never would have called me without knowing I was a black man and, therefore, that he was looking specifically to hire a black person. But I didn't want to interject race into our discussion. Not yet anyway.

"I'm a Southerner, from North Carolina originally," I said. "I miss living in the South." That was the truth, but I said it calculating he would like to hear it and hoping the comment might forge a geographical bond between us. I continued to trace my career for a few minutes before he cut me off.

"We think it's important we have a diverse staff and there are no black editors on our desk," he said. I was surprised by the abrupt way he raised the issue of race without any prompting, apropos of nothing. I began then to appreciate John Maynard as an honest man.

Even if I didn't want the job, I wanted him to like me. I wanted him to evaluate me, to determine whether I was worthy of being hired and to offer me the job. Selling myself on Maynard became a goal because my race was important to him. I wanted to prove I had worth as a newspaper staffer who happened to be black—and at that very moment the best way to prove it lay in convincing Maynard to make the offer. It was an important point for me.

I had learned shortly after becoming an editor on the city desk at *The Sun* that a roster of white reporters working at other papers had been identified (albeit not told or contacted) as "most wanted" potential employees. The black pool, by contrast, had to be dredged anew every time a *black hiring* possibility presented itself. Bluntly stated, I discovered that white editors don't trust themselves to hire the *right* black person for the job. They agonize and second-guess themselves over and over concerning the basic competence of nearly any black applicant whose résumé crosses their desk. These editors will only consider hiring a black person when compelled to do so and, then, will only consider that black candidate capable and qualified if he or she has earned notice from some white-controlled institution or trusted (white) person.

At *The Sun* nobody tracked potential black hires until the need arose. Then a mad scramble began. I would be called in and asked if I knew of any "qualified black reporters" we might hire. I was asked this question by editors in nearly every department at the paper, regardless of whether I worked there or whether I had ever had a conversation with anyone who worked there. Dutifully, I would offer names and numbers of friends and acquaintances in the business. I convinced myself that if I didn't do this, no black people would be considered for job openings. Little difference it made. When I later talked to these friends, most of them reported that they had never received a call. Nevertheless, the department managers would say they had gone out of their way to recruit "qualified minorities" but couldn't find any. Or, they moaned, the best (black) prospect couldn't be persuaded to leave the *New York Times* for a job that featured a pay cut and a demand to relocate to Baltimore.

What they really meant was they couldn't find the blue-chip black, the rare and overqualified African-American who came highly regarded by some other white person. Recommendations from white colleagues were vital because they sanitized the black job seeker, separating those applicants who were more adept at *going along to get along* from those who were likely to develop bad attitudes. They had already proven themselves to at least one approving white authority.

So the same set of black names was passed along from editor to

editor and a few of them were hired. I knew my name was on a potential hire list circulated among editors at various other newspapers. Perhaps that was how Maynard found me; I never knew why he called me
in the first place. I discovered my name was in circulation after my
friend Wilma Randle, a very fine business reporter at the *Chicago Tribune*, called one day when I was still reporting for the business desk at
The Sun to ask if I had received a call from the business editor of the
Washington Post.

"As a matter of fact, I just did. How did you know?" Wilma's
knowledge of my business startled me. I had hung up the phone on the
business editor's call less than an hour before she called.

"I got the same call," she said. Although she was laughing, I felt a
blade of anger slicing between her words. "We're on the black list."

"What black list?"

"That's the list of black folks who work for big-city newspapers
that editors use to make calls whenever they have a black spot open."

I had never heard of such a thing until then.

"I'll bet he used the same damn approach as he used with me,"
Wilma added. "Did he ask if you were ready for a change, ready to
come work for a real newspaper?"

"Damn right, Wilma."

"And then he talked about how the *Post* wanted to have a diverse
staff and how you were one of the fine black business reporters in the
nation, how he had been following your work for a long time—"

"—and how coming to the *Post* at this time would be the right
move to make at this point in my career," I said, overlapping and
completing her sentence.

Wilma and I laughed hard at the absurdity. When she stopped
laughing, her anger waxed with curses and outrage at having been
taken less than seriously.

"Sam, I think I would have been interested if, just for one moment,
he had made me think he was really interested in me and my work,"
she said finally and softly. "All he wanted was to hire a black business
reporter. Not me."

I felt bad as I hung up the phone. I wasn't as angry as Wilma, but her emotional outburst made me feel sad. I knew that the editors didn't get it and, worse, that they would never understand why Wilma was furious. In the end, it didn't matter. What she felt or what I felt changed nothing.

Affirmative action—or this malicious distortion of it—was intended to persuade managers to extend their hiring networks so that the pool of qualified applicants included people from diverse backgrounds. But it didn't work that way. Even when black people were fortunate enough to get hired, they were made to feel undeserving of what they most likely were overqualified for in the first place. Years later, a white colleague at another newspaper told me that the same *Washington Post* editor told him, "Just between you and me, you would have gotten the job, but, well, you know, the *Post* has to diversify its staff." As outrageous as I or Wilma might find this, there was virtually nothing to do about it. The offending white boss man called the shots, hiring whomever he deemed "qualified."

The incident is tucked away, never to be forgotten or forgiven, in my memory, where it stands like a monument to the race-conscious unfairness of most white newsrooms. For me, in fact, it remains unchallenged that whenever a black person is hired into a newsroom, he comes into the job carrying a racial stigma hung over his head by his new boss and visible to all his colleagues. Nothing is said overtly, but volumes are shouted in the quiet gestures, such as the notice on the bulletin board announcing the hiring of a new black reporter. Rest assured the new hire is a blue-chipper, but rarely recognized as such because the blackness of his skin is the most apparent feature of his being.

Even as I warmed to Maynard, I was not deceived by his candid approach. Had I been white, I believed, Maynard would have been certain of my abilities and there would have been no question. Or he wouldn't have called at all. But he was making a special effort to hire a black editor, which implied that he had qualms about just how qualified I might be.

Later that night, I told Cynthia about Maynard's call. "I kind of liked him," I said. "I also think it might be worth looking into the situation in Atlanta. What do you think?"

She was seven months' pregnant and had taken a disability leave from her public communications job at Johns Hopkins University Medical School. With all that going on, I was surprised when she said, "I wouldn't mind moving to Atlanta. After all, it is closer to our parents in Charlotte and Columbia. It would be good for the baby to grow up near grandparents.

"And, I've always wanted to live in Atlanta," she added, grinning broadly. "It's a Chocolate City, you know."

For sure, Atlanta was no backwater, no hick town. It was urban, just as much as, maybe more so than, Baltimore. My yardstick for testing whether a city is urban can be summed up in a three-question test: Is the city home to professional sports? Can you tell people where you are from without appending the name of the state? Does the city have an impressively awesome skyline? While Baltimore technically met the minimum requirements, Atlanta was an overwhelming winner in each category.

But more than that, as Cynthia had remarked, Atlanta was a black city, booming and black, big and black, bad and black. It had become a haven for middle-class black folks from across the nation, owing largely to the election of lawyer-cum-politician Maynard Jackson. He put Atlanta on the map as the best place for us to live in America. In the cliques we moved among, Atlanta was widely hailed as the model city, perhaps the only place in the nation where black politicians and black business owners had teamed up to produce an American ideal, a success story for black-owned enterprises, the "Black Mecca," as *Black Enterprise* and *Ebony* magazines separately dubbed it.

Such a perception stemmed from the pro–black business leadership of Jackson, who in 1973, at age thirty-five, was the first black and the youngest of any color to be elected mayor of a large Southern city. Armed with the political support of a 54-percent black population base and watched by a national audience, Jackson, a wavy-haired, yellow-hued man with an outgoing personality as broad as his roly-poly girth, set about changing the way business was transacted in the halls of the nation's increasingly black urban centers.

In 1973, the City of Atlanta's contracts with minority-owned businesses amounted to $40,000, less than 0.1 percent of the city's budget. This would end, Jackson ordered, and during his two-term administration he redirected nearly a quarter of the budget, about $33 million, to black-owned companies through an inventive contracting set-aside program for minority business enterprises.

This had two predictable results. First, it attracted black entrepreneurs and middle-class strivers from around the country to Atlanta; hence "Black Mecca." From small towns across the South and urban areas in the North, ambitious college-educated black folks rushed to Atlanta. Many came seeking an opportunity to hit it big in the emerging black political and economic energy in this New South city.

The second result was white backlash, as the city's business establishment, called the "Big Mules," at first refused to cooperate with what they considered the black mayor's brash and heavy-handed moves. They complained loudly about "reverse racism" and "social experiments." They stalled and continued to do business as they always had, within their tight, white circle of old-line cronies.

But times had changed in Atlanta. From 1973 on, black voters had placed political power in ebony hands. There was little the "Mules" could do except bray in protest when Jackson and the city council demanded they give black entrepreneurs at least 20 percent of the city contracts for the $400 million in municipal funds to be spent building Hartsfield International Airport. He also threatened to pull $450 million in city funds from local banks if they did not grant loans, jobs and promotions to black Atlantans. The construction of new runways and gates at Hartsfield was vital to the city's business image and economic future, so the whites backed down and Jackson became a national political hero to millions of middle-class black Americans.

I was one of them. By 1987, when John Maynard called me, Jackson's two terms as mayor were legend. He had been replaced in 1981 by Andrew Young, who had continued to advocate government-backed black business participation and greater black hiring and promotions in white-controlled firms doing business with the city. A pattern of strong problack political leadership was enshrined in Atlanta. I was in awe and felt something like pride in Jackson's early political victories and in their continuation under Young. Atlanta had to be the best place in America for black people to be.

While I had doubts about the big picture at *The Sun*, my standing with my bosses was secure and optimistic. I had been promoted to the first rung of newsroom management and there were vague suggestions, offered discreetly, that in time—always in time, never at present—I would move up to more and more responsible managerial jobs. I might even have another shot at overseas reporting. I wasn't unhappy with my job, though since South Africa I had felt I would never be totally happy with any job. But what the hell, isn't that the nature of work no matter where you are or who you are? The inertia of daily life had settled over me, and the routine and the familiarity of the people around me at *The Sun* seemed comfortable, far more comfortable than the unknown down in Atlanta.

What should I do? I did what any good reporter would do. I called one of my most trusted sources for advice. I had met Ernest Holsendolph, then business editor of Cleveland's *Plain Dealer*, when I was writing editorials on the federal budgeting process for *The Sun*. We were the only two black journalists attending a two-day business and economics symposium at the Watergate Hotel in Washington. Almost from the first time I set eyes on him, I sensed there was something magical and otherworldly about this plump, elfin black man with a stubby laurel wreath of hair that wrapped around the sides and back of his head. Ernie and I became friends almost immediately.

Among the first wave of black reporters to work for white newspapers in the 1960s, he told great stories about meeting famous and interesting people on his journalistic travels. For most of his career, he had been either an urban affairs reporter or a business writer at a variety of East Coast publications. He had won awards for his work at *Fortune* magazine, the *New York Times* and *The Evening Star*. Ernie had always taken a special interest in me and my work life. We called each other frequently to discuss articles, current events, books, movies, whatever caught our attention. Whenever he was in the Washington area, we would have lunch together. I always looked forward with great anticipation to these talks because of the dearth of senior black journalists in my professional life. At one of our long, wine-soaked lunches, he asked if I had any interest in coming to work for him in Cleveland. Ernie was the closest thing I had to a mentor, sort of a distant patron whose phoned-in advice more often than not served as my only professional lifeline to sanity. The idea of being closer to him was attractive, but I declined because I didn't want to move to Ohio. However, the thought of working for him never left my mind.

When I called Ernie to report to him about the Atlanta job, I was shocked when he told me he had had conversations with Kovach about going to Atlanta himself.

"It's a good opportunity," Ernie said. "They're doing great things down there. I'm not able to go down and work there. Not right now, at least. But Kovach is a fine editor and I suspect he's going to try like hell to put that paper on the map."

"So what are you saying? Should I go down and talk to this Maynard guy?"

"I don't know him. But what can it hurt?"

"It won't hurt anything," I said. "But if I get down there and don't like it, I may be making a mistake by leaving a good thing here."

"That's life," Ernie said. "Sam, you just have to do the job wherever you can and keep your eyes open. That's about all you can do."

If I keep my eyes open, I can make do in Atlanta, I thought, after hanging up the phone. Indeed, I was ready to accept the job, sight unseen, if I could convince Maynard and Kovach to hire me.

Yet, to temper my enthusiasm, I forced myself to make another call, one that I knew guaranteed a counterweight to the euphoria of a potential career change. I called Momma. I recalled a conversation I had had with her just before I left Charlotte for Baltimore. "You should never change a good job unless they're about to run you off," she said back then. "A good job is hard to find and you should hold on to it until you can't anymore."

Her advice had not changed since then. "Are you having problems there in Baltimore?" she asked.

"No, of course not," I answered. "It just sounds like a better opportunity, a chance to advance in my career."

"Are they going to pay you more money?" Momma was concerned about my being taken. She didn't trust white people, and that question about money suggested she didn't trust me to understand white people well enough to ask for a bigger salary if I was to relocate.

"Well, I've only had one phone conversation," I said. "But certainly, if I take any new job, it would be for more money. I was just calling to see what you thought about it."

"I don't think anything about it," she replied. "You young people seem to have all the answers nowadays and nobody can tell you what to do. It just doesn't seem to make a whole lot of sense to me to be jumping from job to job. I think you'd want to settle down and work in one place toward your retirement."

This conversation had spun out of control. Retirement was years away. Momma had worked one job for the major part of her life, with her teacher's pension, backed by the state government, as the holy grail. She was right, there was nothing she could say to help me with this decision.

"Okay. Okay, Momma," I said, drawing the phone call to a conclusion. "I'm going down to Atlanta for an interview in a few days. I'll let you know how it goes."

A week later, I was standing in the street-level lobby asking a security guard for directions to John Maynard's office. The guard was a black man. He appeared to be younger than I and was dressed in his firm's dark blue trimmed in gold with a silver badge shining on his chest. He smiled when he saw me approach. I suddenly felt conspicuous in my blue suit, white shirt, red tie and black wing tips.

"Don't tell me," he said. "Let me guess. Advertising?"

"Nope, newsroom," I said.

"Not many of us go up there," he said.

I smiled back. That's what I missed about the South. Friendly, nosey, chatty, outgoing black folks. "If they hire me, there'll be one more," I said.

"I hope so," he said, passing me a badge to wear while visiting his building. "Good luck."

I took the elevator to the sixth floor. When the door opened, the first person I saw was a receptionist who pointed toward a cramped cubicle situated in the far northwest corner of the floor. I walked past her station and surveyed the landscape. It was an enormous newsroom that stretched as far as I could see. Along the far wall was a series of glass walls, behind which white men were pecking away at heavy computer terminals. Editors, I thought.

Just outside those offices were queues of desks that looked like a massive fleet of gray battleships sailing on a brown carpeted sea. Most of the desks were empty, but some here and there were occupied by busy men and women, talking on beige telephones or fingering keyboards. Their work produced a sort of hum, a background noise common to offices but apparent only to someone new.

I looked around for black faces and saw none. I was neither surprised nor disappointed. It was about 10 A.M., early morning for a newsroom, and I would get to know who worked there—and who didn't—in time, perhaps.

This place is huge, much larger than the Baltimore newsroom, I thought. Is that good or bad? I didn't have to decide that right away. For the moment, I wanted to calm myself, take deep breaths and go meet the man.

Maynard was affable as he greeted me at the entrance of his cubicle/office. He wore gray trousers and a heavily starched white button-down shirt. His tie was tightly knotted, but hung loose around his neck. I noticed a handsome tweedy sport coat on a hanger as I entered his office. He was stylish in a preppy kind of way.

Maynard looked to be only slightly older than I, although his prematurely graying hair gave him a more aged appearance. His face was unlined and he had the trim build of an avid tennis player. I sensed a casual air about him that reminded me of some of the white guys back at Carolina: in their polo shirts, khakis and Weejuns, they practiced familiarity and reckless abandon as they cupped a foamy mug of beer in one hand and clasped their free arm around your shoulder in a tight, plastic greeting whenever they were among their friends and saw you alone. I had never trusted them.

I couldn't tell whether it was Maynard's flesh or mine that was cold and damp when we shook hands. I believed it to be mine and rubbed my right palm on the side of my trousers when his two fists stopped vigorously pumping my hand. I hoped he didn't notice and take offense at my wiping away his greeting.

"I'm so glad you could get here," Maynard said, closing the cubicle door behind me. His cramped space was a jumble of family photos, newspapers and general clutter.

"Thanks," I said. "I'm flattered you wanted to talk to me."

First impressions are the best, I thought. So far, so good. We seemed to be getting off to a fine start. He began to brag about his department and the work various reporters had produced; I tried to repeat what I had said over the phone. As we jockeyed back and forth, I peered deeply into his eyes, looking for clues as to how I was faring and hoping my eyes were inexpressive. I still didn't want to reveal too much eagerness. At one point during that first hour—it's hard to say when or why precisely—I sensed Maynard warming to me.

"I've looked at your clips and I'm impressed at the range of your work," he said, referring to the stack of newspaper stories I had sent him.

"Which did you like?" I said.

"The one about dockworkers losing their jobs was pretty good," he said. "There was the one retail story that showed how hard it is for stores to create traffic in downtown department stores. We have that same problem at Rich's here. That's the kind of story we could have done. You also had a nice profile of the executive at McCormick, the spice company. We would have run any of those."

It surprised and pleased me to know that he had actually read my clips and could make specific references to them.

"But more than the clips," Maynard went on, "was the fact you sent them so quickly after we had talked. Shows you can get organized in a hurry."

I smiled. This is going very well, I thought, so I decided to repay the compliment by showing more interest in his department's work. "You know, I would like to see some of the business sections you put out," I said.

He nodded and seemed happy I had asked about the paper. "Sure, I can get one for you right now," he said, bouncing up from his desk to rush out to the newsroom. He returned seconds later with an unwrinkled copy of that morning's newspaper. "The department puts out two newspapers every day—a morning paper, the *Constitution*, and an afternoon paper, the *Journal*," he said. "Same staff and same stories. You will be responsible for supervising the production of the business section of the morning paper."

Did he say *"you will"*? Do I already have this job? Am I imagining things? I tried to relax, pretend I didn't hear what I wanted to hear.

I had been in Maynard's tiny office for about an hour and a half when he jumped up from his seat. I hadn't noticed it before, but nearly all his movements were sudden, jerky maneuvers, as if something had just dawned on him or he didn't quite remember the best way to get from one place to another. "There's someone else I want you to meet," he said, rushing out the door.

A few minutes later, he returned with another white man. He was the most ascetic person I had ever seen, thin and sinewy, as though he had once lived a robust life but now, like a religious convert, was refusing all earthly pleasures to gain admittance to heaven. He was a head taller than Maynard, with bulging eyes and a mane of loose, curly brown ringlets that were flecked with gray and fell to his shoulders. He looked like one of the Gorgons I had read about in a mythology class back in high school.

"Sam," said Maynard, "this is Thomas Oliver, another editor on the business desk."

I held my breath as he followed Maynard into the now overflowing cubicle. I exhaled audibly and felt my palms go sweaty all over again just as I extended my hand.

"We're glad to have you in Atlanta," Oliver said. His Dixie drawl was stronger than Maynard's, more robust and booming than any I had ever heard.

"Thomas is going to take you to lunch," Maynard said. "That'll give you two an opportunity to talk and get to know each other."

We walked to a small diner in a bank building not more than two blocks from the newspaper's offices. It was a down-home kind of place that looked as if it had been built for an episode of *Matlock* or *Green Acres*. Oliver explained that he was a simple Georgia boy and that fancy restaurants held no particular allure for him.

"Fine by me," I said. "I'm here to meet and talk with you. Plus, I can't get this kind of cooking in Baltimore."

Oliver's grin brightened his gloomy face like a jack-o'-lantern on a dark October night. He opened the diner door for me. Inside, the place was elbow-close with people who looked like lawyers and bankers, construction workers and secretaries, messengers and truck drivers.

"You must be a basketball fan," Oliver said after we took a seat and a waitress plopped tumblers of ice water before us.

"How did you know that?" I asked.

"Well, I've never met anyone who went to UNC who wasn't," he said.

I was impressed. He had paid attention to my résumé and made an accurate guess.

"I went to Georgia," he continued. "Not much of a basketball place. But we play a mean game of football."

"Oh, I don't know that Georgia basketball is anything to bad-mouth," I said. "Dominique Wilkins went there and he turned out pretty good. On the other hand, I guess people down here still think Hershel Walker walks on water."

So much for small talk. By the time our lunch arrived, we had moved on to discussing news judgment and potential story ideas. He, too, had seen my clips and could cite specifics about what I had written. I commented that the kind of journalism I liked explained how and why things worked, did not just say that something happened.

"That's what I think too, Sam," Oliver said. "I was a business reporter here for a while and that's what I always tried to do. But I had more success at doing that after I became a business columnist."

"You were a business columnist?" My shock had to have registered on my face.

"Yeah," he said. "You seem surprised."

"No, not really," I said. "I just didn't know that about you." Well, yeah, I was surprised. He didn't seem polished enough to be a business columnist, at least not to my prejudiced view of what a business columnist should be. Oliver struck me as a good ol' boy who had made good on his home turf. Not broad and varied enough to be a columnist, but capable enough to be a solid local reporter.

"There's a lot about me you probably don't know," he added. His tone was still upbeat, so I wasn't troubled. "Did you know I wrote a book on the Coca-Cola Company?"

"No. Didn't know that. Did you?" I thought maybe it was a trick question.

"Yep," he said. "It did really well. It was about the business of new Coke and all that trouble."

"Oh, in that case, I want to read a copy of it," I said.

After lunch, Oliver escorted me back to the newspaper building, where I was deposited once again in Maynard's office. The newsroom buzzed with ringing telephones and animated conversations. Maynard was not in, so I took the liberty of looking from his office into the business department. As best I could tell, there were about a dozen reporters. Earlier, I had noticed two black people in the department, though no one introduced us. Both seemed young, and I noticed that at times they looked at me as if they were curious about why I was there. I wanted to go over and strike up a conversation, but decided against it. There will be another time, another place, I thought. Plenty of time to get to know everyone.

"Sam, Thomas tells me he likes you," Maynard said, closing the door behind him. "He said talking with you was like talking with a mirror image of himself."

That was the strangest comment I had ever heard a white man make about a black person. White people, I had come to believe, never saw themselves reflected in the face of a black person. I must have really made a favorable impression for Oliver to say such a thing.

"He wants to know how soon you can start," Maynard said with a sly laugh. "We can't offer you a job today, but it's a good sign that he likes you because you two would be working closely together."

Maynard then explained to me that Oliver was feeling overworked because he was responsible for both the morning and afternoon editions of the business section. It was too big a job for one person. Maynard said he was looking to hire two editors, one to have full responsibility for the morning paper and the other to supervise the afternoon paper. Oliver's job would be to look after the large Sunday edition.

"We'll be a team," Maynard said. "You will report to me. But all of us will have to work together to put out the paper."

It all sounded great to me. I left Maynard's office and the newspaper building feeling reasonably certain that I would be offered the job. I had proven myself to them, and left Atlanta elated at having accomplished my mission.

Three days after the interview in Atlanta, Bill Kovach called me at *The Sun*. I had been looking forward to meeting him during my interview, but he was out of town the day I came in. On the phone, he sounded like a cut-to-the-chase kind of guy and I took his call as a sure sign I would be offered the job.

"I heard good things about you from John Maynard," Kovach said, "and we would love to have you come down here and help revitalize the business pages of our newspaper."

I was now all the more euphoric, since I could tell the editors and my colleagues at *The Sun* that no less a luminary than Bill Kovach had called to persuade me to join his band of newspaper pirates in Atlanta. In a way, it was anticlimactic when Maynard called the next day to formally offer me the job.

He said I would be production supervisor for the business section of the morning daily, the *Constitution*. He said I would make editorial judgments, story assignments, and staffing decisions, and troubleshoot to ensure the smooth flow of the morning operation. He also repeated that I would report directly to him. All that sounded fine and consistent with what we had talked about in Atlanta.

He then turned to the subject of my pay. "We'll pay you $35,000. That is slightly more than what the job description calls for, but we were so impressed we wanted to convince you to come to Atlanta."

Uh-oh, I thought. His offer was the going rate for what the union at *The Sun* required for a journeyman reporter. I had been promoted into management at *The Sun* and my salary was $42,000.

I had been so excited by the opportunity to move to Atlanta that I overlooked Maynard's failure to talk more specifically about salary during our interview and during any of our later conversations. Now Momma's warning about getting more money was coming back to haunt me. I had assumed that money—or, more specifically, quibbling over an increase in salary—would never be a problem in our negotiations. The only time I remembered it coming up had been Maynard's casual comment that he would better my current salary. But he had never asked what I was making and obviously had no idea how much dough he would have to roll out. It would be a no-brainer for me. Atlanta's bright lights alone could not compensate me for a pay cut.

"I can't accept your offer as it is," I said. "I make more than that now."

"Oh?" Maynard said, surprised. "Well, how much do you make?"

I told him, and heard a stifled gasp. "That much!" he said. "Let me get back to you tomorrow."

He called two days later, once again sounding excited. "Sam, just to demonstrate how much we really want you, I'm going to break the bank. I can pay you $45,000."

I had been hoping for $50,000. But, hell, I also wanted the job and it seemed he had gone all out to make it happen for me. And it was more money than I had ever imagined making in journalism. I figured $45,000 in Atlanta would buy more creature comforts than it would in Baltimore. Better yet, I believed Maynard had sincerely sought more money for me and was doing all he could to make me happy working in his department. If nothing else, I could look Momma in the face and say I was making more money than she and Daddy ever did. I was happy to accept Maynard's offer and agreed to take the job.

"Good," Maynard said. "You don't know what I had to do to get that for you. I had to raise someone else's salary as well."

"What?"

I guess he was surprised by his own comment and thought better of being so candid with me. "Oh, never mind," he said, and changed the subject.

Lord knows, I wish to this day I had pursued that slender thread of a comment at the time. What I now believe was that Maynard came close to telling me he had paid Oliver more money because I was being hired at a salary higher than what he was already making. I am convinced this would be a sore point for Oliver in his dealings with me henceforth.

But at the time, I knew nothing about any of this, nor did I believe it my place to poke into whatever deals Maynard had struck to get me on the staff. After all, I thought, what did it matter what others in Maynard's department earned? I was getting what I wanted. Everything about making this move seemed right. If I loved the city, if the Atlanta newspapers were on the rebound, if I was going to have a major role in shaping coverage of the city's business community, if the editors had confidence in me, then why should I remain in Baltimore?

With the money talk out of the way, one more matter remained to be resolved. When would I start work? I explained to Maynard that Cynthia was not due for another month and would not be up to traveling for several weeks after giving birth. She was willing to move as soon as possible after the baby was born, but her doctor was not sure when that would be. Maynard suggested I come early and bring her later, a request I quickly rejected. I wanted to be with Cynthia for the entire pregnancy. He would have to wait until after she gave birth.

Katherine Amanda was born on June 18, 1987. Falling in love with her at first sight unnerved me. It was a new, transformative love that came from deep within an untouched place in my soul. It made me recognize that my reason for being on earth was to love her and be loved by her. Though only seconds in this new, strange and wondrous world, my daughter rested in my hands. Like the religious convert in the grasp of rapture, lacking the words to express understanding or meaning, I was reborn and felt in her birthing cries the breath of God.

From that moment on, I was a different person. Journalistic careerism mattered less and she, my Amanda, claimed top billing in my life. I wasn't turning away from the work world. Far from it, in fact. I now had a better reason to go to work, to do a good job, to earn lots of money. I had a daughter to live and strive for.

It all seemed so proper—a renaissance for me and my family—to leave Baltimore after Amanda was born. I felt something, maybe the spiritual essence of a fresh start, which made this major change seem so right. My family had expanded. I had a new job with greater responsibilities and fatter pay. I was moving back to the South, to Atlanta, a place where opportunities abounded for middle-class black families like mine. From where I sat, all was right and just with the world when, two weeks after Amanda was born, we were packed and moving to Black Mecca.

Our first task, after settling into a two-bedroom apartment in Atlanta, was to find an alternative to that cramped space. We wanted a house. But finding a place to live in Atlanta proved harder than Cynthia and I had ever imagined. We knew what we were looking for, the same thing most families in a new city say they want: an affordable and attractive house in a safe neighborhood with low taxes, good public schools and close-to-home retail services. We preferred a racially mixed community with friendly neighbors and lots of kids as friends for Amanda to grow up with. It should be easy to find in Atlanta because of the city's demographics, I thought. With so many people claiming they want the same thing, surely we can discover the perfect community.

Wrong.

There were pitifully few racially integrated neighborhoods in Atlanta. That's not to say black people and white people didn't live side by side in some communities. They did. But that wasn't the same thing as integrated, where a significant number of black homeowners—say, more than one every five blocks—lived in harmony and parity with white homeowners. If such places existed in Atlanta, we never found them. Nevertheless, every weekend we looked and looked and looked for what was in our mind's eye, in a ritual that took us from close readings of the real estate listings in the newspaper to cruising neighborhoods for "open houses" to, finally, exhaustion and frustration at finding neither our imagined home nor the perfect community that invited my young, expanding and black family.

One Sunday afternoon, after several weeks of peering into other people's homes and finding them lacking for one reason or another, Cynthia and I found ourselves at Brook Glen, a suburban housing development in DeKalb County. The ads in the *Constitution* heralded the subdivision as "Where Dream Homes Still Exist." Whoever was responsible for marketing Brook Glen knew what he or she was doing. Without fully comprehending why, I was smitten by the model home with its subtle, subliminal persuasions aimed at racial pride and feelings of estrangement from white neighborhoods. That house was calling my name and the names of other black professionals new to Atlanta. Indeed, I had never before seen a model home that featured decorations aimed at middle-income black buyers. The book with Dr. King's image on the cover was one item in an upstairs bedroom made up to simulate a child's fairy-tale fancy in cheery, bold primary colors. There on the bookshelf along with storybooks and a black-faced rag doll was this slim book about the life of Atlanta's most famous civil rights native.

"This would be little Amanda's bedroom," said the realtor's agent. She was a reed-thin copper-colored woman. She smelled like fresh flowers and spoke in a soft voice. The engraved name tag on her breast labeled her CAROL ELLIS, BROOK GLEN COMMUNITY SALES ASSOCIATE. I trusted her at first glance.

Cynthia and I immediately fell in love with the model home, imagining ourselves in its bedrooms and family areas and kitchen. We could feel the warmth and comfort of the community and knew without meeting any of them in advance that we would enjoy making friends with the neighbors. This was a community of some hundred homes, most of them under construction or recently built, Carol Ellis explained. She could see we were hooked, so she stoked the sales pitch by telling us that after we made a down payment and qualified for a loan, the builder could have us in our own place in ninety days or less. "You will love this community," she said and I believed her.

I felt a tug at my heart that quickly moved to my right hip pocket. My wallet throbbed. I was being manipulated by the sales hype, and enjoying every minute of it. Of course we would love this community. I had noticed the steady stream of eager home hunters who oohed and aahed, interrupting our sales chat with Carol Ellis. They loved this model home too. Like Cynthia, Amanda and me, they were black professionals with the income to buy anywhere in Atlanta.

If I had stopped to consider, which I didn't, I might have realized there was a sinister reason we had not found anything like Brook Glen sooner. We had failed to find a neighborhood that we liked because no one had made us feel wanted.

We had not been rebuffed or made to feel discriminated against. But we had not been made to feel welcome either. Nobody had gone out of their way to demonstrate that we would have made good neighbors in their community. But so lost was I in my dream of living large in this city of high black achievers that I had not yet realized why these details mattered.

The clues were right in our faces: subtle color-conscious marketing strategies employed by the real estate business made it clear who would be welcome and where they were wanted. Even in Black Mecca, residential segregation steered black people to communities south of I-75, while white people gravitated toward the northern suburban areas. Of course, there were always exceptions. But as I stood there in that Brook Glen model home, it was plain as never before. The builder of this community had folks like me in mind and he didn't mind making a production of it. It was good business. It made me feel good to be wanted as a consumer, someone worthy of the little merchandising details that were reaching for and grabbing my attention, and saying, *Buy here. Move in here. You are wanted here.* I had never felt anything like it. No wonder black people of means celebrated Atlanta so much. White people knew how to make you feel special down here, if only to get your money.

I imagined that the people who lived in this neighborhood—nearly all of them black, middle-class and professional—had at one time been exactly where I was, seduced by the siren call of a marketer who knew what to say and how to say it to a black consumer. This community of two-story Colonial and neo-Colonial homes with expansive and well-trimmed lawns, two-car garages, soaring entrances and gourmet kitchens was nothing if not an attractive locale for Atlanta's newly arrived blue-chip blacks. Yes, this was the place for the Fulwood family to homestead. Cynthia and I agreed to purchase a gently sloping lot at the corner of Seton Hall Drive and John Carroll Drive on which to build a four-bedroom house.

It would cost $134,000 to build that house, more than ten times the money Daddy and Momma had spent to build their dream home in McCrorey Heights. The $12,000 home I grew up in proved to be a sound investment and a source of great memories. I just knew in my bones that this house would be more of the same, a generation later, for my family.

I looked out the window of the model to see what style homes the neighbors had, hoping to catch sight of people luxuriating in Atlanta-style black suburbia. I saw no one on the streets, but I did notice that all the homes had two-car garages. I tried to extrapolate from that one fact what kind of people lived in Brook Glen. Well, two-car garages suggested that most of my new neighbors were two-career families, like Cynthia and me. I guessed they worked hard to meet the mortgage payments and car notes.

Carol Ellis reached into her desk drawer, pulled out the loan application papers and offered me a fat ballpoint pen with a faux tortoise-shell barrel. I deliberately touched her hand as she extended the pen I would use to fill in the blanks. She was tastefully dressed in linen and silk, the right fabrics for that cool, collected and professional appearance on a hot Sunday afternoon. I looked out the living room window once again, this time to see what kind of car she was driving. It was a white BMW 320i, the prototypical buppiemobile.

Chapter Ten

PARADISE LOST

Any big-city newsroom is a chaotic jumble of egos, deadlines and jangled nerves. The one in Atlanta was no different. Like everyone else, I arrived every morning at my desk impervious to most events going on outside the warren of glass-walled offices, but arrogantly confident that whatever was said within them—whether the latest on world conflicts or gossipy trivia—truly mattered. Those of us working in the newsroom defined truth and pronounced its significance for others. By the end of every day, as if by magic, what we had agreed upon became common knowledge for thousands of people who brought our product into their bedrooms, kitchens and bathrooms. In the best of times and the worst, people unfurled their newspaper unaware of the attitudes and drama required to publish it. In the end, all that really mattered was what appeared on the printed page.

As far as I was concerned, my career had reached its apex. I was now an omnipotent and omniscient assistant business editor at the *Atlanta Constitution*, where I did more than simply put words on a page every day. I was commanding a journalistic mission. I viewed my role—assigning and editing stories, working with reporters and whatever else it took to put out my part of the paper—as a calling, one just as sacred and dedicated to truth telling as what Daddy did every Sunday from the pulpit.

The power of a newsroom lies in its ability to cast light in certain directions. What gets reported is by definition important news and, conversely, what is not covered is irrelevant. So the person or team that makes these decisions creates, shapes and preserves reality. I liked being in that mix of ideas. It made me feel immortal. In all honesty, I felt I had greater impact on people than any preacher because my work was seen every day by thousands across the entire South, not just heard once a week by those who attended Sunday services in a church.

Between the time I arrived at my desk at about 10 A.M. and when I left the office at shortly after 7 P.M. or so, I spent most of my day sitting at the corner of a cluster of desks that made up the department's editing station. All day, our assignment and copy editors would come and go from this central point. Thomas Oliver sat to my left, his desk at a right angle to mine and overlooking the configuration of editors. Dave McNaughton, another assistant business editor, who had started about the same time as I and was responsible for producing the afternoon *Atlanta Journal*'s business pages, sat directly across from me and to Oliver's left. The three of us, all assignment editors, formed a conversational triangle at the head of the editing station. Because each of us reported directly to Maynard, who sat in a corner office across the room from us, I considered Oliver, Dave and me to be a team of professional peers. Since Oliver predated us on the scene, it seemed reasonable that he took the lead in showing the two newcomers the department's procedures and practices.

My daily tasks ranged from the necessary but perfunctory, such as monitoring the flow of stock market tables from the wire services into our computer system and from there to the composing room, to the more enjoyable, such as discussing story ideas with reporters. On occasion, when Maynard was busy with other tasks or there was a story I felt a personal stake in, I would attend the mid-afternoon page-one story conference.

For about thirty minutes every weekday, this conference room with its too few chairs seemed even smaller as it swelled with the egos, naked machismo and sarcastic put-downs of editors from all departments who described their stories and attempted to belittle the offerings of others in hope of gaining prime real estate for their reporters' words. These meetings were one of the few times editors competed against each other in open combat (other contests were quiet, stealthy battles waged behind closed doors), preening to catch the eye of Kovach, trying to position the story that would have all the city talking the next morning.

As a newcomer, I didn't attempt to show off in these meetings. When I spoke, it was always to praise the work of one or another business reporter, and rarely did I question proposals from other departments. While I didn't feel in the least intimidated, I felt my strongest contribution to the paper was the work of my reporters. I preferred to think up stories, to help writers sort through a myriad of options or sources, to pull together an article that would reveal something about Atlanta-area commerce.

When I arrived in Atlanta, I was proud, and more than a little smug, because I was one of only a few black assignment editors at the newspaper. I felt an exhilarating sense of being special, of accomplishing something rare, of being in places where few others like me were invited, such as story conferences and page-one decision meetings. I relished these perks of power because they made me feel included in the newsroom.

The realization that all was not well in my corner of paradise grew slowly, in increments so minute that I failed to notice anything wrong. Though I didn't hear him at first, Eric Elie, one of the black reporters on the business desk, tried to warn me. "Don't trust 'em, Brother Fulwood," he said one afternoon. "I don't trust many of them editors at this paper and you shouldn't either."

Eric had a buffed-bronze complexion and wavy hair that he cut close to his head, giving him a monklike appearance. He was slightly built and in his middle twenties, which made him both the least physically imposing and the youngest person in our department. Initially, and erroneously, I chalked up the boulder on his shoulder to his youth and slight physique. He always made sure I was aware of something or other going on at the paper or, more often, something out on the streets that didn't make it onto the news pages. I usually listened to whatever Eric said, not so much because I thought he was always right but because he was connected to the reality of common folks.

Eric played a wicked guitar, jazz mostly but blues and R&B as well, in various locales around the city. He was plugged into vibrations that most people in our more staid world never felt. I liked it when he talked to me in conspiratorial whispers—with the cadence of those who hung out in dark, smoky clubs and accepted boozy philosophies as the real truth—about the world "the man don't want to put in his paper."

Eric had been the first person in the department to cozy up to me, offering advice on how I should cope with "the white man down here in the New South." While I thought his views were fine for him, they didn't fit how I saw myself. His exuberance was appropriate for him, someone with a decade's less life experience. But as much as I liked and bonded with him, I never saw myself in Eric.

"What do you have for me?" It was a Monday morning and I was standing over Eric's desk. Since both of us were in early that day, I took the opportunity to rap with him. I was also looking for a story idea, something that might give the two of us an opportunity to work more closely together.

"Bro Fulwood, did you go to see Minister Farrakhan's speech over the weekend?" Eric was teasing me. He knew perfectly well I hadn't been there.

"Nope," I said. "Couldn't make it. I was home with family all weekend. I don't like crowds and I heard there were ten thousand people at the Omni for that speech. Did you go?"

As I spoke, I noticed Eric's face light up as though something had startled him. "You knew there were ten thousand brothers and sisters there?" he asked.

"Yeah, I heard about it at the barbershop," I said. "Some of the men in there said he had quite a large number of people attending on Friday night and some said there were more attending on Saturday."

Eric nodded. "I'm shocked that you would've known Minister Farrakhan was in Atlanta," he said. "There wasn't a word in the paper about it. If you weren't there, you know, I figured the uptown folks wouldn't have known what was happening on that side of the street."

"You're right, the Metro desk should have covered that meeting," I said.

"Damn straight," Eric said. "They would have covered it if goddamn Billy Graham had been there laying hands on ten thousand white people. I didn't go myself, but I was talking to people who went and I got an idea for a story from Minister Farrakhan's speech."

I liked Eric's suggestion and told him to begin reporting it. In the meantime, I would grease the path for his story with the other editors. Eric was humming, sounding like Coltrane, when I stepped away from his desk.

When the three business assignment editors gathered later that morning for an informal meeting, I took great joy in describing Eric's project. "It seems the Nation of Islam wants to start a hair-care business in south Atlanta. Farrakhan, who was in town over the weekend, mentioned the business at a rally. Eric has seen some of the products in stores in the black community."

Neither Oliver nor McNaughton commented on the idea. I continued talking, selling them on the story. "So, I told Eric to go ahead and find out what the Nation of Islam is planning. He said he thought it might be a good story for the morning paper."

Oliver raised an eyebrow. "Is that anything more than a brief item?" he said.

"A brief?" My voice squealed as if I had been pinched. I didn't expect that comment about what seemed to me a fine story concept. "Well, yeah, I think it's more than a brief. Eric was telling me that the

Black Muslims used to have quite a few businesses in Atlanta. If they are trying to revive their community-business infrastructure, it might be an even bigger story. Actually, I am hoping that Eric will stumble on to a national story, because I would doubt the Nation is starting new business only in Atlanta."

Nothing more was said. I figured I had answered all their relevant questions. When our meeting broke up, I rushed over to Eric's desk.

"Proceed with your story," I told him.

"The man said I could?" Eric said, mocking my authority. Damn, if he didn't have a devilish wit.

"I'm the man and I just told you do the story."

"Okay, boss," Eric said.

I turned back toward my desk to see Oliver standing nearby, wiggling his index finger in a beckoning summons. "Uh, Sam, could I speak with you?" We moved off to the side of our work spaces for a private conversation. "I didn't want to say this before, but I don't think Eric's story idea has much potential to make the paper as a full story," he said. "I think it's a little narrow-focused for a business story. Eric could probably find something better to spend his day working on."

"I don't know that I agree with that," I said. "Why don't we let him do the reporting and then find out whether there is a story there or not? After all, we don't know what he will find until he looks."

Oliver's bug eyes narrowed into gashes cutting across the top half of his face. He cleared his throat again. "I don't think you understand. We're not going to do that story. Tell Eric he should do something else. Okay?"

It wasn't a question anymore. He was issuing an order, one that I had no intention of following. From that moment on, Oliver and I were moving in opposing directions and would never be peers. But I didn't fully appreciate that fact. Not yet anyway, because it required time and repetition for me to believe that Oliver might not consider me his equal.

Eric assumed this and had tried to tell me. But I wasn't listening to this young and angry black man, nor was I paying attention to the little signals Oliver had been sending me. I had ignored the conversations he'd had with McNaughton that abruptly ended when I took my seat. It had not mattered enough to me to challenge him when he arbitrarily changed my work schedule to accommodate his vacation plans. Even his subtle but corrosive criticism had rushed past me without too much notice. I imagined it to be something other than a personal attack.

"You're not listening to yourself, Bro Fulwood," Eric said. I had gone over to him to suggest he continue working on the Black Muslim story, something he considered unwise. "Let's not make an issue of this one. Oliver runs this place. You might not have noticed. But he does, not you. He just wanted you to think you were a part of the team. He's the team. The white man don't ever see the black man as his equal, even if both of you have the same title."

Eric was making more and more sense to me. "That's how racism works," he continued. "It creeps into this place and you don't even notice when they're doing a job on you."

I had been overlooking the hidden messages Oliver was sending me. I began to replay past incidents that now were freighted with new meaning.

"Sam, I noticed you were talking to one of your buddies on the telephone." Oliver's drawl had risen over the typical business department din one day in the recent past.

"Yeah?" I answered. Work rules in every newsroom I'd ever been in were lax and no one had ever questioned my use of the telephone.

"Well," Oliver continued, "I don't think that is a productive use of your time. You ought not do that."

Just who did he think he was? He had no authority to say anything like that to me. I had never heard him say anything remotely similar to a white person in the department. I later recalled that Maynard had been standing nearby as he said it and didn't seem the least bit perturbed.

But ignorant and blissful, I said nothing, gave no sign of protest, as my better self was being demeaned. Just as my father must have done three decades earlier when challenged by the guy selling tickets to ride the donkeys outside Clark's, I swallowed hard and looked forward to the day when I could laugh at Oliver's indiscretion. I even visualized how he and I would be sitting in a bar, tossing back beers and joking over the comedy of erroneous assumptions imbedded in a misunderstanding that would never be repeated.

Fat chance. Oliver and I would never share a beer. Worse, he made new and differing demands that seemed as outrageous as the first: "Sam, you took too long for lunch." "Sam, I think you're leaving the office too early." "Sam, you didn't average this set of numbers correctly."

At every turn, I responded with a stoic nonacknowledgment of any transgression and tried to imagine him disappearing right before my eyes. Oliver's behavior began early in my tenure at the paper and continued for weeks. As far as I could determine, he was the only one suffering anxiety over my work. I just could not fathom what the hell his problem was.

"Maybe he's just insecure and feels threatened," Cynthia said after hearing me complain.

"Naw," I said. "That can't be the problem. I don't see how I'm any threat. I guess it's more personal than that. I guess he just doesn't like me, plain and simple."

"Well, so what if he doesn't?" she responded with a shrug of her shoulders and dismissing my office politics as unimportant. "It's not like he's your boss or anything."

Fact of the matter, he knew he was indeed my boss. I just didn't know it. This revelation hit me one day about six months after I had settled into my job. I took my seat and answered the phone ringing on my desk. For the next twenty minutes or so, I chatted with Momma about something personal enough to require a whispered conversation. When I replaced the phone in the receiver, Oliver was agitated. He glared at me and stalked away from our work station. A few minutes later, as he left the office and entered the elevator, my phone rang again.

"Sam, can you step into my office for a minute." I was surprised to hear Maynard's voice on the telephone. I dropped whatever task I had begun and walked back to his corner office.

"Thomas is very upset with you," he said, meeting me in his doorway. "He's taking the rest of the day off to cool down."

"What are you talking about?" I was incredulous because I had just arrived at work and couldn't imagine how I'd managed to piss him off so early in the day. "What did he say I had done?"

"Well, I don't want to get too far into it," Maynard said. He was looking all over his office, anywhere but at me. "You know, he hasn't been very happy with your work for some time and he thinks you are being insubordinate to him."

I was lost. I thought for a moment that Maynard was blaming me for something that someone else, one of the reporters who was directly under Oliver's supervision, might have done.

"John, there's some mistake here," I said. "I don't know why Thomas would feel I have been insubordinate to him. I don't report to him. I report to you and you've never said anything like this to me before."

Maynard wrinkled his brow and looked at me full-face for the first time since I had entered his office. It was a pained, constipated expression that crossed his face. "Is that what you thought?" he said. "Oh my god. I thought you knew. Oliver is your direct supervisor."

Whatever had griped his stomach was now biting mine, clawing its way through my gut and trying to force its way out. I clenched my butt. "Say what!" I shouted. "Nobody ever told me I reported to him. All this time I thought I reported directly to you. That's the arrangement you and I agreed to when I was hired. I have a letter from you saying that."

I was not only shouting but on the verge of tears. No wonder Oliver thought I was insubordinate. I had been ignoring his stupid comments and directions because I was trying to avoid a confrontation with him. For me to have ignored him must have been enough to give him a migraine and send him home. No wonder. But that was his problem.

My conern was how I had been duped. "I just don't understand any of this," I said.

"Well, I guess I just forgot to tell you that I changed his job description before you arrived," Maynard said. "But now you do report to him and he reports to me. That's the way the desk is set up."

Maynard was just now getting around to readjusting my work agreement. The letter he had sent outlining my job responsibilities meant nothing, nothing that he was willing to honor now. I wanted to take the remainder of the day off too, but I didn't dare because I feared I might never come back. Instead, I went back to my desk and glared at my computer screen and the telephone on my desk, which had started this mess in the first place.

Oliver and I never spoke of that incident. Not very long afterward, Maynard was fired and Oliver inherited his job. My problems escalated. Sometimes he was pleasant, chatty even. At other times, he declined to make eye contact with me for days. I never knew how to read his moods and that made me tentative around him and made working in the department increasingly difficult.

Within weeks of his taking over, I was reassigned to the Metro desk and given the responsibility of supervising the reporters who covered the Georgia state legislature. Although everyone said it was a promotion, I knew Oliver had engineered my departure from his domain. Even before my transfer was completed, he stripped me of all duties in the Business Department and gave them to a young, white and male reporter he had already begun to groom. "You're a part of the past and I'm looking to the future," Oliver said, explaining his reorganization. "Until you move to the other side of the newsroom, I don't care if you come in to work here or not."

I no longer felt important in my job. I was still a newsroom manager, in title at least, holding what is considered a prime job in one of the best cities for black people in America. Yet I was miserable. I was one of the few black managers in the entire newsroom, but that was not enough because I had no one, no mentor or senior advisor, with whom to discuss coping strategies.

On one occasion, over lunch in a Chinese restaurant near our offices, I agreed to a mutual defense pact with Nathan McCall, an editor on the Metro desk, and one of his favorite reporters, Larry Copeland. Both McCall and Copeland were assertive, outspoken and race-conscious black men in a newsroom that they felt oppressed their spirits. We had decided to have lunch because we feared that at some time in our careers at the Atlanta newspapers, a white editor would call one or another of us a "nigger."

"I think we should be prepared to respond," Nathan said, bringing the issue to the lunch table.

"So what should we do?" I asked.

"I know what I would want to do," said Nathan. "I'd want to bust the motherfucker in the mouth."

"Nate, man, you can't do that," said Larry. "That would be the end of you in this place."

"I know," Nathan said. He was laughing and shaking his head. "I'm not about to do that. I just said that's what I would want to do."

"If we want to be practical about this," Larry said, "we should agree to support each other. If one of them racist editors calls anyone of us a 'nigger,' rather than attacking right away, we should go to whoever is around and tell them to hold us back. I mean, if it happens to me, I'll look for you or Sam. And if it happens to one of you, come look for me or the other. We'll have each other's back. Bet."

"Bet," I said.

"I'm down," Nathan said.

Even then, I considered our pledge ridiculous. Still do. But it seemed then, and does even now, a logical and natural thing to agree on. I don't think any of us felt uncomfortable about who we were, but we worried about how easily a foolish comment might tempt us to strike out. If that happened, I feared I might lose all self-control.

Just thinking about it made me sick to my stomach. Why in the hell did I have to consider and measure my response to the possibility that a simpleminded white editor might call me a "nigger" in the newsroom? Did white people ever have to consider anything so asinine? I can understand why black people snap, forcing those whites around them to wonder how and why even the most acute of us, the ones who want and try so desperately to make it in the white world, appear bitter and angry for no apparent reason.

It was difficult and inappropriate to talk of such things with most people in the newsroom. The few black reporters, like Eric, were subordinates in the newsroom's pecking order and I wanted to be an example for them, not burden them with my own problems. As for discussing it with my white colleagues, well, that was so far out of the equation I never gave it a moment's consideration. I never tried because I knew I could never explain that they were what troubled me most. So this is what it is like at the top, I remember thinking to myself.

For the first time in my career, I no longer enjoyed going to the office. I knew it had something to do with the friction between Oliver and me, but it was larger than he was. I felt very tiny, a small speck sitting on top of a giant desk with no real authority or responsibility.

I was alone on the job in Black Mecca.

To the extent that we upscale and isolated buppies nurture a common identity, it is the myth attached to our jobs. Status comes from a paycheck, we think, convinced that getting and keeping a white man's salary insulates us from his oppression. Money buys freedom. That is why education—superior grades, advanced degrees, extracurricular honors—looms so important among upper-middle-class black Americans. The more you learn, the more you earn, as Momma used to say.

But somewhere in this process, the white folks who ran the newsrooms in Atlanta and elsewhere did not get the same message. As I struggled to make sense of what to do about Oliver, it dawned on me that my status as a well-placed assistant business editor afforded me no greater protection than that enjoyed by a construction worker or a gas station attendant.

As all of this madness was going on around me, I packed my bags in August 1989 for the National Association of Black Journalists convention in New York. These were my people, professional peers who understood me and what I felt on the job. My friend David and I were sitting in the convention hotel's lobby bar when I told him the sorry story about Maynard and Oliver and how I felt deceived by working at the Atlanta papers.

"We're all on plantations," David said. "Some plantations are up the river and have kinder overseers, and other plantations are down the river with meaner slave masters. The ultimate goal should be to get off the plantation, but that's not possible in America. You can only improve your fate by finding a better plantation to work on. It might be time for you to find a different plantation."

"You may be right," I said.

My home in Brook Glen was a sanctuary where people like Oliver could never reach me. My neighbors felt much the same way—beleaguered at work, relaxed at home. Pam Harris, an accountant with an Atlanta real estate management firm, was someone in the neighborhood with whom I shared work stories. During a backyard conversation one evening, I told her of my frustrations at the newspaper and expressed a willingness to leave Atlanta.

"But where would you go that is any better?" she said.

Pam had lived in the subdivision a year or so before I arrived, making a conscious decision to seek out a community of black doctors, attorneys, executives and college professors. "This is the best place I can imagine living," she said. "All of us have been made to feel that we have to be validated by whites to be good people and good at what we do." Her pretty brown face was creased with knotty lines and her eyes blazed with hostility as she spoke about trying to live up to standards she felt she would never meet for the sake of white employers who didn't appreciate her or her work. "But I don't want to be validated by them," she said. "By living in an all-black middle-class community, it lets us know that we're good. There are not any white people around here staring us in the face and trying to prove we don't matter. So much goes on at the job that we have to endure, the slights and the negative comments and feelings that we're unwanted. When I have to work around them all day, by the time I come home I don't want to have to deal with white people anymore."

Hers—and mine—was a form of self-isolation, not segregation, which implied an external force dictating our choices. Isolation was our choice, a defense against the pain of being rejected or misunderstood. Karen, another friend, coined the term "white folks overload" to explain the fits of frustration that black people experience from prolonged exposure to white people. With that in mind, she and her husband—both fair-skinned and affluent African-Americans—consciously sought out View Park, a predominantly black neighborhood in Los Angeles, as a place to begin a family. "I can't see whites every day," she explained. "It's not that I dislike them or anything, but there is a membrane of coping that you have to wear to be around them all the time."

I understood what she meant. That was my lesson from Black Mecca. White people, I understood for the first time in my life, had never been at ease in my company unless they were in control of the environment. By outnumbering me at virtually every turn, they compelled me to adapt my view of the world, even my own sense of self, to their majoritarian biases. Trying to explain myself to Oliver or any other person in any other newsroom, none of whom seemed genuinely to care, was taxing and not worth the trouble. I did not want to bother with trying anymore. It was so much easier to retreat into myself and into a self-made buppie bubble. No matter where I lived, I would search out that space for me and my family.

In a peculiar, indescribable sense, I was unnerved by the force and rapid approach of this new awareness. I fully understood the rage of some black folks, those who earlier would have provoked a cluck of my tongue and a shake of my head, like the brother in the newspaper story who in a drunken rage shot his mother, his pregnant wife, his toddler child and then himself. The story said neighbors heard him arguing over burned ends of toast before the shooting started. Crazy nigger, I would have said of him. But not anymore.

I recalled with oppressive sadness the words thrown at me over the dusty South African township air. I now felt the insanity of racism, its crazed toxins flowing through a race-fearing, status-seeking society. I knew how black folks propelled themselves in a mad dash from screaming birth to shrieking death in search of reason and meaning in lives that society has predetermined to be worthless. So that is why, I thought to myself, some of us snap without apparent cause into violent outbursts.

I began to identify with those black folks who never wanted to belong within the man's system. I could share in their outrage at the hypocrisy of trying to be a round peg in a square-hole society. If I no longer believed I would become like white people by impersonating them, then I would be free to do or be anything my resources could purchase. I would never become accepted by their definition of mainstream America. I was a black man in a white, racist society. That fact would never change, no matter what I did or how hard I believed otherwise. Fitting in—or pretending to fit in—was a fantasy that required surrendering too much of how I honestly saw myself. I had tried to fit into their world. I had cultivated an image, a personality and a set of career trophies that I assumed would be eagerly embraced by the larger, white society.

But I had been rebuffed at the moment when I most wanted inclusion. Now I didn't want to belong as much. I was certain the color black would be the foremost thing that whites saw in me. I was reminded of the words of the black sergeant in Charles Fuller's *A Soldier's Play:* "You got to be like them! And I was! I was—but the rules are fixed . . . It doesn't make any difference. They still hate you!"

If the world was fair, as I had expected it to be when I was younger, I would have been more grateful. Compared to most Americans—black, white or whatever—I had what many would consider the perfect life. Family. Career. Home. These are the superficial symbols of the American Dream. And I had them all in spades.

So why did I feel estranged from the white mainstream? Couldn't I just as easily swim in a black mainstream of America? And to hell with anyone who argued that it was a less valid choice.

I decided to find another job, far away from Atlanta, where I could make a fresh start with a new attitude about life and myself. I was a determined and professional networker, having diligently glad-handed white folks as far back as my first job at Webster's Men's Wear. For added insurance, I called Larry a few weeks before the convention to discuss how best to approach potential employers.

By this time, Larry was a crackerjack salesman in the household products division of Mobil Oil Co. I respected his ability to convince people to buy whatever he was selling. "Just make them think it's their idea to close the sale," he said.

Larry also offered a job lead that was even more practical. His wife, Jeanne, was the head recruiter for the *Washington Post* and knew all the recruiters at the top newspapers. She suggested I might look up Karen Wada of the *Los Angeles Times*, who agreed to meet me at the black journalists' convention in New York. My interview with her went well enough that within a few weeks I had an offer to become a correspondent in the paper's Washington bureau.

Deciding to relocate to Washington was easy. I was offered a larger salary and could escape the hostility I expected to find at work by withdrawing into a new home and a new life. My goal was to exchange masters while trading up on creature comforts. I planned to fill my new home with toys and furnishings, thinking that maybe material possessions would take some of the sting out of the racial ostracism I assumed would dog me for the remainder of my professional life. If I cannot put distance between me and white folks, I thought, I'll make them pay for my lack of ease among them. It might not be a fair bargain, but it is the best one I can negotiate; lacking liberation, I'll accept dollars to build a fortress around me and my family. Otherwise, I think I will go crazy trying to deal with white folks at the office.

In late summer of 1989, I entered the *Los Angeles Times*'s Washington newsroom and took the desk that had been occupied by the lone black reporter, whom I was replacing. I felt myself being perceived as the recipient of the bureau's one affirmative action slot. Nobody said anything of the sort. My colleagues and bosses were too polite to express what I was convinced they were thinking in silence. Rather than this being a crowning moment in my professional career, with new challenges and new opportunities, I felt no genuine pride or satisfaction arriving for work.

During my first few weeks at the *Times*, my soul turned inside out. Over the course of my life, I realized, so much had changed in me, but so little had changed in the outside world. Racism surrounded me. I could perceive it, but I was powerless to prove conclusively to anyone who was not black how corrosive it could be.

I was not relaxed. I would never be comfortable, never feel at ease at work again, I thought. Racism, or the fear of racism, works like gravity. It grounds black people's thinking and aspirations, pushing our spirits toward the center of the earth. For most of my life, I had chosen to ignore its weighty presence. But now I felt it surround me like a second skin, tight and uncomfortable. And no matter how hard I scratched or rubbed, I could not scrape away its clinging presence.

Thanks to my experiences in Atlanta, I no longer trusted white people, no longer expected them to be honest or fair with black people. I knew, of course, this was a gross and sweeping generalization—a prejudice in conflict with everything I had been taught or had believed. Surely some whites would be genuine and decent, while others wouldn't. Worse, they might appear trustworthy, but hypocritically hide their true feelings beneath a veneer of civility. How would I know the truth? Why should I have to take the lion's share of risks for promoting racial harmony? Why couldn't white people do right? The pain of not knowing, of misjudging, was too intense. I would never again lower my guard around white folks for fear of being hurt once more.

Shortly after I arrived at the paper, Cindy Loose, one of the five editors in the bureau, rang me up from her home to tell me that she had just started working at the newspaper as well.

"We have a lot in common," she went on to say.

"Oh. What's that?" I said. I didn't know this white woman and doubted she knew me well enough to be so forward.

"I think we're both outsiders here," she explained. "This place is so white and male and clubby. I just feel like you and I should get along together for mutual support."

She had noticed the exact same thing that I had when I arrived for my interviews. I had been invited to Washington to meet with the bureau chief, Jack Nelson, and the other desk editors. Those meetings went well enough that I was invited back for another meeting, with Mike Miller, the paper's national editor, who, based out of Los Angeles, had business in Washington a week or so after my initial interview.

During both trips, I saw no other black faces in the newsroom, and though there were a few women working there, I talked only to Diane Spatz, whom I had met at the NABJ convention.

Diane had sheepishly confessed to me that I would be the only black reporter in the bureau during my interviews. "We haven't done too well on that," she said. "But we haven't done too well on hiring women either. There aren't too many of us in here." I had guessed she was trying to be sympathetic, in the same way she later seemed so contrite when she assigned me to sit at the same desk with the same phone number that had been assigned to Lee May.

I replaced Lee when he was transferred to the paper's Atlanta office. Lee had been the only black reporter in the Washington bureau. And now I had his spot—the Adam Clayton Powell, Jr., Chair for Negro Reporters in the *Los Angeles Times*'s Washington bureau, as Lee and I called it.

I did wonder, however, noting the lack of gender and racial diversity in the bureau, whether I was doing the right thing by moving to so white a newspaper. After all, the *Journal-Constitution* did have a much larger contingent of black reporters and editors than this place seemed to have. I ignored my doubts, pushing them out of my mind, because I wanted the new job.

I took Cindy's phone call at face value and we went to lunch a few days later. I learned that she had grown up in a working-class family in hardscrabble Pennsylvania, or, as she described it, "a paper-mill town that stunk to the high heavens." She had worked odd jobs to pay her way to attend Penn State. One of those odd jobs took her to a newspaper office, which, in turn, led her career to journalism and a job on a newspaper in Detroit.

I remember a few years later, when I won a Nieman Fellowship to study for a year at Harvard, Cindy offered me a bit of insight from her own fellowship year at Stanford. "At the beginning of every course," she said, "the professors would be handing out their syllabus and telling the students how brilliant they were to be attending Stanford and how they were expected to become the future leaders of the world.

"These professors kept doing it over and over at the start of every class. It made me want to scream out at them, 'You're not any better than me. You're just richer than me.' But I have to confess I have mixed feelings about that experience. It made me angry that these students were being indoctrinated for future success, deserved or undeserved or whatever. Yet I wished someone had told me the same things when I was eighteen. I didn't know what opportunities were possible for me after high school and college. It would have helped me to have had that kind of guidance far more than it would have helped them. They seemed to have plenty of options available."

I had thought the same thing myself. In different circumstances maybe, but the idea that some people had been trained to think of themselves as future leaders of society was not new to me. I understood what those professors were doing—my teachers back at Oaklawn had done the same thing—and I also understood how angry Cindy had felt at being excluded. I had felt that as well.

My new job—reporting on politics in Washington—was a clear step up from where I had been. However, that was the least of my reasons for agreeing to take it. I was fleeing a lost cause in Atlanta, burying the whole two-year episode in the deepest folds of my brain. I felt defeated. I was running away.

Chapter Eleven

LOS ANGELES FIRE

"Sam, what do black people think of Colin Powell?" Cindy Loose asked me one Monday morning in February 1991.

It was one of those stupid questions that white people seem never to tire of asking black folks, as if we're telepathically linked to one another. I wanted to ignore the question or to humble her with a sarcastic remark. *We'se all think he's a good nigger, Miz Loose.*

But that's not my nature. Besides, I liked Cindy. She had proven herself to be a friend and had extended herself to me in an honest and open manner. White folks like that deserved straight answers, even if their questions were repetitive or offensive to me.

"I don't know what black people think of Colin Powell," I said. "Why?"

Cindy shoved that morning's *Washington Post* at me. On the front page was a story about a news conference from the previous day during which Powell explained the military strategy for defeating Iraqi forces in the Persian Gulf War. Above the story, stretched across three columns, was a large photograph showing the general pointing to a chart. That photograph appeared on page one of most major newspapers across the nation, including the *Los Angeles Times* and the *New York Times.*

"I watched him during that news conference," Cindy said. "I thought he did a masterful job. He was in control and seemed so confident. He even put some of the reporters in their place when they asked some dumb-assed questions.

"I thought he was so good," she continued, "that it made me wonder whether there is a story in what black people think about him. I don't know, but I suspect Colin Powell is the kind of black person most white people wish all blacks were like."

Even now, years later, that casually offered commentary by a friendly white person still buzzes in my ears like a swarm of summer gnats. Cindy had no reason to know how offended I was. Her comment wasn't intended to be upsetting, and she would have been shocked had she known I wanted to grab her by the throat and shake her like a rag doll.

I was less hurt by her saying it than by the truth of her honest insight into her own people, which made clear to me the doubts I carried to and from work. It validated my worst fear and the greatest anxiety of middle-class black professionals: that we are still stigmatized by white people.

And the worst part of enduring these little murders of our souls is that any rational attempt to deal with them risks the dreaded specter of being considered too sensitive or of having a chip on one's shoulder.

I have a boulder of racial attitudes on my back, and at work I must toil among white people and pretend that the dead weight is not there. Cindy's comment—*"the kind of black person most white people wish all blacks were like"*—reminded me of the attitudes I had to swallow to coexist in a white-controlled job. It seems ironic to me now that the one place where black people and white people have the greatest chance for social interaction and improved communication—at work—has become one of the most tense, confrontational and frightening spaces we inhabit together.

The next day, I began reporting the Colin Powell story. After my initial doubts, I discovered contours to it that I had overlooked in my first reaction to Cindy's proposal.

I had been worried about the lack of black American voices commenting on the war as I noticed President Bush and other national leaders—let's not overlook the nation's leading newspaper and network news executives among them—march determinedly toward a military confrontation with Iraq's President, Saddam Hussein. We were being ignored as the nation went about its business.

This feeling was exacerbated one night as I listened to endless television news chatter about the war's implication for the entire globe. The commentator, as usual, was a white man speaking with the authority of Moses, while a line of soldiers filed past him en route to the theater of war. Nearly every face in that military parade was black.

Where were the black reporters, military analysts, commentators and experts? Where did the families of these black troops, who would fight and die in disproportionate numbers, have an opportunity to talk about their freedom and rights in this country? As far as I could see, this was not news that a nation hell-bent on keeping the rich white folks' oil flowing wanted to hear.

I had never felt more depressed as a news professional than I did during the buildup to the Gulf War. Decisions about its coverage were being made by a "war desk," set up in the Los Angeles newsroom and staffed by reporters and editors drawn from across departmental lines.

Shifting the gears of a massive newspaper for war coverage requires Herculean effort and enormous resources. The *Los Angeles Times* is a newspaper that suffers the journalistic equivalent of penis envy when comparing itself to heavyweight competitors on the East Coast. The war enabled the paper to fight for its respect and dignity in press-to-press combat with the *New York Times* and the *Washington Post*.

Additionally, there is a personal, human element in covering big and important stories. During times of conflict, careers can be made. Individuals sent into combat return as heroes; generals directing successful campaigns are awarded medals and accolades. In the newsroom, reporters and editors can have their individual reputations enhanced by stellar performance in wartime. For the most part, and in ways that mattered, no black people had a role in presenting, defining or shaping the paper's Gulf War coverage.

I had been concerned enough about this to fly out to Los Angeles and discuss my concerns with Shelby Coffey, the paper's top editor. In hindsight, I consider this effort to have been rather foolish on my part. Why, with all that must have been swirling around his desk, did I think he would take seriously my complaints about an underrepresentation of black voices in our coverage of the war?

But he agreed to see me. So I assumed he was interested enough to do something about the imbalance.

Coffey is a tall, graying and courtly man, with the manner that mixes Virginia plantation gentility with the ramrod inflexibility of a Southern military education. After I waited briefly in his office, he rushed in. He greeted me in a restrained, yet familiar way, as though I were a college fraternity brother he didn't quite remember.

"You're doing great work," Coffey said. "I especially like the writing in that story you had in the paper last week."

I had written only one story the previous week, a quick-hit article that even I had forgotten. It couldn't have made an impression on the senior-most editor of the newspaper. I imagined him preparing for our meeting by asking his secretary to give him a list of my most recent stories so he could toss a casual compliment my way. It seemed so tacky and transparently phony.

I began to feel as if I was intruding, a feeling akin to being one of the Jehovah's Witnesses suddenly appearing at his doorstep in the middle of the morning. Executives often say they have an open-door policy, but make employees with complaints feel that they are distracting their bosses from more pressing concerns. I wished then I hadn't flown three thousand miles to get this feeling. I wanted to say my piece quickly and get the hell out of Coffey's office.

After I outlined my concerns, the conversation became even more upsetting. Coffey, ever the noble gentleman, said he understood my concerns but that he had already contacted some black reporters about joining the coverage team. "We asked Lee May and David Treadwell, two very experienced black reporters, to go with the troops to the Persian Gulf," he said. "Neither wanted to do that."

Now I was humiliated. In preparation for my talk with Coffey, I had spoken with both Lee and David to double-check my perception of the paper's coverage against their own. They had agreed with me. In fact, both were feeling left out. Obviously, Coffey hadn't expected me to do that; otherwise, he surely wouldn't have dropped their names—in error—as examples of black people who had refused to join the war party. I felt humbled because I believed that Coffey with little or no respect for my concerns, thought he could turn them aside with so blatantly false a statement. Didn't he know that we, the few black national reporters, talked and commiserated among ourselves? I left his office thinking he just didn't care.

My idea for the Colin Powell story was to allow a wide array of common black people to speak in their own voices about the general's role in the buildup to the desert confrontation. How interesting! It might be revealing to *Los Angeles Times* readers to hear how black people felt about the war. My approach was as old-fashioned as reporting could be. Journalism 101: a man-in-the-street story. I selected a strip of Georgia Avenue in northwest Washington where Howard University students and longtime neighborhood residents mixed in corner stores, barbershops and fast-food eateries. More often than not, whenever people from this community make the pages of a newspaper, they do so as victims—of a drive-by shooting, a robbery or some similar horror story. I decided to make them experts, folks who would relate to my readers whatever perspectives they had about the biggest news event of the moment.

After spending an afternoon beating a path up one side of Georgia Avenue and down the other, I had talked with more than three dozen brothers and sisters—an assortment of black people that far exceeded what I would need for my story, including students in a Howard political science class, a buppie couple from the suburbs having lunch in a soul food restaurant, dudes hanging out at a liquor store and a group of men and women getting their heads together at a barbershop/beauty parlor.

While the last group I talked to proved most pivotal to my story, I learned a great deal on the way there. My initial stop, the political science class, was divided on the subject of Powell. Some trusted him implicitly because he was a black man. But a large and vocal minority had doubts about whether the general could be trusted because, as one student put it, Powell "was in cahoots with President Bush" and had come into public life during the Reagan administration. "They [Reagan and Bush] never meant black folks any good," he said, adding that he shared a form of racial solidarity with anyone who wasn't white, like the Iraqi people and their leader, Saddam Hussein. After leaving that class, I considered making their discussion the centerpiece of my story. But by the end of the day, I had visited Joseph's Hair Salon and changed my mind.

Joseph Ray, who owned the barbershop, said his customers expressed great antipathy whenever Powell's image appeared on the television he kept on all day. Most—that is, a significant majority—felt Powell had betrayed the black community by supporting the Bush administration's war call. Ray shook his head sadly. He didn't know what he believed about Powell, but he was concerned that he had heard so many black people say they didn't feel Powell was living up to his special responsibility of championing issues of primary concern to black. "That's a hell of a note—to get such a great job and have to reject your blackness," said Joseph Ray. "But it seems that's the only way a black man can get ahead in the white man's world."

I was struck by the honesty and candor of his comments, which were echoed time and time again by others I interviewed. I decided to lead my story with an anecdote about the frustration expressed by Joseph Ray and his customers.

The top of my story read:

> WASHINGTON—At Joseph's Hair Salon, a black-owned barbershop in Washington, conflicting opinions bounce from chair to chair concerning Gen. Colin L. Powell's role in the Persian Gulf War.
>
> Refecting views shared by black Americans across the land, some customers expressed great pride and admiration for Powell, the first black man to head the Joint Chiefs of Staff and the highest-ranking military position in this time of war. But many others point to Powell as a source of internal confusion, doubt and sometimes bitter controversy.
>
> "He would make a great white general," said a customer at Joseph's. "He's had to overlook his blackness. They wouldn't let him get there otherwise."

The story went on to quote a varying array of black people with comments—pro and con; virtually nobody I interviewed seemed neutral—concerning Powell. I was very pleased with the result and pleased with myself for having turned what I initially had thought a stupid question into a revealing glimpse into the confusing perspectives of black Americans.

"Sam, your story on Colin Powell is well reported." The soft, almost whispery voice of Ted Mitchell came up from behind me. "You got some good comments. I made some changes to the top. Take a look and let me know what you think."

Oh shit, I said inside my head. Ted would be editing my story. He was the last person I wanted tinkering with it. He had only recently been reassigned as the bureau's weekend and projects editor from a reporting position. This had triggered an enormous backlash from several reporters, who refused to allow him to handle their copy because of his heavy-handed mangling of it and his way of adding conservative spins or incorrect details to their stories. I had never worked with him on a weekend story and so had not experienced these problems. However, I was wary of him based on what I had heard in the newsroom.

His edited version of my story began:

> WASHINGTON—By any measure, Gen. Colin L. Powell ought to be a hero to black Americans.
> But for many black Americans, the luster of Powell's four stars is clouded by a constellation of racial and political concerns.

How dare he take it upon himself to say what black people should think! I charged over to the editors' work station, seething at the cavalier manner in which he had rewritten the top of my story. But before confronting him, I slowed down and took a deep breath.

"Ted," I began slowly, biting my words to mask my angry desire to rip out his lungs. "I have a problem with the way you edited the lead of my story. I don't think we can say Colin Powell *ought* to be a hero to black people."

"What? Why not?" he said, seeming surprised that I was challenging his authority.

"Well"—I struggled to make myself clear—"well, I don't think a newspaper story should tell readers what they ought to think. I think the way I wrote my story shows readers what other people are thinking. What I was trying to do was to show readers what black people are thinking and allow them to say it for themselves in their own language. The way you rewrote it, the *Los Angeles Times* is telling them to like Colin Powell. That's not what the story is all about."

Ted nodded as if he agreed with me. "But back in the 1960s, when I was covering the Civil Rights Movement, black people would have been proud to have had a person like Powell as their leader. Has that changed? Wouldn't you think most black people would be proud of him? Wasn't that what the Civil Rights Movement was all about?"

Now I was livid. I was being lectured about 1960s history, a white man's dream version of it no less. "Ted, that's not the point." My voice grew louder. Other editors snapped their heads around toward us. "I'm trying to let the people in the story tell us what they think. I just don't think we should be telling them what to think. This is a story where black people speak for themselves."

"But, Sam, that's not how we write stories," Ted argued. "You can have your sources make their points, but we have to make the story clear from the top for the audience who is going to read it. Otherwise, they will think it's something they don't want to read. Let me show you what I mean."

He pointed for me to sit in a chair next to his. I remained standing over him. When he realized I wasn't sitting, he turned to his screen and called up my story on the computer.

"I don't think you understand who the audience is for this story," he said. "We don't write stories in black English, because that would turn off most of our white readers. The way we organize a story is that we give readers a way of understanding what is going on. The way you have written this excludes many readers. They won't see themselves in this story. You have to write stories in a way that allows the majority of our readers to see themselves in the story."

"What in the hell are you talking about?" My voice was a barely contained scream. "What readers? Are you talking about white readers? Why can't black readers see themselves in a newspaper story. And, black English? This story isn't written in any damn black English. You're the one missing the point. I have written a story that explains what black people are thinking. White people or black people, anyone can read this and understand what I'm writing."

"Okay. Okay," Ted said. "I'll take a look at your version. We'll see."

I was being dismissed. The whole episode had proved embarrassing. He didn't like the idea of my screaming at him with the other editors looking on. Worse, I had accused him of editing in a racist manner, though I never used the word. But, hell, he had started the whole matter by lecturing me on how to write for some fictitious white reader that, I suppose, he imagined living in suburban Los Angeles— one who would feel shunted aside by not having his views considered in a story involving black people's opinions.

Cindy, who had assigned the story, turned away from her work to look on directly. Neither she nor anyone else in that pod of editors intervened in our debate over my story. I wheeled away from Ted, stalked back to my desk, where I grabbed my jacket, and left the office.

It was lunchtime and I wanted to decompress and commiserate with someone who might understand what I had just experienced. But there was not a soul in the newsroom I wanted to eat lunch with at that moment. I ate alone, in anger and silence.

When I returned to the office, Dick Cooper, the assistant bureau chief, asked me into his office. He said he had heard about the blowup and had read my story. He liked the reporting and had no problems with the writing, but suggested I work with Ted to get the story in the paper. "He's new to editing in this department and is having some trouble making the adjustment from reporting to editing," Cooper said.

"I don't think he meant anything racial by his comments, but I think he has his own way of looking at the world. It might not be the way you or, for that matter, the way I look at the world. But I hope you two can work together to get this story into the paper. It's an important story and deserves to be in our paper."

I said nothing. I left his office thinking I had been ordered to back down, to allow Ted to edit my story the way he saw fit. I felt the white editors had rallied around one of their own.

A week later, on February 17, 1991, my story, which had been scheduled for page one, ran on page A8 of the Sunday paper. Underneath a three-column headline—TO BLACKS, POWELL IS A HERO AND SOURCE OF CONTROVERSY—and a subhead—LEADERSHIP: ADMIRATION FOR THE CHAIRMAN OF THE JOINT CHIEFS AND HIS ACHIEVEMENTS IS CLOUDED BY RACIAL AND POLITICAL CONCERNS—the top of the story read:

WASHINGTON—Gen. Colin L. Powell, chairman of the Joint Chiefs of Staff and the highest-ranking military officer in this time of war, has the ear not only of President Bush, but of the world.

In press conferences, his telegenic good looks, military bearing and quotable style make him a media darling. He is mentioned with increasing frequency as a possible vice presidential candidate in 1992—or even a presidential candidate in 1996.

But for many black Americans, the luster of Powell's four stars is clouded by a constellation of racial and political concerns. Although they point to him as a

> source of pride, his celebrity and
> success also generate internal
> confusion, doubt and sometimes
> bitter controversy.
>
> In effect, says Harvard Law
> School professor Randall Ken-
> nedy, many blacks are "embrac-
> ing him while criticizing him at
> the same time."

This was a compromise, a newspaper story crafted by committee. I successfully torpedoed the line ordaining Powell a hero to black Americans, but the final piece fell far short of my aim: to offer the opinions of common, everyday black folks. Instead, it drew attention to Powell's charm and great-guy qualities and made the first voice heard that of a Harvard Law School professor—someone Ted Mitchell's imaginary *Los Angeles Times* reader could easily relate to.

Reading my byline above this watered-down version, which I no longer recognized or cared to own, I was reminded of a strange daydream I used to escape into as a child. In this fantasy, I was riding a balloon filled with helium. The balloon had a parachute-cloth skin made up in a tattersall of jewel tones that sparkled like fire and ice when the sunlight struck them. There were people below, on the ground, applauding my ability to pilot this craft and waving congratulations.

Usually, in my younger days, the daydream would end there. But this time, with the newspaper article in my hands and my mind racing back to childhood, the serene visions of youth turned into an adult hallucination. This time, I noticed that the people on the ground were not waving at me. I had been mistaken. I could hear their voices below. They were angry, shouting curses and brandishing pitchforks.

The nightmare ended with the sound of air rushing by. It was a low and steady noise, the hissing sound of death, coming from somewhere above my head. I looked up and saw a hole in the balloon. The invisible helium was pushing its way out, escaping in a slow, steady stream. Just as I began to notice my brightly colored balloon going limp and losing its luster, I returned to the real world. Shaking my head as if to clear away the dream's fog, I reminded myself once more that I shouldn't care so much about the stories I wrote.

I received few whippings as a child. So few that I remember each of them vividly. One stands out from the others, less so for its severity or enduring pain than for the lesson it taught me about Daddy and his self-image in comparison to other black people. When I was about eight or nine, my father took me with him to a Western Auto store in uptown Charlotte. I liked Western Auto because, in those days, they showcased rows of shiny red-and-chrome bicycles in the front window. The bicycles were there to catch attention, and that strategy worked to the max on me.

"Daddy, I want a new bike."

"Son, you have a perfectly good one at home," Daddy said.

I knew that. But several of the neighborhood kids had new bicycles, the kind with exaggerated upswept handlebars and banana seats that made those dudes look as if they were pedaling a chopper, not a kiddie bike. For reasons I can't remember now, we called them Spyder bikes. Mine was the more practical kind with straight handlebars and a traditional seat. I wanted the latest style.

"I'm not buying you a new bike," Daddy said. "I can't afford to buy you a new toy every time someone else gets something. You don't want to keep up with the Joneses."

I knew that I wouldn't win. Protesting his decisions, once he had made up his mind, never worked. If he was going to buy the bike, he would have agreed immediately, though probably with a sigh. So, I guess, I only wanted to shame him when I said, "You can afford it. You always said we were rich."

That smart-assed retort enraged Daddy and led to the memorable whipping. "Don't ever let me hear you say you think you're rich," he said over and over between recoils of his skinny belt. "We're no better off than anyone else."

In the late 1960s, about the time my father was whipping me for embarrassing him, some 266,000 black American households earned an inflation-adjusted $50,000 or more, the government's definition of affluence. By the early 1990s, when I was earning $65,000 as a reporter at the *Los Angeles Times*, the number of such households had grown to more than a million. Within a generation, prosperity for middle-class blacks had soared so fast and so high that some of us no longer remembered the way things used to be.

Momma and Daddy never forgot. For all of their life, poverty and black were synonymous. When they married in the early 1950s, about 55 percent of black Americans were living below the official poverty line. Although their lives were comfortable, well beyond grinding privation, they always associated themselves with the underdog existence of the majority of black folks they grew up around. Today, although Daddy knows that only a third of the nation's blacks dwell below the poverty line—with less than 10 percent confined to the so-called "underclass"—he, who lives in relatively affluent retirement, considers himself poor because he is black. Always have been black and poor and always will be, he says.

I thought about Daddy's simple explanation of race and class on Monday, July 1, 1991, when President Bush nominated Clarence Thomas to the Supreme Court. Bush had arrived at his summer home on Walker's Point in Kennebunkport, Maine, the preceding Friday. I had gone with him, a loaner and a substitute on the White House beat, filling in for the two reporters from the bureau who regularly covered Bush. The President was so peripatetic that he wore down many of the reporters assigned to the White House. I got the assignment, happy about my first extended opportunity to be in the mix of the President's entourage.

Normally, this stint would have been nothing more than a death watch, except that Bush had a remote possibility of making news. The day before the President left for his vacation, Thurgood Marshall, the first black ever to sit on the Supreme Court, announced his resignation, giving Bush an opportunity to appoint his second justice to the High Court. No President had ever revealed his nominee when outside Washington. The betting among the reporters covering Bush was that he would cut his vacation short, return to Washington and make the announcement. Or, he would wait a week or two until his vacation ended. The latter option seemed unlikely, given that there was little time before the Court's new term in October and Bush probably would want to have someone in place by then.

On Sunday, Thomas, expecting no more than a second-round conversation with Bush about the job, sneaked onto Walker's Point. During a face-to-face chat in Bush's bedroom, the President stunned Thomas by offering to nominate him for the vacant seat on the Supreme Court. Thomas accepted on the spot.

Like the majority of Americans, I knew nothing of this until much later and, even then, had no idea of the conflagration that would erupt. But there I was among the working press elite vacationing in Kennebunkport, Maine, with President Bush, who on that Sunday strode grinning from a New England clapboard guesthouse to show off his new Supreme Court nominee.

I was expecting a Hispanic, most likely Emilio M. Garza, a jurist on the U.S. Fifth Circuit Court. But instead, out walked a dark-skinned black man whose muscular paunch strained against the navy suit, white shirt and red tie. Clarence Thomas spoke of his humble origins in a place called Pinpoint, Georgia, and he choked up a bit as he thanked his late grandfather for having delivered him to that historic moment.

Looking back with the benefit of history and hindsight, I should have realized from the start that Thomas was a lock to earn the nomination. I had only to think about my Daddy, that whipping or how my family of lifelong Democrats had always identified with the political underdog. Especially if the dog was black. These clues, if I had been paying attention, would have helped me understand why so many black folks struggled against themselves to justify their support for Thomas. He was black and poor, always had been and always would be.

There exists a code of conduct, or rules of engagement, to be followed strictly in this murky space where race and class intersect. Middle-class black people are not permitted to express their feelings of superiority over other, poorer blacks. In private, they do so. But their comments and attitudes are what my parents used to call "house business," which is never supposed to escape the four walls of one's home. To do so exposes a serious error in judgment and risks ostracism based on "being too big for your britches." It is especially grievous for a black woman to assume she has a right to a superior place, ahead of or at the expense of a black man. Worse, these dirty secrets of middle-class black angst are closely shielded from the snooping eyes of white people, who, it is feared, will use our weakest link to set us against ourselves, like crabs in a barrel.

Black folks like Daddy could empathize with Clarence Thomas no matter what Anita Hill said he had done to her. Much of Thomas's support among blacks—especially those who had no letters behind their names, lived in the South and/or had very formal relationships with whites—stemmed from his oft-expressed up-by-the-bootstraps background. In contrast, Hill's prissy and polished demeanor was perceived by many working-class blacks as elitist, something they couldn't identify with, something they associated more with white people than with appropriate behavior for a black person. Especially a black woman.

Thomas was, after all, black and male. He might have been the race's only chance for a seat on the Supreme Court. Bush knew what a double bind he had placed black folks in. We could never go against one of our own, no matter what he had or had not done.

Since that first moment when I stood outside the Bush family's summer home, I have spent many hours replaying the entire chain of events in my mind, its impact on how black folks began to debate among themselves ("Just how important is it to have a black on the Supreme Court, if it's the wrong black?" "What's a wrong black?"), on how black folks began to see themselves ("Are we liberals or conservatives?") and on whether racial solidarity was more important than gender, class or civil rights?

I have since decided that the painful debate over Clarence Thomas's ultimately successful confirmation provided a service to the race. It lifted a curtain on a series of morality plays always in production at center stage of black people's consciousness. The drama unfolds in the private dark space at the heart of our souls where we allow only the closest of kin and never outsiders (and, of course, not white people) to witness our worst fears. Those fears came true during the televised hearings.

We can indeed thank Clarence Thomas—by way of President Bush and, later, Anita Hill—for ripping away our facade of unity. At tremendously expensive rates, black America's internal phobias were psychoanalyzed by arbiters of popular culture. Media personalities, civil rights activists, politicians and a motley crew of celebrities from hip-hoppers to Hollywood sitcom writers lobbied their points of view as the common folk sat in judgment by their telephones and called in to Oprah, Geraldo, Donahue and every local black radio talk show host. Eventually, the word from the grapevine snaked its way to media pollsters. The public speaks via opinion polls. Politicians, in this case the all-white Senate Judiciary Committee, with its key votes residing in black-vote-rich Southern states, paid dutiful attention. This is how the system worked: in the space of seventy-two hours, black folks watched, selected and voted for their favorite actor in the movie-of-the-week confirmation hearings that starred Anita Hill and Clarence Thomas.

On Tuesday, October 16, 1991, after all was said and all was done, fifty-two senators gazed at the overnight polls and felt comfortable enough to cast their votes for Thomas. Black folks all across the nation believed, or said they believed, that Thomas should be confirmed. An ABC News–*Washington Post* poll, conducted over that weekend, showed that 70 percent of black Americans supported Thomas. The *Los Angeles Times*'s poll was only marginally less ebullient, with 61 percent of blacks behind Thomas.

I witnessed this morality play from my perch as a Washington-based reporter. I was supposed to be objective and evenhanded, one of the many lies we tell about journalism. Nobody in the nation was objective over that weekend, especially nobody black. For me, the hearings were all too real and all too painful. The plot twists and turns peeled back several layers of my skin. Nearly every one of the old and dreaded stereotypes of black men, of black women, of blackness came into civic review—our group-think identity, our primordial sexuality, our fear of white people, our persistent quest for acceptance in the white man's world on his terms and, ultimately and most painfully, our feelings of helplessness at being used and abused for the entertainment of a white nation. We knew in our marrow that white folks were looking and laughing at us.

"For us as black people, anything that occurs within the race, whether in the workplace, within our families or private lives, it's a deeply personal and private affair," Kimberlé Crenshaw, a professor at the UCLA Law School, told me during a break in the hearings. "For that to be made so very public is a sense of violation of our collective privacy."

Those hearings, Crenshaw told me, rubbed all of black America raw. We ourselves, naked like a newborn jaybird, were bared for all America, white and black, rich and poor, to see. And we were embarrassed as our private pain erupted into public exposure.

Since that summer, black attitudes toward Clarence Thomas have changed. "We knew he wasn't going to be a Thurgood Marshall," said Royce Esters, president of the Compton (California) NAACP branch, which broke with the civil rights organization's national office to support the Thomas nomination. "But the fact he was black, we assumed he would have to be sensitive to black people. But now we feel betrayed, let-down and frustrated.

"Clarence Thomas has turned out to be the house Negro," Esters told *Emerge* magazine in 1993. "Here is a man we thought we could have some faith in because of his humble background, but now I feel foolish."

I have a theory about what happened to Thomas after he won his seat on the Supreme Court. Nothing happened. That's right, nothing happened. He was, in the words of his black conservative fellow traveler Alan Keyes, "reasonably conservative in terms of standard liberal views of civil rights" and continued to be so after he joined the High Court. No, what happened occurred within the collective psyches of black Americans, whose view of Thomas's place in history has been reshaped by those of us, liberal and middle-class, within the news media.

I take credit for my role in this bit of stagecraft. A year after the confirmation hearings, on a nationally broadcast segment of the Public Broadcasting Service's *Frontline* series, I accused George Bush of lying when he said he picked Thomas without considering his color. I told documentary filmmaker Ofra Bikel that Thomas owed his nomination and confirmation to the accident of his being born black, despite the protestations of the Administration and others. "This whole thing was fraught with race," I said. "Race was an issue. Race was an issue out front, first and foremost. Everybody knew that. Nobody wanted to acknowledge it. Nobody wanted to deal with it as such."

Later in the broadcast, I noted that the irony of Thomas's "accusing the Senate of a high-tech lynching is the same thing he's said he has been opposed to all of his life. That is falling on the race card to say that it is 'them' doing things to you when you can do it for yourself . . . He did it because he was in danger of losing the nomination and he wanted to be on the Supreme Court and he knew it would work. And it did work."

I was playing a role. I said what I believed, but I represented a specific point of view the producers wanted on their show. I was one of many actors in this political theater. Point and counterpoint. There I sat representing the political left: black, liberal and professional, pontificating about how black people like me saw through Thomas and his white conservative backers. Juxtaposed on the right were Thomas's black, conservative and working-class supporters, emoting over how any black man is better than no black man on the Supreme Court.

Bikel had journeyed to Pinpoint, Georgia, to find Thomas supporters in a rural beauty shop and in down-home church services. The broadcast was a showdown: Ivy-educated buppies versus working-class proles. It was no contest and the intent of the show left no doubt of the victor. In the media-ruled court of public opinion, a year after the Thomas-Hill hearings, the buppies beat the proles hands down.

While Thomas will remain on the court, we will have the last word on everything he does. We didn't make him, but we can break him. We will define him. We will caricature him. *Emerge*, a national publication targeted to an upscale black audience and describing itself as "Black America's Newsmagazine," put Clarence Thomas on its November 1993 cover. There he was in a lifelike full-color portrait, smirking, cutting his eyes to the right and wearing a white Aunt Jemima–handkerchief do-rag on his head. The cover lines declared: BETRAYED: CLARENCE THOMAS' FORMER SUPPORTERS.

That's how perceptions are shaped, nurtured and entrenched. I didn't think of it that way when I agreed to be interviewed for the PBS show. I wonder, knowing what I now know, if I would do it again? My opinions are the same as ever. But now I see far more clearly how my opinions were leveraged to move other people's opinions. So much so that opinion polls now show that a majority of black people believe Anita Hill over Clarence Thomas and believe that Thomas should not be on the Supreme Court.

Recently, I called Daddy to ask him what he thought of the Thomas-Hill affair after some time had passed and Thomas's court opinions had revealed his true, conservative and antiblack colors. "I still think what I thought before," Daddy said. "There's a black man on the Supreme Court. That's what matters most."

I was surprised by his inflexibility. He was not surprised by mine.

"You people in the press, whether you're black or white, you don't know what the average [black] man thinks," he said. "You don't have a lock on what's right. You just have the ability to define your version of reality and make it stick. Poor black folks have a reality, a different reality. But we don't have the power to make ours stick to nothing."

• • •

It confuses people when I tell them I work for the *Los Angeles Times*.

"You live in Los Angeles?" they say.

"No," I say. "I work for a newspaper that is based in Los Angeles."

"Oh, I see. You're their reporter in Washington."

At this point, I usually smile. I have another stock response, depending on whether the person asking the question is black or white. For white people, I explain matter-of-factly that the bureau is large, some thirty-five or forty people. "I am one reporter among many."

But for black people, there's a different story line. Back before Jube Shiver and Marc Lacy, black reporters who cover business and regional news, respectively, transferred to Washington from the main office in Los Angeles, I answered in the affirmative. "Yes, I'm the paper's Washington bureau," I would say.

No need to explain about the white folks. For the most part, the black person asking the questions was interested only in what I did. Of course, some black folks' eyes would swell when I said this. Incredulously, they couldn't believe my bosses would entrust me to run their Washington office all by my lonesome. "You mean, you're the only person in their bureau? You're all alone?"

I would be busted, forced to 'fess up. "There are about thirty-five whites in the bureau. But I'm alone. I'm the black reporter."

I stopped playing this game in March 1991 when a suburban Los Angeles plumber named George Holliday turned over to a local television news show a grainy home video shot from the balcony of his apartment. The tape captured a clutch of white police officers in the glare of their cruisers' headlights beating the hell out of Rodney King. Fifty-six blows—to King's head, his legs, his back—shattered the black man's right eye socket, fractured his right cheekbone, broke his right leg, damaged his facial nerves and gave him a concussion. Fifty-six blows etched on Holliday's eighty-two-second amateur videotape. Fifty-six blows in eighty-two seconds.

I can't get that out of my mind. The scene of King writhing on the ground as baton-wielding cops teed off on his body, hammering over and over at him with metal nightsticks, is my worst nightmare. It is every black man's worst nightmare. I could have been King. There he was on that videotape (or was it I?), fearing for his life—and reaffirming my already sinking distaste for the Los Angeles way of life. This was no Hollywood movie set and L.A. was no longer a punch line.

A year later, in early May 1992, I visited Los Angeles. Less than a week had passed since a mostly white, conservative and police-loving jury from Simi Valley returned not-guilty verdicts for the four white police officers accused of criminally beating King. When my USAir jet landed on a Tuesday night, no fires were burning against the night skyline, but LA was still smoking.

I checked into Le Bel Age, a posh West Hollywood hotel frequented by movie stars and celebrities. Hotel staffers told me that during the riots guests met at the rooftop lounge, sipping champagne in the hot tub and watching plumes of smoke blanket South Central. I didn't ask, but wanted to know, if any of those guests were black people. I doubted it.

I went to Los Angeles at the request of an editor who was supervising a special section on the three days of rioting. I joined a team of reporters and editors drawn from various sections of the newspaper who would be interviewing a wide assortment of people. Narda Zarchino, an assistant managing editor, told me I had been picked for this assignment because of my interest in middle-class black people; I was to interview that population group, she said. Other reporters would talk to other Southern Californians, representing the area's rainbow of people. Our tape-recorded interviews would be transcribed and run verbatim—albeit edited for space reasons—in a special section of the *Los Angeles Times.* That section would later be woven into a novel-like narrative written by four reporters and published in a book, *Understanding the Riots: Los Angeles Before and After the Rodney King Case.*

"So they bused you in all the way from Washington." The voice belonged to Andrea Ford. If a casting director ever needed someone to play a firebrand black woman, say Harriet Tubman or Sojourner Truth or Zora Neale Hurston, Andrea would fit the bill perfectly. She is a pretty jet-hued woman with a dazzling smile that makes her oversized red-rimmed glasses jump to the bridge of her nose. And like a good race woman, she is often angry at white people.

I was standing over her desk, located in the middle of the news-room. "Bused?" I said. "You know I didn't ride no bus all the way cross-country." She was trying to be funny, but I didn't get the joke. I had known her a few years before I joined the *Times*. Andrea had a great sense of humor that found the absurd in white folks' inconsisten-cies. She laced her observations of their behavior with irony and ex-pressed them in urban black patois.

"You haven't read the bulletin board, have you?" She plunged a hand into the stack of papers on her disheveled desk. Her hand disap-peared, and reappeared clutching a sheet of paper. "You need to read this. See what Linda Williams said to the *Oakland Tribune*." Her hand, paper and all, shot toward my face.

An article in that morning's *Oakland Tribune* mentioned that Linda, an assistant business editor and another outspoken black woman at the *Los Angeles Times*, objected to the way its editors had deployed black reporters during the riots. Her comments, quoted as part of a panel discussion on blacks in white newsrooms at a regional NABJ conference in Oakland, cited her objections to the *Times* having "bused" in black reporters from suburban bureaus and used them as "cannon fodder" in the rioting areas.

Linda's comments were obvious hyperbole, but they pierced sensi-tive areas in the *Times* newsroom, where the unsaid rule is to speak softly and never negatively about the newspaper. Linda didn't feel a part of the "white boys" establishment, so she spoke her mind when asked.

"Linda has caused quite a stink," Andrea said, still smiling. "She fucked them white boys up."

By this time, I had grown to appreciate Andrea's keen insights into the *Times* corporate culture. On my rare visits to Los Angeles, I made a point of having extended face-to-face chats with her. At other times, we shared long-distance confidences and swapped company gossip, mostly about the doings of other black folks in newsrooms across the country. Though we were separated by three thousand miles, she was a part of my professional network of colleagues and personal friends.

In one of our phone chats, Andrea was outraged that some *Times* editor had dismissed one of her story ideas. As she explained it to me, her teenaged son complained that the police in Long Beach, where they lived, hassled young black boys. Andrea thought the perceptions these kids held about police brutality might lead to a story.

"That asshole," Andrea said, referring to the white male editor who killed her proposal, "said he didn't believe the police were hassling young black guys. He said the police are 'our friends' and wouldn't do anything like that."

Several months later, on March 4, 1991, when the videotape of Rodney King was broadcast around the globe, Andrea was still angry about that exchange with the editor. "That didn't happen because the cops are our friends," she told me in our first conversation after the King beating.

On this trip to Los Angeles, I noticed that while Andrea was elated that Linda had fucked up the "white boys," she was ambivalent over the riots. Her role in the coverage was minimal. Black reporters were among those involved, relaying quotes and anecdotes from the riot scene, but the glory jobs—writing the stories and earning the front-page bylines—fell to white reporters. That was the point Linda was trying to make, Andrea said.

From the editors' point of view, the aftermath of the riots was the worst possible time to complain about race relations in the newsroom. Many of them were hurt. Some took Linda's comments personally, sending her angry messages over the office computer system. Worse, her comments were picked up by an assortment of publications and trade journals, heaping more reproach on Los Angeles as well as its leading newspaper. The editors, mostly white men, were embarrassed. Linda had exposed an institutional weakness at the *Times:* the subtle racism that exists even as employers claim no responsibility for perpetuating and fomenting discord among their minority staffers.

"The quotes were accurate as far as they went," Linda told me years later when I called her to double-check all the rumors associated with what she had said and the newsroom reactions to it. "The context of what I said wasn't reflected in the quotes all by themselves. I was commenting to a question about how blacks were being used at the *Los Angeles Times*. I was saying that whenever there is a big story, like the Gulf War, which was a very important story to this newspaper, black reporters and editors are not solicited for their skills.

"But the riots were the first time an aggressive effort was made to use black reporters at the paper," she said. "What I was objecting to was the fact that a comparable effort to recruit black staffers for other important stories has not been made by the largely white male editors at the *Times*. What does that say about this place? What does this say about equal opportunity? Why in this instance did you make the effort, but not in others? Could it be the most distinguishing aspect of black reporters is their color, not their reporting skills?"

People like Linda and Andrea are rarities. They toil in professional white-collar establishments. They are not go-along, get-along blacks, which makes them troublemakers. In the vernacular, they're not team players. Neither of them is among the most popular people in the *Times* newsroom. I would also guess that neither cares, and wouldn't change who she is to make anyone like her.

I asked Linda if she felt the brouhaha over her comments had curtailed her career at the *Times*. She chuckled sarcastically. "Not more than a week or two after I arrived here, it was very clear to me that I was not among the chosen," she said. "I have never thought I had a real career here, so that incident did nothing to hurt me. I never had anything to lose."

Why not move on?

"I have no reason to leave," she said. "The fact that some people here don't like me may even be more of a motivating reason for me to stay put."

The day after Andrea told me about the discord in the newsroom, I visited Holly Echols to see how the riots had affected her. Holly was another of my NABJ buddies. A thirty-three-year-old former local television anchor and reporter, she had given up journalism for a career in public relations. She lived with her nine-year-old daughter, Aja, in a three-bedroom bungalow on a well-kept street where a mixture of the unemployed and the working class and the professional, mostly African-American, maintained a quiet distance from one another. She recognized the people on her block in the Crenshaw District of South Central Los Angeles well enough to nod a respectful hello, but not much more than that.

Holly said she knew there would be a bad reaction in the community after the verdicts. Preparing for the worst, she joined her sister and mother in a three-way call to commiserate with one another over the jury decision; none of them could believe it. "It's going to be worse than '65," Holly's mother predicted. "There's going to be trouble tonight."

By that time, people were honking their horns in protest as they drove up and down Crenshaw Boulevard, just two blocks away. Holly could hear shooting. She turned out the lights. On the television screen, the violence escalated, with people being yanked from their cars.

"Where are the police? Where the hell are the police? I don't believe this!" Holly remembered screaming at the television. "This is not a tape. This is live! And there are no police. There's no ambulance. There are no firemen. What the hell is going on?"

I left Holly troubled. She was black and middle-class, living among her people and trying to make a contribution to the neighborhood. None of that mattered when the bullets flew. I flashed back to Alexander Montoedi in Duduza. He had warned me not to think being middle-class offered protection. I feared that he might have been prescient. It might very well be the black briefcase toters in America being burned out when the fire rages the next time.

Epilogue

THE PERFECT LIFE

"Daddy, I love you," coos Amanda. My six-year-old daughter is a cherub when she is fast asleep. But she hates the nightly process of getting there. I have always had a knack for soothing her to sleep. As a wrinkled-faced newborn, she cried at her mother's breast, only to be passed into my arms, where she would fall into limp slumber. That is how putting her to bed became one of my chores.

"And I love my room in my house and my family. I love my life and everything in it," says Amanda. Tonight, as usual, she is stalling by flattery. She knows which words pierce my soul, triggering an extended father-daughter chat. I am a sucker for her charms. She knows me better than anyone else on this planet. I am compelled to delay bedtime long enough to ask what has brought that comment to her mind.

"Oh, Daddy, I was just thinking about how lucky I am to have you and Mommy as my parents. Don't we have the perfect life?"

Simple question. How do I answer? I think of the ingredients of my

life: I am a black man; I am married; I am a father. I like—no, I love—
each component. Is that the definition of the perfect life? Something is
missing in that definition, so I search for another.

Am I what I own? What I surround myself with? Whom I associate
with? I'm no longer sure. Was I ever certain? I can describe it, but I
don't know what's for real. I live in a dignified two-story Colonial
house on an acre of suburban Washington, D.C., real estate. Like me,
most but not all of the people in my Prince Georges County, Maryland,
subdivision are black professionals. Although I am friendly with the
majority of my neighbors, I know only a few well and am sincere in my
appreciation of their presence whenever I see them tending their gera-
niums, washing Volvos or jogging in Nike apparel through the community.

How happy I am with my neighbors dawned on me one morning.
As I backed out of the driveway, I paid closer attention to the chubby
black man who lives next door. Kenneth Edwards eased himself down
the three steps off his front porch. With calibrated movements, he
walked along the twenty-odd feet of his driveway and, with a creaky
groan, bent to one knee to pick up his morning newspaper. He and his
family had moved into their house a few months before Cynthia and I
closed the loan on ours. They were among the first in the neighborhood
to greet us as the moving van, packed with our furniture, idled in our
new driveway. Kenneth said he was as excited to see us move our beds,
dishes and clothes into our house as he had been to place his belong-
ings in his own. "I always wanted a house in the suburbs," he said,
adding that now his kids—a son and daughter—were approaching college age with excellent prospects for scholarships. "Why not buy now
and enjoy what's left of my life?"

Kay, his round-faced and level-headed wife, said there was another
reason. "We wanted to live in a saner place, somewhere we wouldn't
have to dodge the bullets." When she said that, I nodded silently. They
were open, honest and friendly black folks, like the people back in
McCrorey Heights, where I grew up—just the kind of neighbors I
wanted Amanda to be around.

On this spring morning, in my recollection, Kenneth was unshaven and wore a tattered plaid robe whose knotted rope barely contained his girth. He wore an athletic-style T-shirt and blue pajama bottoms beneath the robe. No shoes covered his feet.

If nothing else, Kenneth Edwards is more predictable, steady and dependable than the digital clock on my car's dashboard. I can chart whether I'll be late for work by his morning excursions. My office at the Washington bureau of the *Los Angeles Times* is in downtown Washington, some sixteen miles from my house. It requires a forty-five-minute commute. If I back my car out of the garage in time to watch him collect his paper, I can be at my desk by 10 A.M. Kenneth works the late shift and sleeps late. He retrieves his paper every day at 9 A.M. precisely, three hours after I have collected and scanned mine. This day, however, I was struck by the fact that his routine, my routine, the ordinariness of our shared morning greetings, made me feel pleased with his dependability. I liked hearing him shout over the azaleas, "How ya doing?" I delighted in returning the welcome with my typical, rhetorical "Fine. And you?" Having him near me in this quiet community of middle-class black homeowners was security and joy. He seemed comfortable living next to me. I felt snug living next to him.

The white couple who live in the house across the street have just planted a FOR SALE shingle in their front lawn. Of all my neighbors, I know these people least well.

I met him once. In my excitement over building a new house, I made several trips to the construction site to examine the builders' progress. On one of these excursions, I noticed him—a reed-thin white man wearing white cutoff jeans, a T-shirt and straw hat—mowing the broad expanse in front of his house. I waved. He did not wave back. Maybe he doesn't see me, I thought. So I walked over to the edge of his yard, to strike up a conversation, making it impossible for him to overlook me. Now he saw me. He stopped his mower, walked over and asked if I needed any help. I stuck out my right hand and said, "I bought this corner lot. I guess we'll be neighbors."

We shook hands and exchanged the few brief, strained inanities common to people forced together against their will or pleasure. I learned only sketchy details. Both he and his wife were nurses who worked odd hours at different hospitals. He said they liked the neighborhood and had been among the first to move in a year or so earlier, when the houses and lots in the subdivision were sold on speculation—nothing more than colored dots on a realtor's sales map.

Since moving in, he said, he and his wife had been pleased with their purchase. However, they did not know much about the neighbors who had moved in on either side of them. My surprise at this comment must have been evident from my expression, because he quickly added, "Well, I guess we work too much to get to know the other people on this street."

That's fine with me. I don't live here to be near him, and if he wants to leave, so be it. I am happy inside my house and he can't touch me there.

Cynthia and I picked this place with a sense of racial community and isolation from the white mainstream in mind. We wanted comfort on our own terms here. This house is larger than the one we owned in Atlanta. Both were built from the ground up under our expectant watch. Again, we picked oak cabinets for the kitchen and bathrooms. I reassembled the dozens of carefully wrapped crystal teardrops on the chandelier in the dining room; we had purchased it for the Atlanta house and decided to keep it rather than buy a new one when we moved.

On the second floor, a quick step from the staircase, is a hall that extends the width of the house and links our master bedroom suite to a private family room at the other end. From the first time I saw it, I was convinced this corridor would make an excellent art gallery. On either side, the walls now display signed and numbered reproductions from the *Songs of My People* photography book—a black cowboy roping a steer from his bucking horse, a black woman and child in graduation robes and mortar boards, a muscular and hirsute black man holding a bare-assed baby in his strong arms—and a framed original painting that incorporates globs of red, splotches of black and swirls of green oils with woven kinte cloth. I hope that hall speaks with silent symbolism—affirming and Afrocentric—to Amanda, bidding her good night and welcoming her in the morning.

Amanda is my only child and I would do anything to make her life perfect. She has her own room off that hall. Her bedroom is chock-ablock with the precious junk common to the suburban child of the 1990s: Pongo and Patch, the stuffed characters of her beloved *101 Dalmations*; a blue genie from *Aladdin*; several chocolate-dipped Barbie dolls and all their wardrobe fixings; a shelf of storybooks with African boys and girls doing childish things; and enough puzzles and game pieces to keep the floor cluttered.

"Yes, we have the perfect life," I say, finally, to Amanda. "Now go to sleep." I switch off the lights in her room. At this point, with Amanda nestled in her small bed with the images of Pongo and Patch romping over her bed covers, I could not be any happier. My Amanda is already falling into deep sleep, shielded by the love of her father and mother, and satisfied with the comforts of her life. As far as she is—or I am—concerned, from inside these four walls, nothing in the world can hurt us.

But I am troubled by her question. I don't know whether I answered it correctly. My answer took too much effort; it required a complicated psychological journey, forcing me to think about issues I don't want to confront.

Amanda didn't notice the nanoseconds of mental calculation. She didn't care. My darling daughter heard the answer she needed to hear. It was the only possible response that would reassure her. But I remain uneasy. I paused far too long, reflecting on and composing a calculated response to her finely layered question. She caught me off guard, forced me to reveal myself. Who am I? What am I? What do I say to her about who she is and what she will be? These questions—or is it my lack of answers?—scare the hell out of me.

Amanda has done this before, declaring that when she grows up she intends to "be white" like one of her nursery school classmates. What do you say to something like that? The wrong answer, an overreactive lecture or a defensive tone might scar her (or me) for a life-time. Allowing it to pass would be wrong, a missed opportunity in the ongoing education of my daughter.

When I began reading, I was about Amanda's age. Not long af-ter, I discovered comic books and became hooked on the DC Action series that featured Superboy. An orphaned baby sent to Earth from his native Krypton, he looked like any other resident of Middle America as he moved among Earthlings in the guise of dweebish Clark Kent. But he was different. There was something about Earth's sunlight and gravity that endowed this alien with abilities exceeding those of ordinary men. He could see through walls with X-ray vision. He had strength and intelligence greater than all those around him. But I was most captivated by the fact that Superboy could soar over the heads of plodding Earthlings. There was some-thing about his ability to fly that forced my imagination to soar along with him. With nothing more than a simple flexing of his knees, he escaped gravity to glide on invisible currents.

I fixated on Superboy and wanted so much to be like him. I saw myself with an alter ego. I felt, without really understanding why, that I was living a life separate and apart from the one I actually experi-enced. I also convinced myself that one day I, too, would leap from the ledge of a tall building and float over the pedestrians below me, doing all sorts of deeds that would otherwise be impossible for someone like me.

This idea took on an air of possibility during the buildup to one Thanksgiving dinner. I remember Daddy telling George and me how wishes made over the breaking of a turkey's wishbone came true. George and I made secret wishes, held the greasy bird's two clavicles and pulled them into two uneven pieces. I actually believed that my wish to fly would come true.

I awoke the next morning ready for my first flight. I pulled on a pair of underwear over my pajama bottoms and tied a beach towel around my neck. I thought that was the uniform I would need to be-come an airborne superhero, ready for practice flights. I began by jumping off a kitchen chair. Then the kitchen table and, later, a countertop. Every try failed. Gravity dropped me on the floor time and time again with a belly flop of a thud.

I never divulged my wish to anyone, because it made me feel stupid to be so betrayed. A few weeks later, I would feel double-crossed again when I stumbled across unwrapped Christmas toys in my parents' closet. Not only would I never fly like Superboy, but now there was no Santa Claus.

I suppose I remember that holiday season for its loss of childhood innocence. I also suspect that it is the reason I have never gone through the charade of Santa Claus with Amanda.

Amanda's question about whether we have a perfect life forces me to explore with her the meaning of race, class and identity. For the moment, all she needs is a simple, definitive response to satisfy her curiosity. But I need more. I want to know what to say to my daughter without myth, fantasy or, worse, lies. Clearly, the time is coming when I will need a larger vocabulary and some better answers. But I don't have the right answers at this moment. Maybe I never will.

I will never forget the last time I saw Momma. I was preparing to return to Washington from the Thanksgiving weekend. Our good-byes have always been prolonged. This one was no different.

"I wish you didn't have to go back to D.C.," she said. "But I understand you have your job."

I smiled at her. After all these years of trying to make Momma understand my work and life, it was clear to me in ways that required no words that she was proud of me.

"You know," she continued, "I didn't want you to do all that newspaper stuff. But it's what you always wanted. You always seemed to know what you wanted to do, had a mind of your own. I never understood that. But, I guess, I just didn't know how the world would turn out for you. Things are so different for you than they were for me."

"Different," I said, recalling the conversation we had had years earlier. "Things are different, Momma, but I don't know if they're any better."

Two weeks later, I was returning from an assignment in Los Angeles when Cynthia finally reached me at a hotel in Chicago to tell me that Momma had died of a heart attack. She had parked her car in the driveway, slumped as if she were taking a nap and never woke up.

Since the last time we spoke, I have grown to understand and accept Momma in ways I never did before. I see myself in Momma. I see Momma in Amanda. And I see my younger self in Amanda. All of us—Momma, me and Amanda—have journeyed from one cocoon to another.

Those riddles of growing up black, middle-class and Southern that have puzzled me for most of my life make perfect sense to me now. I know why Daddy and Momma didn't suggest going to the March on Washington on my seventh birthday, why they didn't talk about race and class and privilege of birth, why they wanted so hard to protect me even when I didn't want to be protected.

They were trying to be the perfect parents in an imperfect world. Their only shortcoming—and it is unfair to label it a failing—was that they didn't know the opportunities and limitations of the world I live in. They didn't know it any more than I know what kind of world to anticipate for my Amanda.

ACKNOWLEDGMENTS

The initial idea for the book you are now holding was not mine. I wanted to write something, lacking my voice or personality, that illuminated the intersection of race, class and opportunity in the post–Civil Rights generation. Fate—and Jonathan Yardley, the Pulitzer Prize–winning book review critic—intervened to persuade me in this direction.

Yardley, who writes a weekly column in the old-fashioned and verbose style of a newsroom curmudgeon, drew my attention with an attack on the impulse of black people to segregate themselves from whites. I disagreed with what he wrote (the details now escape me; all that remains is its essence and my objections) and I called him to challenge his opinion. Yardley embraced my criticism and suggested a lunch and a face-to-face debate. I accepted.

That lunch led to a series of midday Monday repasts and in home visits during which Yardley and I talked of many subjects. Despite our obvious differences—he's a generation older than I am; he's white; he thrives on major league baseball (the Baltimore Orioles) and I crave college basketball (Go Tar Heels!)—we found much in common. He graduated from the University of North Carolina and edited the *Daily Tar Heel*, both were rest stops on my life's journey. He shared my affection and fascination for the South in all its complexity. We talked of these common concerns and, of course, race and journalism and the fates that united/separated us because of skin color and history.

"I don't often say this to people as young as you," Yardley said as we finished coffee one day, "but you should write a book about your life. I think you have something to say about race that's not being said."

"Maybe one day I will," I replied.

The seed so planted bears its fruit.

Nobody writes a book alone.

I owe a huge debt of appreciation to a cadre of supportive people, like my friend Jonathan Yardley, as I toiled in the garden of reading, writing, rewriting, rewriting, rewriting and editing this book.

Thanks to Susan McHenry, the kind of intelligent editor/good friend every author needs. Susan was there from beginning to end. She read everything I wrote (the proposal, countless drafts, a final manuscript, galleys and proofs). She answered silly questions, phoned in at all times of day and night. She volunteered to me her living room couch, library of popular literature, encyclopedic knowledge of black people's ancestry and her friends for whatever strange need I had of them. Best of all, she complained only when I ran out of Good Earth tea.

I also deeply appreciate the wise counsel and backroom insights I got from Bridget Warren and Todd Stewart and the rest of the gang at Vertigo Books. Stay in the bookselling business because I need you.

My colleagues in the Washington bureau of the *Los Angeles Times*, including my bosses Jack Nelson and Dick Cooper, heard much about this book, but saw nothing of it. Yet they and many others at the newspaper tolerated my slackness for long stretches of writing at home or while I was away on leave. Noel Greenwood's early help, which was instrumental in giving form and structure to my manuscript, is greatly noted and appreciated. And I counted on David Shaw's acerbic comments to keep my ego in check.

I offer a special note of love and appreciation to Pam Shaw and Emily Tynes, two of my best friends, confidants and sounding boards during the ordeal and self-doubts of writing. You listened to me and offered valued insight and guidance that I continue to heed.

Many thanks, too, to Bill Kovach and the great people at the Nieman Foundation at Harvard. An academic year in Cambridge was the perfect place to sit and think and write.

Arabella Meyer, my editor at Anchor Books, and Martha Levin, publisher of Anchor Books, saw the potential in the manuscript that others missed. Thanks to both for your insight, support and encouragement.

I give a special standing ovation to my agent, Faith Childs, who is a no-nonsense professional, a keen student of human nature and a valued adviser. I will always appreciate her ability to read and comprehend this book even when it was nothing more than an image in my mind.

Of course, none of this would have been possible if I had not grown up in the cocoon of love and support provided by the Negro Community Guardians of my youth in Charlotte. Through it all, there was—and continues to be—my family. Thank you, Momma in Heaven, Daddy and George.

Finally, I am compelled to express my bottomless love and respect for Cynthia, who went to bed many nights as her husband typed. And to Amanda, who insisted on never missing a good-night kiss: Daddy loves you more than anything in the whole wide world.

November 1, 1995
Fort Washington, Maryland

About the Author

SAM FULWOOD III is a correspondent for the *Los Angeles Times* in Washington, D.C., where he created a race relations beat. A former Nieman Fellow at Harvard University, he wrote award-winning stories on the Clarence Thomas hearings and contributed to his paper's Pulitzer Prize–winning coverage of the Los Angeles riots in 1992. He lives in Fort Washington, Maryland.